PEACE

PRESENCE

POWER

Helen Alcock

About the Author

Helen Alcock has motivated and inspired people for nearly three decades. She has presented life-changing seminars and healing meditations through Agape Encounter, a not for profit organization, which she co-founded in 1999 and continues to lead. The keys, practical guidelines and principles shared in these seminars over the years have equipped and empowered people to change their lives. She has also been involved in mentoring, writing, team building and has developed and presented a TV series called *The Way to Freedom*.

Helen's extensive experience has been gained over these years through many courses, developing and leading groups, presenting seminars, group and personal healing meditation sessions, and her personal journey of transformation. Her passion is to share this information with people from all backgrounds who desire true freedom, peace, healing and restoration.

She has three beautiful adult children and five grandchildren she cherishes. Helen lives in Melbourne, Australia with her childhood sweetheart and husband Bruce, who she has been married to for over 45 years.

Copyright © Helen Alcock 2015

National Library of Australia Cataloguing-in-Publication entry

Creator: Alcock, Helen, author, illustrator.

Title: Peace Presence Power / Helen Alcock;
            Renée Purdie (editor);
            Helen Alcock (designer and illustrator);
            Helen Sparrow (photographer);
            Bruce Alcock (publisher).

ISBN: 9780646937366 (paperback)

Notes: Includes index.

Subjects: Self-actualization (Psychology)
            Inspiration--Anecdotes
            Peace
            Healing

Dewey Number: 158.1

All rights reserved. Apart from any fair dealing for the purposes of study, research, criticism or review, as permitted under the Copyright Act 1968, no part may be reproduced by any process without the permission of Helen Alcock. Initial enquiries can be made via email to: peacepresencepower@hotmail.com.

Every effort has been made to trace and acknowledge copyright material. Should any infringement have occurred accidentally, the author tenders her apologies.

The quotes from the Bible were taken from the New Revised Standard Version Bible, copyright 1989, by the Division of Christian Education of the National Council of the Churches of Christ in the United States of America, Thomas Nelson Publishers. Used by permission. All rights reserved.

Dedication

To all people seeking true Peace

Liability/Disclaimer

Although the stories shared in this book are true, some of the names and details have been changed for privacy and protection reasons. The purpose in using these real life experiences is to give examples that show readers how Peace, Presence and real Power can be experienced by anyone! The writer and publisher take no responsibility whatsoever for how this information is used or how it may or may not affect the reader's life. We do encourage people who need further assistance to seek professional help.

Contents

Acknowledgements   9
Foreword   11
Introduction   16

SECTION 1 PEACE

1. Overcoming Struggles—An Adventure Begins!   21
2. Understanding Feelings and Using Them Constructively   33
3. How Negative Feelings Can Lead to Peace   49
4. Transforming Life by Transforming Thoughts and Beliefs!   57
5. Blockages and Obstacles—Discovered and Removed!   72
6. Resistance and its Influence on Your Life   87
7. From Breakdowns to Breakthroughs   92
8. How Fears, Terrors and Trauma Can Dissolve!   96
9. Finding Your 'True' Self Versus Roles and Masks   111
10. How Being 'Right' Can Be 'Radically Wrong'   121
11. The Power of Words   126
12. Healing of Body Pain   134

SECTION 2 PRESENCE

13. Discover What You 'Really' Want   145
14. Discover True Treasure   150
15. Discovering the Loving, Powerful Presence Within   154
16. The Healing Meditation—   168
    A Step-by-Step Guide to Peace
17. True and Lasting Happiness   173
18. The Power of Love Languages   180
19. Becoming Free To Be Me!   186
20. How 'Really' Listening Melts Hearts   193

21	How to Develop Healthy Relationships	199
22	Relationships with Healthy Boundaries	209

SECTION 3 POWER

23	Powerfully Resolving Conflicts	219
24	The Power in Acknowledging, Allowing and Asking to Receive	227
25	The Power of Curses and Blessings!	231
26	Using Anger Powerfully and Constructively	241
27	How to 'Really' Forgive	253
28	Questions That are Empowering and Life Giving	259
29	Freedom from Stress … Practical Keys	265
30	Change Your Focus and Change Your Life!	271
31	The Power of Decisions That Can Change Your Life	275
32	The Power of Expectations	281
33	How to Gain an Empowering Perspective	285
34	The Power of Attitude	290
35	'What if…?' A Powerful Question	294
36	How to Attract Good Things into Your Life	298
37	How to Attract the 'Right' Friends and Partner	303
38	How to Develop Healthy Habits	308
39	Empowering Destiny Keys	314
40	Angels and Their Power to Help	318
41	When 'It' Seems Impossible!	334
42	How to Maintain Peace, Presence and Power	339

Expanded Contents for easy reference	348
Afterword	361

Acknowledgements

I want to acknowledge the special man in my life: my husband, friend and soul mate, who has made it possible for me to dedicate my time to helping others experience real freedom and peace over 28 years. He has been there for me, giving his quiet support, helping out with the family, and assisting me with aspects of running Agape Encounter, a not-for-profit organisation. *It is through this organisation that I have presented the material contained in this book through seminars that have been life changing seminar for many over the years.* My husband has also been the publisher of this book for which I am truly indebted.

There are too many people to mention by name, to whom I am deeply grateful. They will know who they are. I experienced unconditional love and a helping hand from them when I first began my personal journey to freedom. They encouraged and guided me, taught me and walked with me to discover the Presence, peace and real power deep within myself, in memories that were transformed from darkness and pain into light and peace. This then enabled me to help others in this way.

I must mention, however, two people who have been on this amazing journey with me for over 25 years: Edna Hatch who has been like a rock for me, never wavering or doubting, and also Dorothy Francis who has stood strongly beside me through what has often been a challenging, sometimes painful, but mostly exhilarating, exciting and inspiring journey. We have been taken on the path less travelled together, assisting many people, from diverse backgrounds to experience Peace, Presence and true Power. What a privilege it has been to have these special people in my life as well as the other team members of Agape Encounter. I thank Trish too for her time and talent as she completed the initial edit of this material before I passed it over to Renée Purdie, with whom I have had the pleasure of working with, to complete this book as my professional editor. Thanks also goes to Virginia Rogers who continually encouraged me to add the little characters to this book as they really spoke to her heart.

This book wouldn't exist if it hadn't been for the prompting to go to a particular seminar over 14 years ago, where I was convicted to write down all I was learning and experiencing that was changing my life and the lives of others. This information was then presented in many seminars over the years, much of which is now shared in this book.

I am eternally grateful for all that I have learned and shared as well as the privilege to witness the transformations that I and others have experienced as they encounter Peace, Presence and Power.

Foreword

When I reflect back, it doesn't seem that long ago since I began my journey of discovery. I was seeking real peace and the power to know how to deal with myself and my ocean of negative emotions and why I reacted as I did. I wanted to know what was going on in me. I felt lost, alone and without direction and wanted to develop *authentic* relationships.

Although I wondered at that point in my life if God really existed, I decided to get down on my knees and ask for his help. I said in my prayer that I felt like there was a great brick wall between us. I had no idea what that brick wall represented, but brick by brick, over time, the wall was dismantled and I discovered a Presence. Each time I encountered this Presence and Light, every negative feeling dissolved. I wanted to know what to do with my life then so I asked this question. Then I heard quite clearly in my mind: 'I want you in my employment.' I had no idea what that meant, but I was aware at that stage of my life that I had been thinking of opening my own employment agency! But now I had a little taste of a Peace beyond understanding … I wanted to know what direction this Presence wanted me to take!

A dramatic change in direction
That was a dramatic about-face for me. Over the next three years, I committed time daily, waiting in the Presence, being still, talking, praying and listening. Wonderful things began to happen effortlessly. That certainly built my faith and belief in the Presence and who I was learning to get to know and trust.

My trust and confidence was being tested too. On one occasion when I was having a 'quiet time,' I heard in my mind: 'Go and tell

Sally I love her.' I thought: 'I hardly know Sally. I've only met her twice in my life and only vaguely remember where she lives.' Was this really God speaking to me? Just in case, I thought I'd better follow up on the request. I found Sally's house and as I approached the front door, I remember feeling reluctant, well honestly, I felt stupid knocking on her door. What would I say? However, I did knock and Sally appeared at the front door. I told her how I was feeling a little stupid, but explained what had happened that morning in my quiet time.

I told her the words 'Go and tell Sally I love her' came into my mind. Sally looked stunned. She said to me, 'You would have had no idea what I have been saying all morning as I walked around the house.' I said, 'What was that?' She said, 'I have been saying over and over again, "God you must hate me!"' She went on to say, 'I believed God hated me because of what is happening in my life right now.' I was stunned too, but then amazed and delighted. I was so pleased I had had the courage to follow up on what I had heard in my mind as both Sally and I were both profoundly moved. I thought, "Wow, that must really have been God!" as the words shared gave Sally hope as she realised that God heard her and that she was not alone in her trials.

These sorts of occasions continued to occur and over time helped build my trust in listening and responding to what was coming to me. At first, it was like walking on water, hoping I wouldn't sink, but the results were always life-giving. Even after years of sharing, mentoring and presenting seminars, I never fail to be blown away when I see people and circumstances being transformed. It's like I'm on this amazing adventure, never knowing quite what is going to happen! I remember being shown an image in my mind of me riding on the back of a horse and buggy with my Friend and Helper sitting beside me. He was in charge of the horses and the direction they were going, but I was invited to take one of the reins whilst he held the other. I was to watch and listen to his directions. I sensed that I was being finely tuned to how he was directing the horses. I love horses by the way, so this spoke to my heart as well as my head. I got the message!

It then seemed like all hell let loose in my life.
One of my children became very ill, and as my husband was working long hours as well as studying, I felt alone and desperate. Again, there were many opportunities to ask for help when I felt so weak and powerless. The results were stunning. You will hear more about this story as you read on.

Now I understand that I needed to face my deepest fears, which I was unaware of, that were negatively influencing my life and flowing over to the family. Opportunity after opportunity came for me to authentically reconnect and come to know my inner self so that Peace, Presence and Power could become a reality in my life. My daughter's health was restored as I was enabled to *really* 'let go'. Now many years later, she is well and healthy and is working as a personal trainer and model. She is also happily married with beautiful children of her own now.

Join like-minded people on this new journey.
Although I was reluctant to join the groups I had been invited to, I agreed, but always sat up the back to check everyone out! I saw, heard and learned a great deal and am forever grateful to those wonderful people I came to know. This was the path that had opened up in my life and I was willing to give it a go. Eventually, it led me into places I never dreamed, doing things that had never occurred to me. People began coming to see me through word of mouth. I was invited to speak at many groups and then developed a not-for-profit organisation to

make this information and experience available to anyone from any background.

Your path may be different. What's important is that we all know how to come to know real Peace, Presence and Power within our whole being: body, mind, heart and spirit which will automatically ripple out to those around you thus beginning to change the world into a better place … as it did in my life.

You will journey through my life and the lives of many others.
The names of people in many cases have been changed and some of the stories have been altered slightly to respect people's privacy, but the stories are true. I share from years of experience working with those seeking clarity and a true and lasting peace. The practical keys and principles to life shared are simple yet practical and powerful as you will read. You will discover how our thoughts and beliefs influence our feelings, actions, reactions, decisions and our destiny. You will read how unresolved memories that have been influencing people's lives in the present are released, freeing people from emotional, mental and physical pain, leaving Peace, Presence and Power!

I hope this book will inspire and enable you to know what is possible.
You may not believe that it can be possible for your life to change—as I once did. However, I ask that you open your mind and heart to the stories you will read … where the seemingly impossible changed.

What if you or your friends could be enabled and released from confusion, anxiety, fear, anger, hatred and powerlessness as well as other negative emotions and thoughts and then experience Peace? What if your life took on a whole new purpose where you felt fulfilled, making a difference wherever you go?

I feel passionately about what I share with you because I remember where I once was and how my life has been transformed as I've discovered the truth about myself and circumstances . I had tried to change my ways and failed, but after experiencing the powerful life-changing Presence in both the past and present, my life began to change for the better through all sorts of challenges. I know I am not alone now and that I have the greatest Helper and Friend of all to be with me at all times to guide me. I know this is available to all of us no matter what we have or have not done because for me the Presence is Unconditional Love.

I invite you to take this exciting journey of learning, growing, changing and experiencing Peace, Presence and real Power until you feel complete, lacking in nothing.

Introduction

What I wanted most of all was peace—a greater peace within me, no matter what circumstances or situations I encountered. But no matter how hard I tried, I found it almost impossible at certain times to suppress the thoughts and emotions I felt and often reacted from them. I hated the disharmony that they caused. I wanted change, but didn't know what to do. This book shares my journey of discovery over 30 years and how my life and the lives of other people began to encounter true Peace. The stories are real, true and inspirational.

I suggest you read the chapter that seems appropriate to your situations when necessary. You could liken the chapters to recipes, each supplying ingredients that *create peace* in some way. But, as you will discover, you can ask the One who *created* the Universe to help you, just like a child has an adult to help him bake a cake!

The information overlaps from time to time because each Chapter has been presented as a separate seminar over the years. I felt led to leave the material as it was presented as reading certain information more than once can reinforce what is being said. Please go gently and discover, as appropriate, the simple but powerful principles, keys and information that has profoundly changed my life and the lives of others … and which can also change your life.

Many years ago I was unaware that the situations that were robbing me of peace and causing distress in our lives were tied to the past, triggering off unresolved, painful memories. But as you will discover in Peace, Presence and Power, the past can gently but powerfully be released and healed. Peace can be restored in memories, even in pain-filled memories that seem blank, grey or dark—often frozen—as Truth, Light, Peace and Presence is encountered. This experience has transformed lives not only in the past but also in the present.

I am grateful that this opportunity to discover Peace, Presence and Power often occurs when people are at their weakest: feeling confused, lost, angry, sad, stressed, empty and alone, often 'hitting the wall' so to speak, and are in emotional or physical pain of one type or another. I now know we don't have to 'have it'—our life—all together, and that it is possible to experience a safe space where we can be authentic about how we feel and what we think and discover Peace, Presence and real Power.

As a result of not knowing what background people have come from when seeking help to experience peace or clarity, we ask them who or what they believe in. I have discovered those who have no faith usually believe in Truth or Love. For me, this is the same as the Presence who I have discovered is Truth, Light and Unconditional Love. Most people have felt *safe* with allowing the Spirit of Truth to assist them, whilst others relate to Presence, Source, Unconditional Love, Divine Counsellor, Wisdom, Jesus, God, Holy Spirit and Friend. Thus, throughout this book, I change my language in the hope that readers from diverse backgrounds will be open to the keys and principles that can change their lives as well as be open to experience Peace in any pain-filled situations or memories. All these names mentioned, from my perspective, relate to the Author of all creation, of the Universe.

I hope that as you read this book, you will use the language that you relate to. It is just like the many names I call my husband who I married in 1969. Although his name is Bruce, I often refer to him as my friend, lover, companion and husband, depending on the circumstances!

Every area of my life has been changed, and still is being changed for the better, as a result of what I share throughout this book. I am grateful beyond words and want other people to know what is possible.

HOW TO CHANGE YOUR LIFE FROM STRESS TO PEACE!

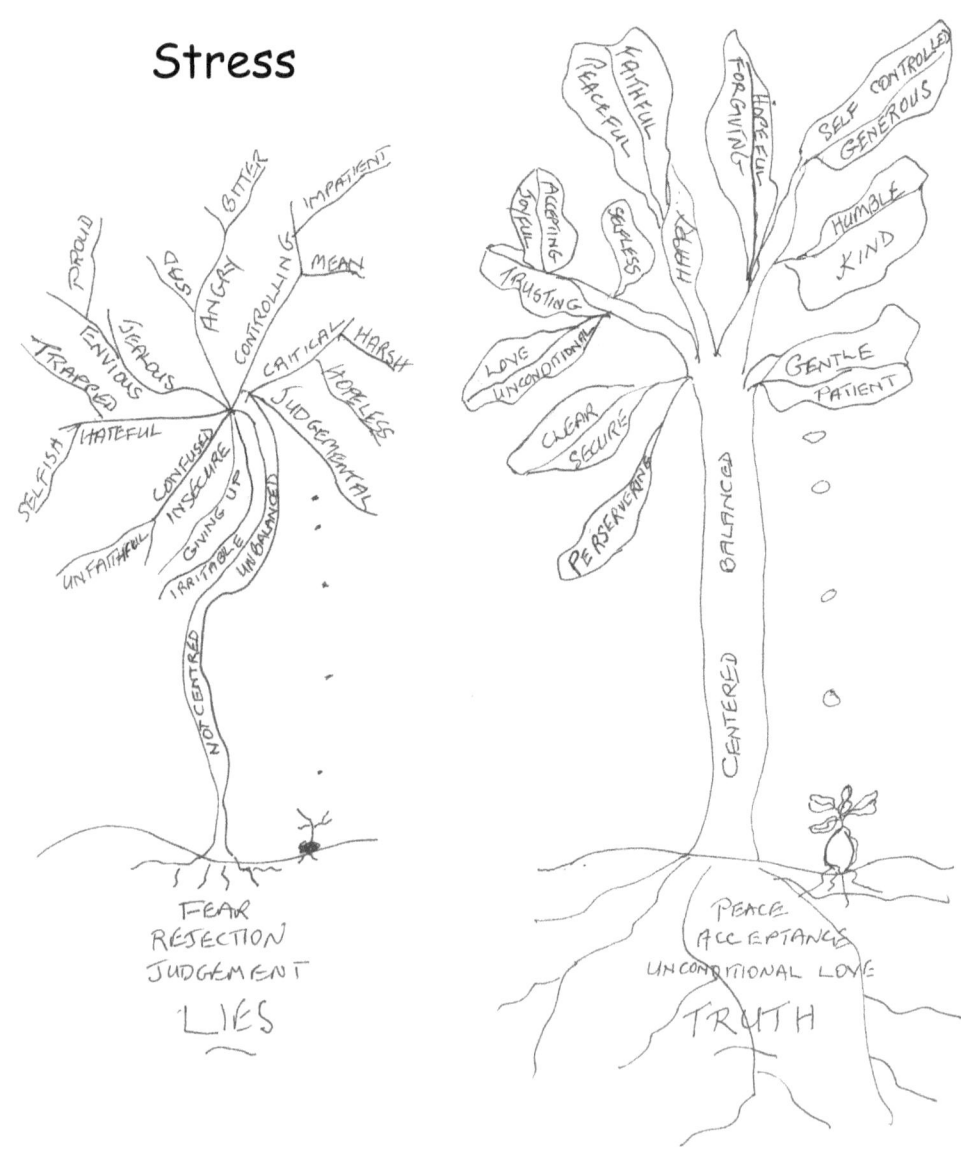

Section 1

PEACE

1

Overcoming Struggles—An Adventure Begins!

It once seemed impossible to bring change to my life and the lives of others. Have you ever felt like that? And are you, like I was, left with the feelings of frustration and anger because everything you try never makes much difference and, in fact, can seem to make the situation worse? Does it seem there is one struggle after another in your life? Then I want to meet you just where you are and invite you to embark on an exciting road of discovery, one I began many years ago. I now know, after facing what I believed were insurmountable situations, that change for the better and transformation are possible for *anyone*, no matter what background!

I had much to discover about myself. For instance, I had no idea how powerfully the beliefs, emotions and decisions I had made since I was very young (which I was unaware of) were influencing my life in the present, despite all my conscious efforts. Most of my struggles, I later discovered, were as a result of unresolved fears and negative emotions that I had experienced throughout my life. But at that point in time, I wanted to know how change could possibly occur.

On the way, I discovered that there was a Power beyond me, particularly in my powerlessness, to do what I couldn't do! I remember sitting in my chair where I would go daily to spend time with my

Creator in the hope for change. I would 'unload' all my feelings when I was in a struggle, saying, 'I'm not leaving here until you do something with the way I am right now.' Peace would always come if I waited long enough, and somehow solutions to my struggle would eventuate. It never ceased to amaze me.

Discovering a powerful Friend to bring order out of chaos
So, as I came to know, over time, that I had a powerful Friend who was always available for me to call upon for help, my life began to become an adventure instead of a struggle. I learned that the battle was not mine alone. The changes have been astounding as you will read.

Every struggle that came along became an opportunity for a breakthrough and an adventure in the sense I never knew what the outcome would be rather than dreading the struggles and battles. Each situation that caused me grief in some way began to teach me about myself, how my mind worked at different levels, the laws of life and attraction and more. In fact, after some time on this journey, I began to get almost excited to see what would happen in each difficulty that I now saw as an opportunity. It became the adventure of all times for me.

As I dealt with, instead of struggled with, each situation with this new perspective, which was a choice each time, my life began to change slowly for the better. This influenced my family, friends and now hundreds of people through journeying with them personally or sharing at the seminars I have conducted over the years. I never would have thought years ago that facing my struggles would lead me and my family from a place of tension, a place that seemed to me like we were lost in a wilderness, to a place of greater peace and enjoyment.

There was a world of difference between using only my human efforts compared to asking my Friend and Helper to *take over* what I did and said. This always brought order out of any chaos in my struggles and battles—and boy I used to have plenty of them!

We're not just a body, but a soul and spirit.

I discovered that we are not just flesh, but rather that we are a body and a soul, which comprises our minds, wills, emotions and spirit. I became aware that my body tends to gravitate towards those things that often decrease my quality of life and bring a form of death in a sense. For instance, I used to struggle with feelings of separation after my boyfriend, now my husband, used to return to his home as I knew I wouldn't see him for another five days. After he left, I would head straight for the chocolate biscuits in the jar and eat them all! I was looking for comfort, but I didn't realise that all the comfort I needed was always available within me. You and I know that finding comfort in this way is only temporary. These biscuits (and for others it might be drink, gambling or sex) only filled my emptiness for a few minutes and then I always felt bad. The struggle would only get worse as I used to turn on myself, judging and criticising myself for being hopeless and fat. This way of responding to my emotional pain only led me down the road to self-destruction.

I realised in my weakness I needed the Spirit of God to strengthen my human spirit to help me resist the destructive ways I used to numb my pain. I also discovered a deep satisfaction and fullness whenever I invited the Spirit who for me is Unconditional Love to fill my need. The struggle to satisfy my body and soul in destructive ways began to decrease and eventually disappeared! It has been quite a journey. So I encourage you to ask for help too as it is a very powerful and gentle way to break bad habits and discover Peace.

What do you do when overwhelmed?

One of my greatest struggles left me feeling overwhelmed to the point of drowning. For three years, I had done all I could to help my daughter who was suffering from severe asthma. She had stopped breathing numerous times. I had doubted that God cared about our situation, as I had been begging him for help. How could he let a child continue to suffer so badly? It wasn't until I totally surrendered my daughter to his will that her recovery began within two weeks. The Helper of all helpers brought the victory when I felt totally helpless.

It reminded me about the story of King Jehoshaphat in 2 Chronicles 20, and what he chose to do when he felt completely overwhelmed. What was vitally important in this looming battle against two great armies approaching their towns was who he turned to, how he listened and responded and the principles he applied. The story shares how he then experienced complete victory over his frightening circumstances.

King Jehoshaphat and every single town in Judah and Jerusalem called out to God for help from the depth of their distress, saying they didn't know what to do. They said to God that they *believed* he would hear them and save them from their overwhelming circumstances. As they were saying this, in the middle of the assembly, the Spirit of God came on one of their sons. (Interesting how God chose a young man to speak rather than one of the fathers!) He told them to listen to him and not to be discouraged or afraid and to face the large armies as the battle was not their battle but his! God told them where to march to the next day saying that they would not have to fight! They were told only to take up their position, (which I believe is a position of having faith in God, my Friend as I call him), and stand firm (in other words don't wobble, procrastinate and doubt). Jehoshaphat bent his head to the ground as did all Judah and those who lived in Jerusalem and worshiped God.

The next day Jehoshaphat told them all to put their trust in God and then they would be able to stand their ground. Musicians marched at the head of the army to sing praises to God, singing his love is everlasting. As they began to sing, God threw the invading armies into panic and confusion and they completely destroyed each other. When the men of Judah reached the spot to face their enemy, they found only dead bodies. What an amazing victory and with so little physical effort! After many years, I have realised that no matter what struggle or battle seems to overwhelm us, anyone can have the success King Jehoshaphat experienced if they do what he did!

Here are the principles I learned from this story that I have now applied in many overwhelming circumstances with great results. I recommend you give them a try next time you are struggling, overwhelmed or in some type of battle. They are:

- *remember that the battle is not your battle but God's battle*
- *ask for his help*
- *wait and listen to what is coming to your mind or from his Word*
- *take a stand with what you read or sense, not doubting*
- *respond or act according to what comes to you*
- *praise and thank God for what he is doing for you and the circumstances, BEFORE you see the results. This is the faith that moves mountains.*

I can remember following these instructions—sometimes grudgingly at first. Even though I sometimes didn't have a whole-hearted response, I still witnessed amazing results as you will hear further on in this book.

There was a time I was struggling with John. I basically wanted *him* to change! When I asked for God's perspective on the situation, I realised I needed to stop focusing on wanting John to change and to instead focus on the One who would change me! So I gave up the struggle to change him. I then listened to what came to my mind which was to stand beside John, focus on God and ask God to help us both!

The shift in John was almost immediate and unbelievable, even though he didn't know what I had done. I now realise John could sense I wasn't loving him unconditionally, but rather judging him. Then I was reminded of the time John had said to me: 'I don't want to change you', and I knew then that I was making him feel as though he was not good enough. What a wake-up call for me!

John drew closer to me shortly after I let go of the struggle to change him. This often happens when you surrender to God's will. I could feel the void between us disappear. I now have an image of us being companions on the journey, both needing help in our weakness, but loving each other anyway just the way we are. There is no more struggle or tension, but rather acceptance and unconditional love. Remember though, we don't have to like what people do and can judge the *things* they do and ask God to help them.

Over the years, many people have shared how they asked for help in their struggles, but nothing ever changed. I wondered if they followed all of these steps and persevered long enough. I sometimes suggest that they ask to be made aware if there is anything in them that would prevent breakthroughs and victories in their lives. I will share more about blockages and obstacles in the chapter devoted to them. After reading this information, you may come to the many ways we can stand in the way of answers and victories in our life.

Discovering the path to life when struggling
I learned to discern whether I was on the path of life by the consequences of what I was 'doing.' The fruit was either sweet or bitter and of course I either became better or bitter in the way I was being. When I began living in and flowing with the Source of life, I experienced life in all its fullness, eventually, through all battles and

struggles. The fruit of living this way always leaves me with an increase in my sense of self-worth; there is a feeling of lightness, peace, growth, movement and flow. I begin to prosper and clarity, freedom and empowerment are experienced. However, as you no doubt know, learning to remain on this path that brings life can be a battle—or you can view it as having an adventure of learning and discovery.

On reflection, Jan came to know she was on the path of life because the results were sweet, despite the horrible circumstances. Jan's husband had left her for another woman; her son had recently committed suicide and she was in hospital waiting to have an examination under anaesthetic to see if she had breast cancer. They said it was possible that they would operate if necessary so she wouldn't know the outcome until she woke up! It was like all hell had been let loose in her life.

The surgery team was delayed in taking her into the operating theatre for a long time. Jan said she was terrified, and felt totally powerless and alone, but then remembered someone had told her to speak the Word of God and it would invoke his presence and power. She began saying these words over and over again: that God did not give her the spirit of fear but of power, love and a sound mind. She said the next thing she remembered was a nurse waking her up. She had fallen asleep. When the nurse held her arm to inject her with the sedative, she commented on how relaxed and calm she was and asked what she did to keep so calm.

Not only did she go into the operating room with a great calm, but when she woke up they told her there was no cancer! What a great victory! Had she dealt with this from a negative point of view, she could have been a blithering mess and would have created more stress than she already had.

Recognising the path to destruction when struggling
I know what it's like to take a different path, operating out of what I call the darker side of my human nature when battling or struggling. I realise now I was reacting negatively, blaming and accusing others and myself and resisting what was happening. I wasn't aware then that I was on a *path leading to destruction* and was being robbed and deceived. As a result, I experienced a loss of Peace and Presence. I became angry, cynical and confused and felt trapped. This way of being always separated me from others and myself. I now realise that I chose this way and turned my back on the path of life. I certainly could not see anyone else's perspective in that state, only mine. What seemed worse is that everything else started to go wrong in my life. Have you ever experienced this when you get 'off centre'? I realised I attracted more of the way I was: more chaos, more disharmony, more battles and more struggles.

How to grow personally from every struggle
What if we could use annoying times to our advantage, particularly when we find ourselves tempted to struggle with ourselves or with our children? Asking constructive questions that make us stop and listen gives us an opportunity to gain another perspective in difficult circumstances. For example, asking this question has made a huge difference in my life: 'What good could come from the situation?' There have been many positive answers. Try it and see the results. It certainly stopped me looking at what was wrong!

One such case was when I had upset Jenny. She was obviously furious with me because she spent the next six weeks expressing her anger about what I had done, not to me though, but to many people far and wide. I know because I had feedback from them! I could actually feel a prickly tension around me for weeks.

Finally, I asked Wisdom what I was supposed to do to stop the slander. I then saw an image in my mind of taking a bunch of flowers to Jenny. At first I struggled with this solution. I thought: 'You are joking! Why should I take this woman who has been slandering me a bunch of flowers?' Eventually, I listened and responded to what came to me.

When I reached Jenny's house with the flowers, I was understandably feeling uncomfortable, as the last time I had seen her she had screamed at me with all sorts of accusations in front of a group of people whilst my family were present. Before I got out of the car, I heard in my mind: 'Write her a note saying you are sorry.' I thought: 'How can I say sorry when I don't feel I've done anything wrong?' Then I had a sense that I was only to say: *I was sorry that she had been hurt*. This I could accept because it was the truth. So I wrote the note, put it with the flowers, approached the front door and rang the bell. I really didn't want to do it, but knew I had to listen to what I had heard in my heart. It was an adventure in a sense, not knowing if I'd be abused again! Anyway, she wasn't home. Thank God!

The next day I saw Jenny at a group we both attended. Although I didn't want to go, I had a strong feeling that I was meant to attend the group that day. When she saw me, she said: 'I see you have learned your lesson!' At that moment, I had a strong sense not to retaliate, as I heard in my mind: 'Don't say anything.' I said quietly, 'I have learned much!'

I actually felt a sense of self-respect, having avoided going into battle with her. I knew that she could only see the situation from her perspective. There was peace from that day forward … no 'fiery darts' being launched at me, no more reports of her criticising me and I could feel the difference in my body—no more feeling those prickles on my skin. You can see what I learned and what I gained, and there was more to gain.

The power of perspective to defuse a battle
So there are cases where no matter what you say or do, some people will want to continue in a struggle with you; that's their choice! However, there can be no battle or struggle between people when you respect that everyone has a right to their perspective and opinion and don't argue with it! Accepting that everyone is entitled to their perspective, even if you don't agree, develops respect and peace. This can defuse arguments and battles.

Perhaps if you listen to their perspective without interrupting, they may listen to your point of view. There could also be a possibility you may see the situation differently after you have listened. Obviously, if they are being abusive, let them know you are open to hearing them but not while they are acting in that way. Then walk away from them as it does no-one any good by allowing abuse to continue.

I had to walk away from Jenny eventually as she hadn't been open to having a conversation and had been abusive. Jenny did see the situation differently six months later at which point she phoned and said: 'Are you still my friend?' She said, 'I now realise that I projected all my unresolved anger that I had felt with my mum on to you. You appeared to me as an authority figure as she was in my life! I am sorry.' I could hardly believe what I was hearing from the woman. I was stunned. That was the last thing I expected, but you can see what is possible if you leave a safe space for people who have abused you to say sorry.

Many years later, Jenny attended a seminar I was presenting and resolved much of her inner tension and struggle with people from her childhood. Within weeks, she rang and excitedly told me that the people she literally couldn't tolerate before the seminar no longer triggered her anger. She saw them completely differently and felt peaceful in their presence. I was thrilled to see how much we had both grown since gaining a life-giving perspective.

I share more information and practical ways to gain perspective in Chapter 33 as I realise people have been unaware of how important this in their relationships and often end up being stuck with only their perspective.

Regaining clarity, peace and unity
To do this, I need to take time away from what I am doing and ask my Divine Counsellor to reveal what I need to deal with in myself to free up a clear space for me to gain another perspective. It is cleaning up and clearing out everything inside of me so there is room made to regain my peace, strength and centre. It's a little like a wardrobe that is filled to capacity with old clothes. Before any new clothes can be put into your wardrobe, you need to make room for them.

I start by becoming aware of how I have been left feeling and what I believe about myself or the situation. All this is better revealed and healed than buried and burning, ready to explode unexpectedly one day and start another battle. I know from experience! Only after I have regained clarity and peace do I make a time that is appropriate with the person I have battled with in the hope of reconciliation. I make sure I never use the 'you' word, as it implies judgement. Then, if appropriate, I apologise for what I said, the way I may have spoken or for whatever has hurt the person.

When I went to apologise to the people in question, I found that they were always gentle with me and very forgiving. In most cases, my actions melted down walls and barriers that had strained these relationships for years. I approached them seeking true reconciliation, not wanting anything from them. I just wanted to 'clean up' anything

I had done to cause disharmony or hurt in them.

I wanted to remain in the Light and was encouraged or rather warned to do so when I was given this image in my mind one day. I saw a house with a veranda that was full of Light and Presence. I sensed I was in this house, in fact on the veranda. I felt safe, secure and very much at peace. But when I looked outside the veranda, it was dark. When I stuck my face outside this veranda, it almost got blown off! The message of this image was very clear to me. I needed to remain within the boundaries of the house that was full of Light. I knew without doubt that this for me was the house of God. In his house and Presence, I felt complete, and had no need of anything else. My attitudes, motives and responses were totally different from this place compared to moving into the darkness. The darkness for me was filled with terror and fear, the absolute opposite of Presence and Peace.

When I remained in the Presence and applied what I have learned over the years, my whole family has changed from suffering, sickness, disaster and disconnectedness to health, blessings and connectedness. This doesn't mean that I don't face what I used to call struggles from time to time but I now see them as an adventure as I know they can be transformed when I ask Wisdom for help.

You can now be encouraged when struggles come your way if you see them as an adventure with Wisdom.

2

Understanding Feelings and Using Them Constructively!

Anger

I used to be scared of anger. I was once totally unaware of what I am about to share with you, but understanding this emotion has enabled me to use it constructively instead of destructively. I discovered that:

> *Anger is the natural emotional response to a wrong suffered (or perceived wrong suffered). It is an emotion that is neither good nor bad.*

That's important to understand, as many people have felt they are wrong or bad as a result of their anger or someone else' anger. There is an appropriate place for righteous anger. *Anger is a powerful energy.* You may have discovered already that used in the wrong way it can very quickly deplete your energy, leaving you exhausted and feeling bad. Therefore, it is vitally important to remember that it is *what we do with the anger* that is important. It can cause harm to others or us by *repressing* it or *expressing* it in a destructive manner. Let's look at the consequences of dealing with anger in these two ways:

Repressing anger can damage you:
- emotionally, leaving you feeling depressed, irritable, frustrated and with an inability to cope
- physically, by leading to ulcers, high blood pressure, colitis, insomnia and chemical imbalances.

Expressing anger in a destructive manner can:
- destroy relationships
- leave you feeling guilty and bad, often leading into judgement and hatred of self, others and our Creator.

Anger can come from *beliefs about ourselves* as a result of a situation. When we encounter the Truth and Presence, anger dissolves. Anger from minor offences can be relinquished when we listen to the other person's perspective and gain God's perspective. Anger can sometimes be resolved through discussion, agreement and forgiveness.

Righteous anger is appropriate and justified at times, especially when we are being treated badly or suffer abuse. There are many wise sayings in Scripture that tell us to be angry, but not to sin (think, say or do harm), to not let the sun go down on our anger, and that when we are slow in becoming angry, we have great understanding. We are also told to put away all bitterness, anger, wrangling and slander towards others. Instead, we are instructed to be kind to one another, even tender-hearted, forgiving one another as we have been forgiven by our Creator through his Son whilst unjustly being crucified.

As I have already shared, when I had sudden outbursts of uncontrolled anger and rage, I would feel better initially, but would later feel bad and guilty, particularly when others were left feeling hurt. I could always tell because they avoided me. This made me frightened of anger and I learned to suppress it. No wonder I found life so painful–I was retaining all the unresolved anger inside myself. June told me when I was ministering to her that she felt her anger as trapped in a room deep inside her. She said the only relief she felt from the suppressed anger was when she cut herself. After a guided healing meditation, peace flooded her and the desire to cut herself disappeared! How to be guided in a Healing Meditation is shared in Chapter 16.

On reflection, I now understand why there was tension within me and my family, as we were all burying our feelings. We were wanting everything to be all right, and at peace, but what we were doing only made things worse. Thank God we now feel safe to express all our feelings in a respectful, non-judgemental manner. The tension and fear has dissolved and there is a peace between each other which is so sweet. This I might add has been quite a journey for us all, but well worth taking! Anger is such an important emotion that I have devoted an entire chapter (Chapter 26) to it in the hope that this information will change many lives for the better.

Frustration
Most of the people I have assisted experience frustration in their lives. It is a very common emotion. In most cases, people feel powerless or helpless and believe they can't do anything about the situations in their lives. This then can build into anger, resentment and eventually a deep sadness and belief that the situation is hopeless. This usually leads to despair.

Can you imagine having the privilege of watching people experience release from all these feelings and beliefs? When they experience the Presence that has everything they ever desired nothing else matters at that moment. All frustration dissolves. There is contentment, security and peace and a deep knowing that somehow 'all is well' despite not knowing what will happen in the future about their situations. Now I call that awesome!

I used to experience a great deal of frustration, wanting others to change. The great news is that little by little I have come to learn the power of acceptance and respecting other's right to be as they choose to be. This is very freeing and powerful for both me and other people.

A turning point came when I had exhausted every means of pointing a member of the family in the 'right' direction. I literally gave up. When I expressed my feelings of utter powerlessness and frustration, I heard a voice say to me: 'I know just what you mean.' It was like a lightbulb going on in my mind, and the frustration just melted away. I knew in my heart at that moment that the Presence who I knew was my Creator really knew how I felt because he had felt the same way with me. He had to wait a long time for me to respond to his ways! All my frustration and self-righteousness melted away at that moment. I sensed that I was to stand by the person and just love them as they were, unconditionally. That action released the tension that came from frustration in our relationship and the very desire of my heart began happening. It's amazing what happens when you let go and let Unconditional Love, take over.

Rage
My experience with rage is that it builds up from unexpressed anger and is like an atomic bomb ready to explode when triggered! It causes devastation as one is often out of control and it can even lead to murder from a sudden, impulsive action. It can terrify others, leaving them in shock. My husband said that he felt like he'd been burnt by a blowtorch after I exploded in rage one night. Thank God I have a forgiving husband and that I have not only learned about my feelings, but have been released from the underlying triggers that set me off. My patient husband is very grateful too!

Hatred
I realise now how many have held hatred in their hearts. It has often been buried and they can be quite shocked to realise that they still feel hatred in unresolved memories that surface. Many feel they have a

right to hate the person because of what was done. I share with them that it is all right to *hate what people do*, their actions, but *not hate the person*. Surely it's better to deal with our hatred constructively and then commit the person to the Just Judge, the Presence. I tell people that if they allow hatred to remain in them, they usually only attract more of what they are harbouring.

Murderous feelings
When the buried emotions of hatred, bitterness, resentment, rage and revenge are triggered and suddenly erupt like a volcano spewing out of control over others (who are often not the real cause of the emotions) they cause devastation. Many people I have assisted have experienced this devastation. They feel crushed, shattered and dead. This affects them in every area of their life. Many others who have been abused emotionally, physically or sexually discover they have deep wounds with feelings of hatred, rage and *murder* 'for out of the heart comes evil intentions, murder...' Left unresolved, these feelings bring 'death' in one form or another to both the victim and the perpetrator.

Some time ago on the front page of *The Age* there was a young man who confessed to murdering his mother. He said he had hated his mother since he was a child. He had been left out of the family photos and believed he didn't matter, and had felt manipulated and controlled by her through her wealth all his life. He had waited until just recently when he could take his revenge out on her. He doped her food and murdered her, bashing her to death. He said he was like a mad dog, out of control, but felt released afterwards. What a way to come to release! If only he had known how to recognise these feelings of rejection and hatred, and deal with them constructively as I share with you in this book, it would have dissolved those murderous feelings. He will now no longer be free to bring up his young son and his wife has to carry the burden of all that has happened as he was sentenced to many years in jail.

We leave ourselves open to torment when we harbour these emotions. Murderous feelings can be a result of abuse happening over a period of time which is usually suppressed. I remember one of my sisters teased, belittled and embarrassed me time and time again when I was growing up. I didn't know how to respond so I tried to ignore what she did, but deep inside I was so hurt and full of anger and resentment.

One day she embarrassed me one time too many and I completely lost control of all the emotions I had buried. I attacked her and grabbed her around the neck. I remember feeling like I wanted to murder her at that moment. Fortunately, my mother turned up and broke us apart. Many years later my sister asked me to forgive her for the years of teasing. I also asked for her forgiveness because of my reaction. We're good friends now, thank God! Have you ever heard yourself or others say, 'I could murder him!' after some injustice or abuse? Sometimes it isn't just words.

I recently had a phone call from one of my daughters who was in shock. She had just heard that her hairdresser was murdered on the weekend. Apparently, the young man she had been with was under the influence of drugs. The police found him with cuts all over his body. What if this young man had dealt with his feelings and thoughts? So many lives are destroyed as a result of unresolved negative emotions that are often projected on innocent people.

Another lady rang me to say she was furious. After listening to how furious and even enraged she felt as a result of what happened with her husband, I asked if she wanted some help in resolving her feelings. After a hesitant 'yes,' I took her through the Three Perspectives Exercise (which is shared at the end of this chapter). As she expressed her feelings to the person in her mind's eye, she said she felt like she could murder him by splitting his head with an axe. As much as you and I don't want to hear this, it is better to admit what's already there than to suppress it, only to have it explode out in a murderous rage. It was stunning to hear the change in her voice and calm replace the rage within as I asked her to listen to Wisdom's perspective. When she had completed the exercise, I asked her how she felt about the person she had wanted to murder. She said she felt sorry for him. Compassion had replaced murder. She had gained clarity as she emptied her feelings and listened to another perspective. Another relationship, and possibly a life, saved!

Fear
So many people experience fear these days. We can become fearful just by watching the daily news which is often filled with frightening stories about terrorism, shooting rampages and people being hurt on the streets. Fear is also experienced in our relationships when we feel judged, rejected or abandoned. Terror is an extreme form of fear that can leave us feeling paralysed, usually through trauma and shock. There is healthy fear, which is meant to protect us, such as a child feeling frightened as her father sternly warns her not to touch fire for her own good. Chapter 8 is devoted to this topic as we need to know how they can be dissolved and how to respect healthy fears.

Feelings of being numb or frozen
Just recently I heard an elderly lady tell her grandchild she was 'too sensitive' and that she needed this 'knocked' out of her. This lady later shared with me how her life had been full of situations where she felt she could do nothing. She said after a lot of heartache and a great deal

of crying she realised how futile this was. She then made a decision never to cry or feel again. She said it was the only way she knew how to survive in life. When asked on another occasion how she felt about some of the stories she shared, she said she didn't feel anything anymore; she just felt numb! That's a terrible way to live from my perspective, but this lady didn't know of any other way of coping. This feeling dissolved as she let go of her decision never to cry or feel again.

Many people I have assisted over the years who have suffered abuse or trauma describe how numb and frozen they have felt in the relevant memories that surface. Some of these people have shared how they feel unable to love, listen, care and empathise with others, and find it difficult to have worthwhile and meaningful relationships. They just exist instead of living life to the full. They have often realised too how controlling and protective they have become almost to the point of smothering those under their care, which tends to drive people away and creates a self-fulfilled prophecy of believing that 'everyone always leaves them.' Through experiencing the Presence and Truth in these memories, the negative, numb, frozen feelings melt away, and these people are left feeling safe, peaceful and unconditionally loved. They usually share some time later how they have been able to develop meaningful relationships.

Sadness and grief
I believed until recently that sadness and grief would only be resolved over time and that can be the case in many situations. However, I am now aware that sadness and even grief can sometimes be released in an instant when we encounter the Presence, our greatest Comforter. When my father died, I felt I was totally alone with feelings of grief and sadness as I was told by some people that I shouldn't feel this way. Although Dad had helped many people, he too had suppressed

negative emotions that would erupt, especially after working huge hours and then drinking, often deeply wounding people around him.

Four days after Dad died, I went to mass, and during the service I silently cried out for help, sharing how alone I felt in my grief, feeling too vulnerable and weak to be able to speak at Dad's funeral service the next day. Within what seemed like a second, I experienced a deep peace seeping into my heart and whole being. As this calm flooded me, I realised all the sadness and grief had dissolved! I knew I was not alone. In my mind's eye, I felt like the hand of God had reached down and dried my tears. It was profound and so were the results.

After the service, a family member apologised for the way they had treated me and for not being there for me. Many people also told me how deeply their hearts were touched after my sharing about Dad, with some being brought to tears. I have never experienced a moment of grief since, but only peace when I think of Dad. It was an extraordinary experience of grace, one I hope many will experience if they only ask for help as I did.

Sadness is also often experienced as a result of believing: 'I can't do anything' about a painful situation. I have heard this hundreds of times. However, when we acknowledge what we believe and feel, and wait to hear the Truth, sadness can just disappear. Some people have even burst out laughing at the end of a healing meditation. I remember one such time when an elderly lady came seeking help. After sharing for some time how devastated she felt, with tears pouring down her face, the very picture of despair, she said she believed the situation was hopeless and that she couldn't do anything. I then asked her to allow the Spirit of Truth to reveal his perspective. A few minutes later, she burst into laughter even though her cheeks were still wet from all her tears. She laughed and laughed. She shared that what she had seen in her mind's eye as she listened was totally opposite to what she had been thinking beforehand. She was left in absolute amazement at the change and at the peace she now felt.

In these cases, and in many others I've seen, these words apply from Scripture: 'I will turn their mourning into joy, and will comfort them, and make them rejoice from their sorrow.'

How feelings can lead to awareness, healing and peace
How eternally grateful I am that I now know how feelings can lead to awareness, healing, freedom and peace. Whenever I am off centre, even in small incidents in life, I deal with myself in this way. Otherwise, everything seems to get worse. I observe, acknowledge and accept all my feelings and beliefs and then ask for Truth's perspective. Waiting, listening or sensing what comes to me usually transforms and dissolves all the negative feelings and beliefs. I'm left feeling the Presence and Peace again. My life gets back on the right track and everything begins to flow. What a difference this has made to my life and to those around me. Thank God I no longer drive off in the middle of the night, lost in my emotions, or suddenly burst forth in anger or rage, often leaving the other person in shock and devastation.

Learn how to deal with painful emotions instead of running from them or projecting them on others. They will lead you to what you believe and then you can gain Wisdom's perspective and experience peace.

As I listened to a young man being interviewed on TV, he shared that he and his wife had dealt with painful emotions by taking prescription drugs. He looked like a zombie. Apparently, he was still smoking cannabis. He went on to share how his wife had died a few years earlier after overdosing on those drugs. Despite still obviously being under the influence, he wanted to alert others to the consequences. Taking drugs to feel good or cover up negative emotions is far too common. If only these people knew how to deal with their negative, painful feelings constructively as I have shared, what a difference it could have made to their lives.

Some steps to discover the Truth which dissolves negative feelings
When you become aware that you are struggling with yourself and/or others in a difficult or painful situation, the following brief guideline can help you use your feelings to lead you to healing. You may not feel your emotions very intensely, but may just have a sense of the feelings. That is enough. Don't judge your feelings; accept all of them. Please go gently as you are dealing with your heart, which can be very fragile. Allow an hour or so and find a private, quiet place.

Be aware of the situation that is causing emotional pain. A memory may occur or you may sense blackness, numbness or blankness in your mind. Ask the Divine Counsellor, the Spirit of Truth, to guide you in every step ... which makes it safer and easier.

Ask what you *feel* as a result of the situation or memory.
Ask what you *believe* as a result of these feelings.
***Accept* what comes to your mind.**
Ask the *Divine Counsellor for his perspective and truth.*
***Wait and listen* to what you sense, hear or feel ...** You may have a thought, hear words, see a light and/or sense a Presence. You may experience a change or breakthrough in many ways. Waiting patiently is important. If you listen to and respond to this truth (not doubting), you will see a change for the better, either profoundly or subtly. The Truth will set you free! All the painful feelings in your mind, emotions and body should be released.

If nothing has changed, ask to be shown any blockages or obstacles. These represent unexpressed anger, rage, hatred, unforgiveness, judgements and decisions. Again allow time to listen to anything that is revealed and deal with what is revealed appropriately. It is possible that you may just need to express your feelings in greater depth, which has certainly been the case with many people, including myself. Refer to Chapter 5 on Blockages and Obstacles for further help. The following Three-way Perspective Exercise can also remove any blockages.

Three-way Perspective Exercise: a powerful freeing meditation
This exercise should only be done in your mind's eye with the intention of bringing peace and reconciliation. You will listen firstly to yourself, then secondly to those who have hurt or offended and then thirdly to the Divine Counsellor's perspective. Then you will have listened to three perspectives. You can use this exercise very effectively in any situation where you are aware of negative feelings towards others and even yourself. Ask the Divine Counsellor to guide each of these steps to gain clarity and peace:

- Ask to bring into your mind's eye anyone with whom you need to resolve your feelings and thoughts.
- Look into their eyes and honestly, either silently or aloud, tell the person/people how you were left *feeling* as a result of what happened and what you believed about yourself as a result. Tell them what you'd like to do to them! (This will release any suppressed anger and is always done with the intention of gaining peace and truth.)
- Ask to be shown what that person/people would say to you in response. Look into their eyes.
- Ask the Divine Counsellor's perspective and truth about the person, yourself or the situation. If necessary, ask for the ability to forgive so you can be released and restored.

Feelings and everyday life
Use all of your feelings constructively, both your negative and positive feelings, but *NEVER* let them dominate or control you, *as feelings are only an indicator of what you are thinking or believing* in any given situation. What if you misunderstood the situation? Use the exercise above to experience the truth. Another simple tool when you are upset is to ask the person what they mean. In other words, listen to their *perspective*.

We are called to live by faith, not feelings. However, we have explored the negative effects of suppressing your feelings so learn to express them constructively and cultivate gratefulness for all of them. I have just read an eye opening book called the Molecules of Emotions, written by scientist Candace B.Pert Ph.D. which powerfully demonstrates the influence our emotions have on our whole being. For me this confirms yet again why we need to process our negative emotions quickly and constructively to avoid disease being created in our bodies!

Let your experience help others
Your heart will be softened as you become real about your feelings, and you will be able to have much more tolerance, patience and understanding with others who struggle. Self-righteousness disappears as you gain Wisdom's perspective and you become aware of how often you may have experienced mercy. You will be able to let others express their feelings when struggling because you will realise how healing this has been for you.

This is exactly what has happened in my family. Boy oh boy, when we began getting real about our feelings, it seemed we were being torn apart! The opposite was true though because we all began to hear each other in truth, and listen to all those feelings that had been hidden.

In Chapter 21, 'How to Develop Healthy Relationships,' I discuss other keys that make a profound difference in relationships. For instance, you will become aware of when to speak, how to speak and body language. As a result of applying what you learn, you will be more confident to not only express your feelings but know how to effectively listen to others expressing their feelings when struggling. Many of us can feel uncomfortable with other people's negative feelings and often don't know what to do to help. All we need to do is really listen to them without judgement but with unconditional love.

The ultimate role model

My first role model as a child was Doris Day, the actress. I loved her happy disposition and songs. In fact, people have said that I remind them of Doris Day. It is interesting how we become like those we focus on. Fortunately, I now have the ultimate role model: Jesus. I am grateful that he was real and expressed all his feelings as I now do. I also encourage other people to do the same.

Jesus experienced feelings of anger and resentment when his temple was being used as a marketplace. He grieved and wept over Jerusalem. He grieved to the point of death in the Garden of Gethsemane when struggling with what was being asked of him. He said that the spirit indeed was willing but the flesh was weak. But he didn't deny his feelings. After expressing his feelings in his struggle, he asked if it was possible that the cup pass from him. However, despite the intensity of the emotions and struggle, he let go of what he wanted and said yes to his Father's will: '… yet not what I want but what you want.'

Do you have a role model? What is their life like? Maybe you might consider Jesus as a role model, or another person who you can identify with who has integrity.

Discovering how *you* deal with your feelings
Do you take time to listen to your feelings when upset or hurt? Who do you share these feelings with? Are you open to sharing them with Unconditional Love who is also the Divine Counsellor, allowing time to experience perspective and truth? This is a productive rather than destructive way of dealing with feelings. Projecting judgements and condemnations on ourselves or others often leads to hatred, resentment, bitterness, jealousy, envy, anger, hopelessness and despair. This way of expressing our feelings only further separates us from love and peace and opens the door to disaster in our relationships. I know because of personal experience …

I helped a lady named Joan who wanted to experience freedom from most of the negative feelings I have just described. But there was still a part of her that was resisting listening in the healing meditation session. This was because she believed that if she let go of her negative feelings and forgave the person involved they would get away with what they had done and there would be no justice. I asked if she would like the ultimate Defence Attorney to assist her. She immediately said yes as she felt justice would be done. She was then willing to listen. Through the healing meditation session she acknowledged all her negative feelings and beliefs, and expressed her anger. As she was willing to listen to her Defence Attorney's perspective, her negative feelings all dissolved and she was left feeling compassion for the person who had hurt her. Peace was restored, and she felt as light as a feather. Her whole appearance changed as she relaxed.

Rejoice and be thankful (You have to be joking!)
In the midst of many difficult times as I felt frightened, frustrated and powerless, I remember hearing a song that said: 'Rejoice in the Lord *always*.' I felt like saying: 'You're joking! How can I rejoice when I

often felt overwhelmed?' But I eventually came to understand that I was to rejoice and be thankful because I could ask for the greatest Helper, someone who could save me, take over and guide me in these situations. It felt like I was drifting in threatening seas, often thrashing around trying to survive not knowing which wave (circumstance) could drown me. Wouldn't you be thankful and even rejoice if you felt like this and realised that help was available?

I also now realise how finding ***anything*** to be thankful for in difficult times helped me change my focus from complaining and feeling sorry for myself to focusing on something I could be grateful for at that time. Being thankful taught me how to see **what I had** rather than **what I didn't have**. As my attitude changed for the better so did my life!

I began believing, despite how I felt, that all things could be brought to good despite not 'liking' what I was going through at the time. I stopped resisting and struggling and began accepting that I didn't understand 'why' I was going through these trials. It wasn't until much later on that I came to realise I had one opportunity after another to face my deepest fears and experience Peace. I also learned to cling to and trust Wisdom. As I gradually grew in faith, thankfully many of my family, friends and those who came to the seminars also experienced Peace. ALL things were being brought to good!

3

How Negative Feelings Can Lead to Peace

'Over the top' emotions

What I am about to share with you may seem 'over the top,' but that is precisely why I *had* to discover why I had all these 'over the top' negative emotions that took me on such a rollercoaster ride throughout my life. When they surfaced, or more accurately erupted, often out of the blue, I was left feeling exhausted and often bad when I had caused a void in my relationships.

To avoid causing an argument and destroying a relationship, I can remember driving off in the car in the middle of the night sobbing. I felt so alone, lost, angry and sad. I parked in a street somewhere and cried and cried, thumping my fist down on the dashboard of the car with anger, asking why, oh why did I feel so many of these horrible feelings. It felt like all of my emotions were gushing from every pore in my body from some internal bleeding. When the emotions subsided, I felt totally empty, abandoned and depleted, so I drove home and went to bed, but nothing was really resolved.

I later felt trapped, unable to justify or rationalise these emotions when I looked at the circumstances that had triggered them. How could just a few words have the power to release so many 'over the top' emotions! It seemed then that I couldn't prevent myself from reacting in this way. It was like I was on a merry go-round with the same emotions being triggered time and time again. I was fed up with feelings controlling me, but I had no idea then how to deal with myself. I then literally cried out for help … hoping that maybe God would be listening. I waited in silence then found myself drifting back to what I now know was the very first time that I had begun believing no one cared for me. I asked for the truth to be revealed in the darkness of this memory and experienced Light and Presence. Peace replaced all the emotional turmoil of not being cared for and feeling abandoned.

As time went by, I realised there had been a big foundational shift within me. Whenever similar situations or comments were experienced that used to trigger all those emotions, I felt at peace. There was no longer a hook to the past. I couldn't be triggered as there was nothing to trigger off within me.

Why we bury our feelings
One of the reasons for burying my feelings came as a result of frequently being told throughout my life that I was too emotional and too sensitive. As a result, I felt like I had no right to express my feelings and I didn't feel there was a compassionate, non-judgemental ear to hear me. I had no voice! As I said before, I learned to be frightened of my negative emotions and hated them. Many people I have assisted have felt the same way. So, it's vitally important to make a safe place for people to share their negative, painful feelings. Being listened to in a safe place is often all that is needed.

Other consequences of burying our feelings

Sudden outbursts of anger or rage
I remember when my husband and I were travelling around Canada,

the US, Mexico and Guatemala in a van with our friend Tim for six months. After a period of four months together, there was a moment at breakfast when Tim was pouring heaps of honey on his cornflakes and I went berserk! Tim fled and we didn't see him for a couple of days. No wonder! You might ask (as I later said to myself), why would anyone go berserk over such a ridiculously insignificant thing? Of course, it was not about too much honey!

On reflection, my husband and I realised how frustration had built up in us over the months as Tim always woke up at least an hour or more after our agreed time to get on the road again. Not only that, he would amble out of his tent and then ask us what was for breakfast, totally oblivious that he was holding us up yet again. Tim was a gentle soul but was in his own world with his own timing! We had a right to be angry, but going berserk was inappropriate. However, after that episode, Tim always woke up at our agreed time!

I now realise how often I have been late for appointments, also keeping people waiting! I too have been in my own world with my own timing! But thankfully, people have been very patient and haven't gone berserk at me! I'll share more about how to be aware of time in the chapter on how to develop healthy habits.

Recently, a young Asian man went berserk, shooting two dead and wounding five others in the very university and room where my son, who wasn't present, has tutorials. Apart from the two lives lost and the wounded, the other people involved were left traumatised. On reading about the perpetrator today, the article said he was prone to outbursts of anger, born out of frustration. He had a great deal of trouble with the English language and found the lecturer hard to understand. People found him hard to understand as well. His feelings of fear and frustration led to anger and rage, and then on the day he was to do a presentation, he went berserk. I wonder if he feared failing and the consequences. If only he had learned how to deal with those feelings and underlying beliefs before it was too late. If only everyone could experience Unconditional love and truth and realise that no one is *a failure* ... we only *fail at some things we can't yet do,* from which we can continue to learn.

Depression

I don't have to look very far these days to see the eyes and faces of what are clearly depressed people. They look lifeless and lost, like the walking dead! I often wonder what they are thinking, believing and feeling and if they have anyone to listen to them. If people have suffered abuse, shocks or traumas for many years, but have made a decision to 'just get on with life' and never listen to their heart or express and resolve the emotions within, they can become depressed and lifeless. They become disconnected from themselves. Other people withdraw and hide from life, not knowing how to communicate their feelings appropriately. They can often fear being hurt yet again. These ways of dealing (or rather not dealing) with feelings decreases our capacity to live, love and learn.

John shared with me how he wanted to run away and hide under a blanket because he couldn't find any solution to his problems, which had been going on for years. In actual fact, the thing he loved most in life was to go to bed. He explained no one could get to him there and he didn't have to deal with any problems. However, he couldn't just lie in bed all day and night and had to eventually face people and life and for him that was hard.

In the process of listening, he became open to allowing the Divine Counsellor to guide us to the root cause. After sharing how he felt in his present situations, memories holding similar feelings came to his mind. He felt the same fear and terror in these traumatic memories that were paralysing him in the present. I asked the Divine Counsellor:

'How true is it that John is all alone to deal with life?' John then became aware of a Presence with him, and at that moment, he knew he would never be alone to deal with life ever again.

When I asked if he still felt all those negative feelings which had been causing him depression, he hesitated for a moment to check. He was amazed, and I was delighted, as he shared that every negative feeling had dissolved. He just felt Peace as he revisited his present circumstances and the memories that had surfaced He said he felt a greater sense of wholeness and freedom. When he thought about dealing with people and problems, it no longer felt hard but rather light as he no longer felt alone.

If you ever feel depressed, be encouraged as you can now deal with your negative feelings and beliefs asking the Divine Counsellor to guide you and then reveal his truth and Presence. But also seek help from a counsellor you can trust and connect to if you need further assistance.

Physical Depletion

You will have read already from the stories I have shared how exhausted I have become, even to the point of burn out, when I don't deal with my feelings of anger, resentment and fear or when I feel that I have to be in control and responsible in my own strength for everyone. Many people have said how they feel like a heavy weight is pushing down on them, which has been released after letting go of judgements. Other people have seen an image of themselves with a ball and chain around their leg making everything hard going, which often relates to roles and decisions influencing them. At the conclusion of the healing meditation session when negative feelings, thoughts and any blockages have been released, I then ask the Spirit who brings life to flow through their bodies releasing them from the *consequences* of all that they have dealt with and restore their bodies. The exhaustion they felt then dissolves.

Other people have come seeking help with body pain. It has become apparent that the cells of our bodies retain memories because that's what is revealed after I ask the Divine Counsellor to drift them into the source of the pain. After resolving all that is revealed in the memory, the physical depletion and pain dissolves. It still blows me away when I witness the change and am able to assist people who are courageous enough to deal with whatever is going on in their bodies and minds.

Tristan came to me crippled with back pain and asking for help before considering surgery. I never know at such times what may happen, but I trust that we will be guided by the Divine Counsellor for the best outcome. As she drifted into the area of pain, she became aware of a memory when she was a little girl and had been badly hurt. She had felt alone and that no one was listening to how badly she was hurting. Two days later, the doctors discovered she had a broken arm. So how did this relate to the back pain?

She remembered then she had made a *decision* to be responsible for other people who were hurting. She didn't want anyone else to go through the pain of not being listened to and not being helped. I asked the Spirit of Truth to reveal 'how true it was that Tristan had to carry this responsibility on her own!' She then sensed the heaviness of this decision weighing her down. As she heard that this wasn't true and felt a Presence, she was able to let go of the decision to 'help others in her own strength *alone.*' She realised she was to ask Wisdom to guide her decisions to help others only when appropriate. She no longer felt alone. The heaviness she had sensed earlier lifted and she felt the pain in her body slowly dissipate from her head down through her spine and out through her feet. She was left feeling a lightness in her body and a peace. Awesome! It is such a privilege to watch people experience transformation in every area of their being.

I was with Chris one day and she sounded desolate. She said that her family had little or no money left to pay their bills and she didn't know what to do. I asked how she felt. At first she resisted sharing her feelings as it was unpleasant having to acknowledge them. Eventually she shared how trapped she felt. She also felt responsible and alone to sort out the problem. She felt God had abandoned her. Then she became aware, in her mind's eyes, of a satchel which was on her back, literally weighing her down and depleting her energies. It was full of all the responsibilities she had taken on over the years. She came to realise that she had to let go of it. The moment she let go, she had a sense of the satchel, which contained all the things she had felt responsible for, including herself, being lifted up into the sky. She realised how light she felt in her body instead of being weighed down. Her voice had even changed and she sounded full of life.

About an hour later, Chris rang to say some money was being sent to her, and another idea had presented itself that could bring money into the household. She had created space to receive. I was reminded of the words in the Bible that say if God looks after the birds of the air, how much more he wants to look after his children–all of us!

When I used to bury my feelings, I suffered from stomach ulcers, bowel problems and arthritis. All of these physical consequences have now disappeared since I began to apply what I am sharing with you in this book. What if some of your physical pain is linked to the stress of unresolved feelings, beliefs and decisions you made in the past that you may have forgotten about? Would you be willing to ask Wisdom to reveal anything in you that is causing you pain?

Over the years, I have seen most people come in physically depleted from fears, anxieties and all sorts of stress. Often in one session of expressing their feelings and beliefs and experiencing Truth and

Peace, they are physically transformed. They look younger, as though the wrinkles have faded and their faces look luminous. It's like a 'makeover' from the inside out! Try it and see!

Trapped and stuck in hurt

I remember walking down the hallway of my house one day and being totally frustrated because I was feeling hurt, yet again, over a particular situation. I didn't want to feel hurt and I wanted to be on good terms with the other person. I had forgiven them for what they had done over and over again, but there was no peace within me. As I called out in total frustration for help, I heard these words in my mind and have never forgotten them: 'You need to tell me why you need to forgive this person.' Immediately I felt at ease as I knew that God wanted to listen to all my hurt feelings and thoughts. It was like revealing a missing part of the puzzle.

It reminded me of a time when I saw a young child being told to make friends with the person that had hurt them without anyone first hearing their feelings. They were resistant and resentful. But as I discovered with a young child who had been hurt, all I had to do was listen to all her feelings, to understand, and then she was happy to forgive and make friends again.

I remember a young women sharing how she felt trapped and stuck but wanted to forgive her father for sexually abusing her. But no matter how hard she tried she couldn't forgive, even after dealing with her feelings. I silently turned to Wisdom and asked for help. The thought came to me that she could ask for the capacity Jesus had to forgive on the cross to flow through her to her father. She agreed to this happening and experienced an immediate release from this traumatic memory. All the pain and shame melted away. She looked so different. That's God!

4

Transforming Life by Transforming Thoughts and Beliefs!

I've heard people say that our life is what our thoughts make it, but we can have lots of thoughts come to our mind and I know not *every* thought can change our lives. However, *it is when our thoughts become our beliefs that our life changes, either for the better or worse and then what we believe often keeps occurring, until that belief is changed.* How important is it then that our beliefs are life giving, rather than negative attracting negative things into our lives.

I have just read an article sharing what stem cell Biologist Bruce Lipton has discovered, after years of research, about the influence beliefs can have in our lives. He says that our *beliefs,* true or false, positive or negative, can affect genetic activity and even alter our genetic code ... interesting!

I was unaware of what I was thinking–I just reacted!
I now know how unaware I was of my thoughts most of the time and their influence on my life. I rarely stopped long enough to discover if what I was thinking was the truth. I was so busy and preoccupied with life, not realising how powerfully my thoughts controlled the direction and quality of my life. I now realise thoughts can become *beliefs,*

beliefs lead to *feelings*, feelings lead to *words*, which lead to *actions* or *reactions* which can lead to *habits.* This is how *we influence and create our life and our destiny.*

I certainly was trapped in this cycle as the way I was acting or reacting to certain situations developed *habits* that controlled the quality of my life. A simple example is when I *thought* someone was judging me; I *believed* in some way that it was my fault. This made me *feel* insecure and defensive. I would act by slinking away or reacting. Whenever I reacted from negative thoughts, beliefs and feelings, it was always a disaster.

So over the years, through many experiences, I discovered that my thoughts and beliefs have the power to build or destroy, bringing either life or death in my life and my relationships. Negative thoughts and feelings appeared unannounced and I wasn't aware or present enough to even question if those thoughts had any foundation. I had no idea at first why I thought and felt as I did, but I was being controlled and dominated by them.

At last I made a decision to ask for help … from my Creator, as I was fed up with being so emotional and upset at certain times. I also felt alone and misunderstood when everyone else appeared to be fine. I wanted to find the path to real and lasting peace within me and needed new and constructive ways to deal with life and certain situations.

I thought I was living from the truth, but I knew something was amiss as there was no lasting happiness and little peace, as you will hear throughout this book. In many areas of my life, I had been travelling down the path that basically restricts, stunts, robs, cripples and kills. This was, as I discovered later, because much of what I thought and believed about myself and life *was grounded on lies* from which grew deception, doubt, discouragement, despondency and even despair at times–even to the point of considering driving into a lamp post one night.

My first attempt to transform my mind was totally unsuccessful!
I began to study the power of positive thinking and was always looking for the positive way to see situations, no matter what was going on in my life. I couldn't be honest about my negative feelings and avoided people who had them. I was living from unrealistic expectations of myself and others. I was trying to make everything 'right' in my life because I felt it had all been so wrong ... including myself! If I reacted to situations in a negative way, I would feel ashamed of myself because I felt I had once again failed to change myself. Have you ever felt like this?

Past unresolved experiences were controlling my mind!
I began to realise that many negative thoughts and beliefs I had, which 'seemed' true, were unable to be transformed in the present no matter how much I tried with one method or another. I know now that certain situations or words were triggering *unresolved* situations from the past. I sometimes felt like I was a time bomb, never knowing when my emotions would erupt.

I discovered these unresolved situations were buried in the inner most part of my mind: my subconscious and unconscious. Sometimes areas of my memories that surfaced were just blankness and darkness. I listened to these 'parts' of my memory as I would listen to myself in any other memory that would surface. I discovered many lies and negative feelings along with decisions I had made about life, which I had totally forgotten about.

Thankfully, as these memories surfaced, were heard and resolved, Truth and Peace were experienced. I then discovered when similar situations occurred, I felt only peace as there was no longer anything in the past that could be triggered off in the present. I was stunned … it was like a miracle. Actually, it WAS a miracle! Later on, as I began assisting others in this way, I witnessed them experiencing this miracle of transformation within their mind and emotions.

Transformation needed at a deeper level
There had been many times I related to Paul in the Scriptures when he said, 'I do not do what I want, but I do the very thing I hate.' I had been shaped by my past experiences and had become a prisoner to them! For example, when my husband worked long hours, six days a week in real estate, as ironically my father had, I would be fine for long periods of time. I would rationalise any thoughts of being abandoned and get cross at myself if I had any negative feelings (which I now realise was denying them!) It was my attempt to be perfect: tolerant, patient and understanding. However, every now and then, out of the blue, I would erupt, exploding in anger and accusing my husband of not caring about me, which of course only separated us further. The emotional pain and tension I felt was extreme—I felt like I was being torn apart. I felt like leaving our marriage. I believed the pain would subside if I was on my own.

However, I remember asking Wisdom at that cross road: 'What you want me to do?' The word that came straight into my mind was: 'Stay!' I gained a certain peace from accepting things just as they were, but I realise my call for help was heard as within two weeks of that day I experienced a deep release. Thank God I didn't run away, but stayed and faced the source of my pain.

Release and blessing
Dorothy, a dear colleague of mine, helped me discover the source of my thoughts of being alone and abandoned through a healing meditation. What a relief and what a change! *I never felt alone or*

abandoned again.

After this experience, my relationship with my husband changed dramatically, as I no longer reacted when he worked long hours. I could now 'see' that my husband was being responsible to provide for us all. His intentions were only for the very best for our family. It was like a light had been switched on in every area of my mind that previously was in the dark in relation to these beliefs. I was able to accept the situation as it was, releasing the circumstances to the Presence.

A short time after this healing experience, I was in the bathroom and heard these words in my mind: 'You are going to hear something, but don't say anything!' I thought, 'Where did that come from?' I sensed it was from God, but didn't really know. I went out to the kitchen and my husband said: 'I've got something to tell you. I'm going to sell my business!' I knew I was not to utter a word! I know now that Wisdom was sorting out how Bruce and I could have more time together effortlessly. I had tried for years prior to this point without success!

Bruce then sold the business and stayed on as an employee. His workload was lightened and he was able to spend more time with me and the rest of the family. As a result of listening to the instructions 'stay' in the marriage, I received release and blessings. This is a perfect example—one I have now experienced many times, as have others—that as my inner world changed, so did my outer world. Our relationship had suffered all those years because I believed the lie that I was abandoned, alone and not loved. Hopefully, my story will help you, or someone you love, see how release from negative beliefs and the associated pain can change.

Changed from a snake into a lamb!
Now I understand more fully the words of Paul in Romans 7 about inner conflict. For instance, when I had felt hurt, often my response would be to judge others and harbour what I thought was justifiable resentment. Some of my sudden biting comments in retaliation would be like a snake squirting venom over the person who I believed had hurt me. But later on, I would feel bad and realise that I needed help; my mind and reactions needed some transformation as I was destroying my relationships!

These words spoke loud and clear to me: 'For those who live according to the flesh set their minds on the things of the flesh (acting how I thought), but those who live according to the Spirit set their MINDS on the things of the Spirit (who gives us all we ever want!) To set the MIND on the flesh is death, but to set the MIND on the Spirit is life and peace. For this reason, the MIND that is set on the flesh is hostile to God; it does not submit to God's law—indeed it cannot.' I know I have at times been like a rebellious young kid, doing what I thought was justifiable!

The snake in me has become more like a lamb ... because the Presence who I believe is the Lamb of God has transformed my mind and my reactions. Now that I know how the negative thoughts and feelings can be dissolved and I can experience Peace, the negative reactions and cutting remarks have disappeared. I deal with them constructively before squirting them out over others. Now, thank God, I have been taught the art of healthy communication, particularly in conflict! Even when I slip up, I now know that this is an opportunity to just say sorry. I found this very difficult to say in the beginning as I was so defensive and couldn't bear to think I was wrong. I now feel grateful for those who loved me unconditionally, even while I was not easy to love.

Allowing our mind to be guided in a superhuman manner

I know people who have used mind-control techniques to change their mindsets so they will prosper financially, physically or in relationships. This is man operating on a human level, guided by human reason, and it can often lack Wisdom's balance—gentleness yet power. People can experience change to some extent, but it can eventually lead them to exhaustion and despair. One young man focused all his mind and will power on becoming physically fit, attending the gym almost daily. He looked amazingly fit but that didn't help his emotional and mental state as he eventually committed suicide. I believe if he had experienced Truth and Peace within, and had allowed Wisdom to guide him, this may not have happened.

I discovered that after spending time each day meditating and being still in the Presence, shortly after my mind would be filled with creative ideas and insights. They came to me effortlessly and influenced and changed lives. I knew this was beyond my normal human capacity but that Wisdom was enabling me to think and act in a superhuman manner. I felt very grateful and humbled. I became aware that our souls (mind, heart and spirit) could be led to levels far higher than those which man's reason could have brought it!

I remember Jennifer coming to me one day feeling frightened, alone and insecure because she felt everyone would be against her at a family meeting she had to attend the next day to decide whether she could visit her mother. As I listened to her thoughts, beliefs and feelings thoroughly, which took about 30 minutes, I asked her to listen to the Spirit of Truth. As she listened, her face changed. She said she felt like she was enveloped in Light. She no longer felt alone as there was a Presence with her. All the negative feelings had dissolved. She knew she wouldn't be alone at the meeting the next day. She burst into laughter as she announced she now felt like *superwoman!* We all laughed. She knew that she would be guided in a superhuman way now. She later told me that she entered the meeting the next day with a calm confidence and feeling totally supported. The meeting went very well!

The influence of our formative years on our thoughts
It is said that during the first five years of our lives, we are basically formed psychologically. It is during this time that we establish foundational beliefs that can influence our life either for good or bad. The trouble is that not many of us realise or are aware just how powerfully these foundational beliefs influence our present day situations. In fact, we have simply picked up by osmosis thoughts and feelings from our parents or others and believe that they are ours.

Our mind, it is said, is the greatest computer of all so the data received, if believed to be true, directs and controls our lives. Whenever there is disorder in our lives, then there may be beliefs/lies in the unconscious, subconscious memories held in one's mind that need to be revealed so Truth can be established. It is truly a divine encounter that is necessary, just as Jennifer experienced. Wisdom, who created us, can change the damaging data in our memory bank and replace it with the truth that will restore our mind with the correct data.

No more 'struggles' with negative thoughts
I don't struggle with negative thoughts anymore, as this used to bring tension and confusion into my mind leaving me feeling exhausted and frightened. I have learned now to be aware of any negative thoughts, never allowing them to harbour in my mind or take root there but rather redirecting them to Wisdom for his truth. They usually then dissolve and so does the tension and confusion. However, if these thoughts persist, then I know it's time to go to the root of the negative thoughts, often in a memory, through a healing meditation.

Daydreaming?
Many of us have experienced daydreaming. Our minds have drifted off somewhere else and we are not present. Have you found yourself listening to another person (particularly if they don't draw breath and just keep talking at you) and although you're physically present, your mind has drifted off somewhere else? If we do this often, it can become a bad habit. In my case, I used to be *unaware* that I often wasn't present but focused elsewhere, daydreaming. I remember occasions where my children would often talk to me, asking me a question and trying to get my attention, but I wasn't present and although I would make little comments like I knew what they were saying, they would become frustrated saying, 'Mum, you're not listening,' and they were right. I know now what it's like when people aren't present to me when I am talking to them and they don't listen!

I have now shared this realisation with my adult children and apologised for the times I wasn't present to them. This will hopefully help them remember to be present to their children. I am grateful I realise how important it is to be present to others now, instead of being lost in my own thoughts, daydreaming.

Out of one's mind ... blank, dark, grey areas of one's memory
Have you heard people make comments like: 'I think they are out of their mind!'? This can actually be true. Let me explain. As we have assisted people in a healing meditation, they become aware of memories that appear as being blank, dark or even grey. (Up to this point, people have often been unaware that this is an area of memory that has held negative feelings and beliefs, usually as a result of terrifying or traumatic experiences.) They have often felt this area of their mind is 'outside' of themselves and somewhat disconnected.

However after the blockages are moved (see Chapter 5 on

Blockages and Obstacles), people experience Presence, Truth and Light in what was blank, dark or grey memories. There is no feeling of being disconnected either as all the negative feelings, beliefs, and trauma they held dissolve. Then people 'see' the situation that had been challenging them in their present life with peace. Changing the past unresolved memories changes the present and hopefully the future.

Finding life hard and difficult!
Those who have discovered they have lost or repressed memories as a result of the effects of trauma, unresolved emotions and beliefs usually find life hard and difficult. It is as though they are journeying through life with only part of their mind present, and other 'parts of their mind' are blotted out from their conscious memory, leaving them feeling only partly alive. A part of them can often feel okay, but they are aware that another part of them feels heavy, lifeless, fearful, powerless and even dead! Some people have said they often feel like an outsider or they don't belong; they do not feel like a part of the human race. This often relates to those aspects of their minds that are separate from their conscious mind. This leaves many people feeling frustrated and in despair not knowing what is going on in them and how to find peace.

That was how I felt. I remember starting my journey to find freedom feeling exhausted. Life was hard at times, when I felt overwhelmed and burdened. I believed somehow that I was responsible for 'making things okay' and 'holding things together.' I remember feeling so tired that it was even hard to talk (which some may have been grateful for!) Basically, I had come to a point in my life where I was burnt out. I felt like I couldn't 'be responsible' for holding things together anymore. My body also showed symptoms of these feelings and was forcing me to stop. I had no idea then that I had taken on the roles of being responsible, guarding and saving everyone around me. I didn't realise I had taken over my Creator's role but eventually I came to experience the reality of the words 'when I am weak then he is strong.'

I realised I had to let go of these roles and in blind faith ask for help from God asking him to take over. I also asked for help and guidance to unravel why I was where I was and how to change. And as you will hear throughout the book, I was taken on the adventure of my life into the innermost recesses of my mind many times to experience release in memories and discover Peace, Presence and true Power.

Where is your mind focused?
I wonder how aware you are of what you are thinking and where you are focused? We can become so pre-occupied and consumed with the things of this world, the things we want and need, responsibilities and worries, that our minds can be on overload, cluttered and confused. Our minds can be only focusing on our outer needs. Then we can become hardened and disillusioned. I used to think, 'when my children are no longer so sick,' 'when my husband doesn't work so hard,' 'when my dad is healed,' 'when my children are happy,' then I'll find peace and can relax! Do you relate to this? This I discovered is a lie. I had to learn to focus on the Source of truth and wisdom.

On reflection, I realise whilst I was focused on and had my mind set on the things of the world only, it was as though a veil was over my mind, as in the days of Moses. As I began to turn within and seek the Source of peace, the veil was removed. I could then 'see clearly.' As I have watched others 'see clearly,' they look like they have had a 'makeover.' Their faces become transformed. They begin to reflect, like in a mirror, the Presence, Peace, Light and Truth rather than the fear, anxiety and doubts that were in their minds to begin with, which were creating a dark veil over their minds.

Some keys to retaining peace of mind
One key to retaining one's peace of mind is being thankful, despite the circumstances and what you think. One such example in my life was the day the healing ministry team I was involved with was closed down due to insurance concerns. I believed wholeheartedly in this work and had dedicated myself in a leadership role to caring for and nurturing the team. We had all seen such amazing results and transformations in people. On this day, I was awakened at 4.00 am and so began to pray for wisdom, as I was the representative of the team. All I heard in my heart was to ask questions at the meeting. These were certainly wise words because as a result of asking questions, I came to hear and understand where the other committee members were coming from and their fears.

During the meeting, I felt what I have come to know as God's presence and peace, as I was thanking him silently for his will. When the decision was made to discontinue the healing ministry, I heard these words quite clearly in my mind, 'Rejoice, I have set you free.' At the moment I heard these words, I had the physical experience of feeling as light as a feather. I also felt like I was being lifted above my chair. I felt totally at peace. This is not what I would have expected to feel under the circumstances!

However, after a few days, other thoughts and doubts began to creep into my mind. Instead of immediately taking these thoughts captive and asking for Wisdom's perspective, I allowed these negative thoughts and doubts to nest in my mind and, of course, they festered like a sore and tormented me as I struggled with them.

One of the thoughts was that this decision was so very wrong (my perspective!) The feelings these thoughts ignited were mainly anger and resentment. They took some time to wade through. It felt like I was in the middle of a whole lot of muck. Eventually the peace I had felt when the decision had been made to close the ministry returned, but it only occurred after I acknowledged and accepted all I thought and felt (emptying my mind and heart) and then asked for Wisdom's perspective. Now I understand why I was told to rejoice! I could have avoided all that pain and struggle if I had listened to this instruction and retained my peace of mind despite the circumstances. Lesson learned!

Another key to retaining peace of mind is not only listening to, but responding to Wisdom's instruction! Not long after the healing ministry was closed, I had another experience whilst away resting one weekend. I sensed a holy Presence, perhaps Jesus, walk past me as I sat on the ground reading. I know this sounds a little odd, but you have to have an experience like this to know what I am talking about! At that same moment, there was a 'knowing' that I was being asked to step aside from every commitment and group I was involved in.

Over a period of months, in obedience, I withdrew from all my commitments and groups. This, I later realised, created space for another wonderful plan that was about to evolve. A group of caring people I had been working with joined me in coming aside from everything to be still and wait in the presence of God. At the same time, we all decided to continue assisting people asking for our help. During this time, the way in which we worked with people changed gently to asking questions and inviting them to listen to themselves and then to listen to the Truth. After many months, the group grew and we felt led to establish an organisation called Agape Encounter, a non-profit organisation, that would go on to assist people from all backgrounds with experiencing Peace from their unresolved past, and equipping them with practical keys and principles for life.

Another key is not to worry!
I had begun realising the truth of these words from Philippians 4:4: 'Rejoice in the Lord always; again I will say Rejoice. Let your gentleness be known to everyone. The Lord is near. Do not worry about anything, but in everything by prayer and supplication with thanksgiving let your requests be made known to God. And the peace of God, which surpasses all understanding, will guard your hearts and your minds in Christ Jesus.' I remember at first thinking it was impossible not to worry. I was just human after all, but then I witnessed and experienced Peace replacing worry as I and others began to apply, practise and preserve with these instructions in our lives. It's worth it. Our lives changed for the better.

How creativity can flow from your mind
Creative ideas flow when you are communicating with the Creator of all things. This for me is the Source of all creativity. In fact, I have sometimes said, 'Slow down! I can't keep up with the flow of ideas!' So if your mind is dull and you feel bored and lifeless, you know now where to turn. Help is within you ... just ask as I did and begin to develop a real, honest and open relationship with the Creator of all creativity. Allow him to release you from the blockages and see what happens. But it is vital to make a decision as I did to take time daily to be still, to chat (pray), to listen to your thoughts and then the thoughts of the One who created everything. I believe you will then become aware of an increase in your creativity too.

What you believe will be done for you!
As only one example of the power of beliefs and how it can influence your life is when people have *believed they are responsible and it's their fault*. Either someone blamed them or they blamed themselves. It becomes etched in their mind and memory as the truth often as a

child. Through a healing meditation, people remember many occasions in life where they have *believed they are responsible and it's their fault.* It only stops reoccurring when these people experience Truth in these area of their memory.

For our life to become better our beliefs need to be founded on Truth in all areas of our mind: conscious, unconscious and subconscious. Dr Bruce Lipton says that only five percent of our lives is run using the conscious mind, and the other 95 percent is controlled by subconscious beliefs and habits.

My hope is that *all people* will become aware of Truth in every area of their mind and memory and will know the power they have to change their lives. I love these words and ask that they become a reality in my life and yours: 'I pray that the God of our Lord Jesus Christ, the Father of glory, may give you a *spirit of wisdom and revelation as you come to know him,* so that, with the *eyes of your heart enlightened,* you may *know what is the hope to which he has called you, what are the riches of his glorious inheritance a*mong the saints, and what is the *immeasurable greatness of his power for us who believe,* according to the working of *his great power*!'

Just think about what you could do if you choose to believe these words now, despite what has happened in the past. Take a moment to say them, perhaps focus on one aspect of these words, ponder them and let them sink deep into your mind and heart. They're meant for us all no matter what our background. I have found that memorising words like this and repeating them helps to *fill my mind with life-giving thoughts.* Give it a try and see the results.

5

Blockages and Obstacles—Discovered and Removed!

Blockages are created by our thinking, beliefs and actions or inaction. Shocks and traumas can also become blockages as they usually influence our whole being. Obstacles are those things we perceive as hurdles in our lives that we can negotiate, if we so choose.

I have discovered that many people are only aware that they are stuck in some way in their present circumstances, but are not aware that their past can be influencing them. The following words relate very appropriately to how I and many people have felt. Many people have seen themselves, in their mind's eyes, in a desolate pit! But as the unresolved, relevant memories are revealed and the blockages and obstacles to Peace, Presence and Power are removed they experienced this change: 'I waited patiently for the Lord; he inclined to me and heard my cry. He drew me up from the desolate pit, out of the miry bog, and set my feet upon a rock, making my steps secure.' When people feel secure, it provides a solid foundation from which to begin to live a life worth living and in fact flourish. I know because I have experienced this transformation.

As a result of my husband and me experiencing release from many blockages and negotiating obstacles, a genuine peace has occurred between us and a rich, alive, authentic relationship has developed. We know *how to negotiate* any challenges that come our way, so they don't act as a permanent obstacle to our relationship. Other people have noticed the change as well. For instance, Tina rang me after my husband and I attended her mother-in law's funeral, commenting on how many of her friends were touched by the way my husband and I were lovingly relating to each other. They are also aware of the huge changes in the lives of our family.

These people now even ask me about my work, which rarely happened before. I was able to share how I help people experience clarity, peace and release from stress. One of these people, Jim, wants to have an experience of encountering the Presence that others have experienced. He is a professor of psychology and has committed his life to helping people in jail. He has a heart of compassion.

Tina said to me, 'And you didn't mention anything about God!' I didn't need to, I thought, as I had asked my guardian angel to be present and touch each person I spoke with that day. Tina and I used to have huge obstacles between us, particularly about religion. They have mostly been removed over a period of time as I have changed in many ways. Also, many people seem more amenable to opening up when angels are mentioned. See Chapter 40 for the many ways angels are able to intercede on our behalf.

Obstacles in my life acted like a brick wall between people, me and my Creator. It was as though I was hiding behind the wall. I realise now I was cut off to some degree from Truth and life. Many people have actually seen images of themselves hiding behind boulders as they don't want other people to know how bad they feel about themselves. This changes through the healing meditation, thank God! Here are some of the things that can act as obstacles in our lives.

Lack of Awareness

A major turning point in my life occurred when I finally became aware of what I was thinking, saying and feeling and how I was reacting. Until then, I was so involved in and focused on what I felt I had to do that I rarely stopped long enough to reflect and become aware. It wasn't until I reached the point where I became overwhelmed, exhausted or sick that I stopped to seek help.

I also *wasn't aware* of my *real* motives for doing things. I often wasn't present to myself, others or Wisdom. The turning point came after I made the decision to make time to become still, pray and reflect. Little by little, I became aware and conscious of the damaging ways I was acting and reacting, particularly in conflict. But I needed some extra help to *stop and become aware* before I reacted negatively as I hadn't been successful leaning on my own understanding. So I asked my guardian angel to help me (see Chapter on Angels) and then effortlessly I was able to stop and become aware before I reacted. I also learned to silently ask Wisdom to 'take over' my response. Sometimes, my negative emotions would soften when I was on the verge of 'losing it' and at other times I 'knew' to withdraw from the situation to process my feelings and thoughts. Then an appropriate time would occur when I was able to respond from a centred, calm place and be able to speak my truth in love. What a wonderful change occurred in my relationships as a result.

Many people often want a quick fix. I understand how they feel because that was what I was looking for at first as I was desperate. I discovered, however, that Wisdom wants to give us more than what we want. He wants to release us not only from the emotional pain caused by our destructive beliefs either in the past or present, but then help us change our ways and destructive habits, so we end up living our whole life from Peace. These words from Wisdom certainly related to me and many others over the years: 'For my thoughts are not your thoughts, nor are your ways my ways.'

Judgements, condemnation, rejection and hatred

I have come to see that some of the most common obstacles are: judgments, rejection and hatred of oneself, others and God. As people become aware of these judgements, they also sense a heavy weight pushing down on their bodies that makes it hard to move. Life and living is hard work! When they let go of what they have done, the weight dissolves and they are left feeling light, in fact feeling as light as a feather which is a much healthier way to live.

It is appropriate to *judge bad behaviour*, and then pray for the person, which can bring change for the better. We are, however, instructed *not to judge people or ourselves*. 'Do not judge, so that you may not be judged. For with the judgment you make *you will be judged*, and the measure you give will be the measure you get.' We are also told '… The Lord will judge his people.' Thankfully, he is just but also merciful as he see the whole circumstance. If you listen to those around you, you will become aware how frequently people judge and criticise others or themselves. This only creates obstacles to developing healthy relationships. To want our lives to improve and be different, we have to act differently.

Why do we judge others? Many judge and criticise others as a result of their own lack of self-worth. It temporarily makes them feel better than other people. I call that distorted thinking. This can be due to jealousy and envy and their underlying negative beliefs about themselves—more obstacles to peace. I discovered I was frequently judging and criticising myself and others until I 'woke up' and became aware of the consequences to myself and others. Acting this way often leads to being self-righteous, another obstacle to freedom. 'Why do you see the speck in your brother's eye, but do not notice the log in your own eye? ...You hypocrite, first take the log out of your own eye, and then you will see clearly to take the speck out of your brother's eye.'

Once I experienced Truth and Peace in the memories that originally held judgements, condemnation, rejection and hatred, I noticed how free I felt even when people judged me. None of what they said touched me anymore. If necessary, I dealt appropriately with the way they were acting, but I responded gently as I was aware they were seeing situations through their eyes and their past experiences. I also apologised to those who I may have hurt in this way, thus dissolving the obstacles between us. This opened the door to mending some fractured relationships.

Control

We often feel we have to control things, people or life itself, usually as a result of some time in our lives when we felt frightened and out of control. It is often the only thing we knew to do to survive; however, while we try to control everything, we are often left exhausted and rejected because people hate being controlled. The need to control is founded on fear and there is no unconditional love in control! We need to let go of this 'role' of being in control and ask for Peace to replace the underlying fear. When this occurs, there is no need to control as we feel safe and secure. We are invited though to accept one of the gifts of the Spirit which is self-control. Then we allow others to learn from their mistakes, instead of controlling them, and can take responsibility for our behaviour.

Pride

Many people have become used to relying totally on themselves. With their words or actions, they have said they can't trust anyone, not even God. These people have had to 'know' or 'understand' what is happening. Often they feel responsible to make everything, and even everyone, right, and they can't bear to be wrong. This is a form of protection and can develop into false pride! Because all this is based on fear and control, no matter how successful they become, it leaves them empty and alone. They and their world often fall apart in the end. Pride DOES come before a fall. That is when we often see people, as they have become humble enough to ask for help. As they experience Truth and mercy in the healing meditation, they leave feeling free and at Peace.

Fear
All unhealthy fears can control our behaviour and reactions to varying degrees. Fears prevent us from being free and experiencing peace. When we react out of our fears, we can try to control or manipulate others and situations, as I did, or we withdraw from people. This eventually brings disaster in relationships. Some of the most common fears are: fear of rejection, fear of judgement and fear of being alone, all of which I have experienced. Facing one's fears and asking the question what if 'this' (the fear) happened, how would I feel and where would I be left, helps to get to the *root belief* that created the fear. Asking Perfect Love to cast out the fear and reveal the truth is an awesome way to dissolve fears, leaving Peace.

Death wishes and 'not wanting to be here'
At one of our seminars, I remember asking people to raise their hands if they had ever wished they were dead. About 70% of those people raised their hands. What was good about their honesty was they became aware they weren't alone in having wished they were dead. Death wishes and wishing that we weren't here or that we'd never been

born need to be acknowledged and then let go of so we can receive life from and out of everything. We need to ask for forgiveness, renounce these wishes and choose life to the full guided by the Spirit of Life! Sometimes we have made these wishes when very young, but the Wise and gentle Divine Counsellor will reveal what we need to let go.

Most people who become aware of a time when they had wished they were dead discover this part of their memory is in darkness and full of fear, guilt and lies. I often discover that what they experienced in life was so painful and devastating that this aspect of them in this memory would rather be dead and remain alone in the darkness. I listen to all the feelings and beliefs and ask for an abundance of grace to make it safe even for a moment for them to let go of the death wish and choose life so they can hear the freeing truth. I always let these people know that they can change their minds at any time as their free will is always respected. They then experience Truth and Presence that literally dissolves all the emotional pain and Light replaces the darkness. Peace in this new safe space is felt instead of fear and terror, which had caused them to make the death wish.

Not forgiving
When we don't forgive ourselves, others or God, the hurt we feel will remain with us and can destroy us in many ways. Forgiveness is necessary for our freedom and to experience the Presence of Unconditional Love. We can ask for the same grace Jesus was given on the cross to flow through us. People who have wanted to forgive but felt they couldn't forgive have experienced a profound and instant release as they allow this grace to flow through them, setting them free from the past.

Forgiving others, I realised, did not mean that those who hurt us would get away with the wrong they had done. Justice would be done by the Just Judge in time! I also remember the words that say that as we forgive so shall we be forgiven. I realised on reflection that I have hurt others when I was in pain. Listening to three perspectives, yours, others and Wisdom's is powerfully freeing as compassion replaces all the negative feelings and beliefs. Forgiveness just happens as Wisdom's perspective is gained.

Decisions and inner vows
We make vows as a way of protecting ourselves, but there is always unresolved hurt behind them. They only lock us away and separate us from the safety of Unconditional Love, deep within us. Vows are statements that often begin with the words: 'I will never…' such as 'I will never tell anyone'; 'I will never forgive'; 'I'll never see you again'; 'I will never love anyone again'; and 'I will always hate you.' These words are powerful and influence our life, even if we have forgotten or never realised we made the vow. Even so-called good vows such as, 'I'll always be responsible to care for you' or 'I'll never let you down' can place us in a lifetime bondage to others that we can begin to resent until we let go of them. Often children who have been abused are threatened and made to swear they will never tell anyone what has happened.

I remember ministering to a young person who was desperate to be healed. It seemed like we were constantly blocked. After a number of sessions, I asked the Divine Counsellor to reveal if the person had made any vows. Suddenly this person said, 'Oh yes, I now remember I said I would never tell anyone.' The moment he renounced this vow and asked for forgiveness, the session flowed and he encountered real freedom from his pain.

I also helped another young woman who had been unable to conceive a baby. In the healing meditation session, she became aware that she had said, 'I never want children.' She was amazed and shocked as she had forgotten she had made this decision. After renouncing it and asking for forgiveness, she conceived soon after.

Logical thinking
We can often rationalise and minimise situations by saying, 'It doesn't really matter … it didn't hurt; I don't want to blame them; they didn't know what they were doing.' By doing this, we can end up being a victim or martyr and this can lead to self-pity. Our 'logical' thinking ignores our feelings and what we really think instead of expressing them constructively. This can poison our bodies, bringing disease. Sometimes we feel bad if we express our true feelings so we say nothing and rationalise our feelings, which are then suppressed. In Chapter 21 on 'How to Develop Healthy Relationships,' I share how to express our truth in love at the right time.

We can't be healed of what we won't reveal. Don't try to understand and solve the problem yourself using only your mind. Always ask for Wisdom's guidance and perspective. Understanding and clarity in our mind always comes effortlessly as a gift when we experience the Truth.

Roles
We develop roles such as becoming a guard or protector and end up being on constant alert as a result of unresolved fears and trauma. Other roles we take on as a result of what we have or haven't experienced are that of being a victim, bully or being super strong. But we lose our true selves as we allow our 'parts to take over. In the end, there is no satisfaction or love experienced but only disenchantment and exhaustion. Most people have said to me that they haven't been successful in fulfilling these roles anyway. Ask yourself, 'what if I didn't guard or protect; where would I be?' The answers often brings

up negative beliefs and emotions in memories of vulnerability or abuse. This is where you can experience Truth, Presence and Peace. The roles then are no longer needed and you can relax!

Most of us that take on roles of one sort or another haven't known what else to do to remain safe at that time. We usually don't let anyone know how we truly feel or what we believe, not even God. Then we are often left feeling trapped, frustrated and unfulfilled. In assisting people who feel unsafe and who have felt unjustly treated, I have suggested that the Spirit of Truth acts as the Defence Attorney, Protector and Advocate. Most people are then willing to let go of the roles they have taken on and experience a tremendous release of tension as they experience a Light, Presence and become aware of the Truth. When childhood memories that need healing surface, people have shared how they sense the presence of angels acting as protectors and helpers. The visible change in people as these memories are released is extraordinary.

Becoming the 'responsible' one is a common role people often take on. When I ask these people how this makes them feel, the answer is always the same; they feel heavy and exhausted! I have discovered that when people feel overly responsible, it often relates to a memory when they were young where they believed they were expected to take on an unrealistic responsibility for their age.

Other people have shared how they believed they were responsible for everything that went wrong. It always seemed to be their fault. There was guilt attached to this feeling of responsibility, which has then made them feel they are also 'responsible' (a role) for trying to make up for the wrong they have done. Again, this makes life hard and heavy and never sets them free. As they listen to the Truth, the *belief* of being responsible dissolves and so does the negative physical effects as they also let go of the *role* they created to be responsible to make all things right. I ask them to listen to what the Presence is asking of them. Most realise they can just 'be' in the Presence and don't need to 'do' anything to make everything, including themselves, all right. In fact, there are no pressures or tension to 'do' anything! I recommend, however, that they become *responsible to listen* to Wisdom's directions and respond. Then life can become light and easy instead of a hard slog. In fact, it can become an exciting adventure!

Sometimes people find it difficult to let go of the roles they have taken on even though they have been a burden to them because they only know themselves (their identity) and their life in this capacity. I always encourage them by suggesting they give it a go for a short time and see the difference. They then discover the truth of these words: 'Take my yoke upon you, and learn from me, for I am gentle and humble in heart, and you will find rest for your souls. For my yoke is *easy*, and my burden is *light*.'

When I begin to feel exhausted or heavy, I always stop and check if I have begun to take on 'roles' again or to do things only in my strength. At these times, I thank my 'role' part, often my responsible role, and then invite this part of me to step back from being responsible and allow Wisdom to take over. This way of dealing with gentleness with my 'role' parts has been very fruitful.

Denial

We can *deny* that we have any problems at all. We may not want others to know we're struggling, weak and vulnerable and so we say, 'I'm okay' or 'I'm fine,' when it's not true. We can often be ashamed to tell anyone. Who is there in our lives that will make it safe for us to let down our guard, let go and just talk without judgement? I found earlier on in my life that when I shared my struggles with certain people, I came away feeling even worse than before I spoke to them! I rarely felt anyone really heard me and could manage to be present to me without trying to fix me up.

I remember once feeling like I would drown as there were so many dramas in my life. A wonderful woman who I will call Mary arrived at my door one day, took one look at me and then gave me a very present, gentle, caring hug. She just held me for as long as it seemed appropriate, without a word, but with unconditional love. This one compassionate hug made all the difference to me. It made me feel safe and accepted in my weakness. I felt this was all I needed. I wasn't alone and I could continue on without drowning.

The Presence, who I believe is the Creator, also knows exactly where we are at and is the source of all compassion. I later discovered he was always waiting for me when I stopped, turned around and began to open up my heart and be honest with him, no longer denying how I felt. *He* also helped reveal what I was feeling and believing and also made me aware, without judgement, of any obstacles in my life to freedom. I experienced the reality of these words in Luke 8:17 where it says, 'Whatever is *hidden away will be brought out into the open*, and whatever is covered up will be found out and brought to the light' and in Ephesians 5:9 we read '… for it is the light that brings a rich harvest of every kind of goodness, righteousness, and truth.'

When people experience the Light, despite what they have or have not done, a great peace and power is experienced by them. So be encouraged to be open, no longer denying how you feel, to allow the greatest Friend a person can have be your Helper.

Doubt
Over the years, although I have seen people experience astonishing breakthroughs as they experience Truth, within a short period of time they often *doubt* what they have heard and experienced. They say:

'How could this release have been so simple after all my years of trying to find a solution?' I remind them of how they felt and the wonderful change that occurred. I then ask them to let go of doubt, and ask for Truth to be revealed again. They immediately experience Peace again, even if they don't understand. Doubt makes us feel insecure and usually leaves us feel tormented in our minds yet again. I believe when God instructed us not to doubt but believe his truth, he was trying to protect us from being robbed yet again. Mountains in my life have been removed, as I held onto Truth and let go of doubt. The same can apply to you as well … if you don't doubt Truth.

Unresolved memories
I have come to realise how much of our life is negatively affected by unresolved memories, where we have taken on beliefs about ourselves and life that create painful emotions and where we have made life-changing decisions. Unresolved memories can prevent us from experiencing peace. The conscious (five per cent of our minds) and subconscious and unconscious (95 per cent of our minds) all need to experience Truth. I certainly was not conscious that much of the emotional pain and stress that I often experienced was as a result of past experiences.

An example of what I am speaking about is when Joe as a young child went to the toilet, opened the seat and saw a mouse swimming in the toilet. He was terrified! Now as a middle aged man, he can't handle people talking about mice without shuddering as this triggers the feelings of terror associated with this childhood experience. Unfortunately, Joe was not open to experiencing release.

When people are ready to process their unresolved memories and experience the Presence, all negative emotions dissolve. Peace is always experienced both in the memory and in the present. There is a sense of being protected and feeling safe.

Blank, dark, grey areas of our mind

I touched on this area already, but it is important so I am revisiting it here. These blank, dark areas of our mind are parts of our memory that we have lost touch with and in a sense have been buried in our unconscious or subconscious. A young woman I will call Susan shared how she suffered from epilepsy since she was a teenager. I asked her what happened at this time. She said she went through the awful experience of her friend dying. When Susan thought of this time, the memory revealed was full of darkness. After processing all the feelings, thoughts and beliefs in this dark part of her memory, she was asked to listen to what the Spirit of Truth and Justice would reveal. As she listened to Truth, the darkness of this memory dissolved as did the negative beliefs and Light filled her mind. She said she now felt comforted in this Presence and was at peace.

People like Susan often have no idea how to resolve these past traumas or that they could still be negatively influencing their life. Susan said her way of dealing with what happened was to bury all that she thought and felt. She just got on with life, but began having epileptic fits after this experience. As with Susan's experience, these dark, blank or grey areas of our memory often contain shock or trauma, pain and unresolved beliefs and feelings.

It is common for people to become aware that this part of their unconscious memory seems to be outside of them. Sometimes reconciliation needs to happen with the conscious part of the person. Often the person has suppressed this darker side of their minds which commonly holds self-judgement and condemnation. When they experience Truth and reconciliation with 'all' parts of their mind, conscious, unconscious and subconscious, people no longer feel empty and alone, but experience a greater wholeness within themselves. They experience Peace, despite the fact there is no change in their outer circumstances as yet. However, this usually follows.

Generational influences

Habits and patterns of behaviour can be passed on from one generation to the next. We can absorb and be influenced by what others are feeling and thinking. People have shared how they have felt a great release as they have prayed for forgiveness for all the generations in their family, asking everyone to be freed from all negative influences, habits and patterns. We also need to take responsibility for any bad habits we have picked up or developed ourselves. I have found a gentle way of doing this is to ask Wisdom what I need to change in my life and then asking for the grace to make the necessary change.

I am very aware that the way I am acting and living can influence members of my family, which may in turn influence my beautiful grandchildren whom I dearly love. My hope is that they will be influenced in a life-giving way by the adults around them so they in turn have a life-giving influence to future generations. This simple act is how we can change the world into a better place.

6

Resistance and its Influence on Your Life

How resistance, based from fear, can stop the flow of life!
I can now see how resistant I was when one of my daughters was sick. I wanted her healed through natural therapies and resisted a drug (for over three years) that helped her recover. I realise now I was fearful of her being damaged by the drug, but the reality was she was suffering terribly with her illness anyway almost to the point of dying. This resistance left me feeling tense and fearful.

It wasn't until I finally let go of controlling the way in which I thought she should be healed and faced my deepest fears of her dying that recovery and life began flowing into her within two weeks and I experienced a deep peace. She later became a personal trainer and is now the picture of health. So letting go of resistance and control, facing my worst fears, choosing to trust the outcome to the One who created my daughter were the keys which opened the door to Peace and healing.

If we are being resistant, like I was, from a foundation of fear, then we will likely attract others who are resistant in this way. As the saying goes, 'birds of a feather flock together.' However, we usually only notice the resistance in others. Being resistant in this way prevents us from being open to listen to other people's perspectives (our perspective is usually the right one, right?) and from learning and growing through *all* circumstances. Having a go at new things is usually avoided as it would mean stepping out of the security of our comfort zone. Intimacy in relationships is difficult because we are guarded. Do you relate to any of this?

Some signs of resistance

- ***Tension***: I find that most of us become tense when we feel frightened as a result of being threatened or challenged. We then become guarded, protective, controlling and resistant, all of which create only more tension and act as a block to the flow of life. We become like a blocked drain!

  I remember feeling tense in the presence of authority figures, sitting for exams, being interviewed for a new position and when I first began presenting seminars. I often felt alone, inadequate and frightened of failing. When do you remember feeling tense? Were you resisting someone's comments or the way they were being?

  My body speaks loudest when I experience tension. My hands become clenched, mouth and jaw tight, my body becomes rigid and my hips become locked. Now I understand why I often used to experience body pain; it was the result of all the tension and resistance within me because of what I was fearing and believing. I am grateful now for any pain which I now see as a 'wake-up call' that reminds me to deal with what is going on in me.

- ***Fears***: We have discovered over the years that most people resist facing their fears. It is usually very uncomfortable as we don't know what we will find; it is the unknown. But those who are courageous and accept the grace to face the parts of them that are weakest, vulnerable, rejected or judged, uncover the lies they have believed, release their negative feelings and reactions and consequently are freed from their fears. What a blessing to experience this, instead of living like Job. He said what he feared overtook him and what he shrank from came upon him.

There is a natural reaction to resist any person or situation where we have experienced fears of any kind so we tend to close the doors to any further contact in that area and bury our fears. One lady shared how she never goes away at Easter time because she is frightened of being in an accident. If this is how she acts every time she is frightened, she will trap herself, which closes a door to life.

Even if we try to protect ourselves from an unresolved fear, it still remains in our unconscious or subconscious and can be triggered off again when anything occurs that has elements of this frightening experience. So let's not build the walls of protection even higher when we experience fear, but rather face it and experience Peace.

How to deal with resistance constructively

- ***Become aware.*** Recognise when you are not 'relaxed and at ease.' Tension in your body often leads to headaches or pain of other forms. Discover what you are resisting.
- ***Face your fears.*** A simple way of doing this is to ask the series of question, 'What if the fearful situation occurred? How would I feel and what would I believe?' Then ask the Spirit of Truth to reveal his healing perspective.
- ***Get realistic.*** Earlier on in my life I believed I was responsible for keeping everything and everyone peaceful and happy. This was my way of coping and trying to prevent my worst fear which was that my family would fall apart and I would be left

alone. I remember what that felt like from my childhood experiences. As a result, I resisted listening to anything that was negative. Everything had to be positive. How unrealistic I was being! Now I realise this prevented me from being present to others no matter how they felt.

- ***Always listen to yourself and others***. By being present to and allowing myself and others to express feelings and fears (no longer trying to close them down), the resistance and fears subsided and respect developed in relationships, even if we didn't agree. Only after we have listened to ourselves without judgement is it possible to listen to others without judgement.

  I recently had an opportunity to practise the power of effective listening with Sally. I was sharing about a product that I thought might help both of us. I felt resistance immediately through her body language and the tone of her voice. The atmosphere was tense and she looked like she was on guard. I asked her what she was thinking. She said she felt like she was going to be pressured into buying something she didn't want. I acknowledged her concerns. Sally was then open to hearing that I felt the same way and was unsure what to do myself. As we both felt heard, all the resistance and tension dissolved. We were then able to discuss the pros and cons of the product peacefully and came to an amicable decision.

- ***Accept the situation.*** No one likes cutting themselves, but the reality of the cut needs to be accepted and dealt with so we don't get infected and become ill! The same applies to any negativity, tension or resistance. Acknowledge it, accept it, and deal with it constructively so it doesn't build into something destructive. Considering asking the question 'What is good or could be good from what is happening?'

- ***Gain a life-giving perspective.*** Remember the saying 'that which you resist persists'! So embrace everything in your life and apply what is relevant from these guidelines and watch how your life will begin to flow with greater ease and grace. We are usually only able to ask for a life-giving perspective after we have gone through the steps already mentioned. This unblocks the areas that have become stuck, allowing space for a life giving perspective.

I was sitting with a few people recently and I couldn't help overhearing one lady talking to her friend about my life with a resentful attitude. I could have easily interrupted their conversation and resisted this woman's comments, but as I knew this way of acting would only create a scene, I chose to do something different.

Later that day, I applied the Three Way Perspective Exercise where I asked the Divine Counsellor to bring this woman into my mind's eye so I could tell her how I was left feeling, listen to her response, then gain the Divine Counsellor perspective. Then all tension, resistance and anger dissolved, and I felt compassion for this woman as I saw in my mind's eye that she was trapped and miserable. Peace came to me as I prayed for her.

So we do need to *resist those things, actions, or reactions that would harm or hurt* ourselves or others, but we need to learn when and how to fight those battles. Otherwise breakdowns in health and relationships occur.

7

From Breakdowns to Breakthroughs

People have said to me, 'I'm heading for a breakdown,' or 'I'm going to have a breakdown.' Others tell me they feel completely broken and don't know what to do. This chapter is a brief overview that has helped many people, including me, experience *breakthroughs.* Let's first of all understand the definition of the words breakdown and breakthrough.

In the *Oxford Dictionary*, the definition for breakdown is 'collapse of health or mental stability.' A breakthrough is defined as 'a major advance in knowledge.'

Elise and her story is a perfect example of moving from a breakdown to a breakthrough. She is trying to obtain custody of her children, as she believes her partner is abusing them. During the *collapse* of her health and mental stability, she sought help from me as she felt totally powerless.

Memories of being abused as a child came flooding back to her. No wonder she was breaking down and overwhelmed. As a child she felt alone and believed she was not good enough as a result of the abuse. She had made a decision to never trust anyone as a means of protecting herself. She had to be in control, yet in truth had little control! This only isolated her even more than before from people who were trying to care for her. She noticed, however, that people cared for her when she was sick and that she was often sick. I invited her to accept the grace to let go of her decision not to trust anyone to enable her to experience the truth and presence of Unconditional Love in this memory. She agreed with all that I had suggested.

As she encountered the truth about herself, she felt a huge weight lift off her. Her laboured breathing became easy. She felt secure and cared for. In her mind's eye, she saw herself being washed clean. The negative feelings, lies and decisions she made dissolved, as she experienced the Spirit of Truth. She felt light and free and empowered in the presence of Jesus to face the battle in the court for her children. She even began laughing. She had experienced a breakthrough, a *major advance in knowledge* about herself. She no longer felt alone but knows from this experience who to rely on for help. The storm within her memory had been calmed. It is truly awesome to see such transformation in a few hours.

A new perspective on breakdowns

How different we would feel if we began to believe, without doubt, that *every* breakdown is an opportunity for a breakthrough, a transformation. The first step to this new perspective is to become aware of what we presently believe about breakdowns. In my case, I needed to face my fear of conflict and my belief that it would break down relationships I valued. I felt I would be left alone in a situation that seemed out of control and I would be devastated! I knew what that felt like because I had experienced it as a young girl many times. When I stepped into the middle of conflict trying to bring peace, those involved often turned on me. At other times, I would run and hide trying to protect myself. What do you do when there are breakdowns? As I began to deal with my fears and beliefs, step out of the middle of conflict and hand over control of the situation to my Saviour (a perfect name in these situations), breakthroughs and transformation in my life began to occur frequently. I then actually began to get excited to see how the breakdowns would turn into breakthroughs as you heard with Elise.

Breakdowns, I came to understand, only meant that life or people weren't operating as they were designed to; otherwise, there would be peace and harmony. So, breakdowns are a wake-up call saying that something is out of order!

Keys to breakthroughs

The following are some keys in a nutshell that have guided me from breakdowns into breakthroughs that may help you:

- *Listen to your body when your health is breaking down.* It is a warning to take time out to rest, recuperate, be restored and find balance. Exhaustion is a doorway to breakdowns. Discover what drives you to push your body to the point of ill health or exhaustion and what your deepest fear is about taking time out. Listen to Truth and Wisdom.
- *Avoid panicking, taking control of situations and becoming the 'saviour'* when you have *not* been asked for help, especially if you are a third party to the breakdown (unless of course there is an emergency and someone is out of control).
- *Ask the Spirit of Wisdom to take over* in breakdowns, as I did. He sees and knows everything, and how to bring about a breakthrough.
- *Do not doubt, but believe100% that every* breakdown can be an opportunity for a breakthrough if you do what these words say, as I have done many times, despite how you feel: 'I trust in the Lord with all my heart, relying *not on my own insight. In all my ways I acknowledge him,* and *he will straighten my path.*' And I have repeated these words until my path, or the path of those having a breakdown, are straightened!

- *Deal with every 'storm' in your life with the help of Wisdom and Love before it becomes a 'tornado' wreaking havoc!*
- *When you or others are angry or enraged,* stop, step back and take time out when possible. People rarely see things as they truly are in this state.
- *Approach situations from a place of being centred and calm.* Remember Jesus miraculously calmed the stormy sea. I have now experienced the truth of these words: 'God is our refuge and strength, a very present help in trouble'. Become aware of the keys in How to Develop Healthy Relationships in Chapter 21 and apply what you think will be of assistance.

This is what I have also done in breakdowns, and perhaps you might consider doing the same: 'Commit your cause to the Lord, *let him deliver you—let him rescue the one in whom he delights!*'

After being privileged to witness people experience Peace in their emotional breakdowns, despite the fact that nothing has changed externally yet, this is what they have come to experience: 'The Lord (Peace and Presence) is my shepherd, I shall not want. He makes me lie down in green pastures; he leads me beside still waters; he restores my soul. He leads me in right paths for his name sake. Even though I walk through the darkest valley, I fear no evil; for you are with me, your rod and your staff—they comfort me.' This is a promise given to us all in our breakdowns, if we will but open ourselves to listen to Truth and persevere to breakthroughs and Peace.

8

How Fears, Terrors and Trauma Can Dissolve

I remember saying to someone, 'I don't have any fears.' However, within 24 hours, I became aware that my life was filled with fears I had denied. At that stage of my journey, I wouldn't allow myself to acknowledge any negative thinking and certainly didn't know how to handle them. I was practising the power of positive thinking which, in itself, is good except when I denied and suppressed my real, often reoccurring, negative feelings. I realise on reflection I was trying to control everything and was not conscious of the fears hidden in the innermost parts of my mind that controlled me. I was blind, as many of the people I have assisted have been, to the buried memories that held unresolved fears and trauma that were still influencing my life in the present. But the tell-tale signs showed in my life by the way I had been acting or over-reacting and the lack of peace and order.

My way of coping with tension and fears
My way of coping with tensions and fears as a child was to try and be like the movie star Doris Day. In fact, she became my role model as I wanted to be like her. She appeared to be carefree and happy. That is how I wanted to be so I would find myself often singing her songs. But despite trying to *be* happy, in reality, I experienced tension, fear

and moments of terror. There were times when I was taken to hospital as I felt I was unable to breathe, feeling I was going to suffocate from the fear and terror I experienced in certain circumstances. I later discovered I had felt these feelings as a little baby.

At a young age when I felt very alone and life seemed dark, a dear aunt came into my bedroom and I experienced tenderness and love. I felt safe. She told me to be a 'good girl.' (Up until that moment, I believed I was bad). So another way of coping with my fear of being alone and being rejected was to make sure I was 'good.' Then I believed I would be loved and feel safe.

This decision led me to have unrealistic expectations of myself. Trying to be 'good' and get things right all the time only added to my tensions and fears and eventually brought me to my knees. After I was married and had three beautiful children, I realise now I was still trying to make everything right in every area of my life. The harder I tried to make everything perfect in my life, the worse situations became (because all my trying was based on fears and tensions). As a mother, I was frightened to say no because then I would feel bad! This didn't help anyone. I was living in a pretend world.

My children became ill and often had a hard time at school and there were times my marriage was fragile. I was full of resentment, judgment and self-pity which brought on the beginning of arthritis. I felt if I let go of control I'd drown and feared that everything would fall apart. Of course, this was a lie.

Then I gave up coping my way and began to often say, 'Take over Wisdom' hoping he would bring peace and order to the mess I was in. I was willing then to also face my fearful feelings and beliefs hidden in unresolved memories instead of blaming others. The turnaround in our lives was gradual but profound.

How do fears start?
I believe fears begin to influence our lives for many reasons. The main ones for many people begin when they have felt threatened or experience trauma and shock, often as little children as I did. Adults in children's lives, mainly parents and teachers, are meant to create a safe environment where children feel secure, where they can learn and grow, making mistakes without fear of judgement and condemnation. However, for many people their experience has been the opposite.

Although my parents worked hard at providing a safe environment, they often acted out of fears and trauma they had experienced and didn't know how to resolve. As you have read, I began life being influenced by my mother's fears and beliefs and so entered life seeing it as a threatening, frightening place. I now know from experience that what we fear and believe repeats itself throughout life. We usually attract what is in our innermost being … our subconscious and unconscious mind. But once we face our fears and deal with them, they dissolve, are replaced by Peace and stop reoccurring in our lives.

Healthy and unhealthy fears
Healthy fears are meant to protect us from hurting ourselves and are there to help us prosper. This is what we were meant to grow up experiencing in a healthy, authentic, unconditional loving relationship with the people in our lives. This then leads on to developing a healthy fear of being separated from these people by upsetting them or disobeying them. As a result, people want to listen to and respond to those who love them in this way. One such example would be of a child wanting to touch the flames in a fire. There is a healthy fear established as a parent very firmly warns or even commands the child not to touch the fire or else he could be burnt.

In any situation where an authority figure instils a healthy fear by setting boundaries, their intention would always be to protect us from the consequences that would cause us pain and even disaster. I now know that this is the intention of our Creator when he gave us his commandments out of love. They are there to protect and guide us. He does know how his creation works best I have discovered! Unfortunately, we often have an unhealthy image of God, as we can make him in the image and likeness of our unhealthy, fearful relationships and experiences.

Unhealthy fears create tension, pressure and separation. Life doesn't flow and there is little harmony. Fearful people are often controlling, which most people object to, especially children. I have seen enough people to realise how exhausting it is to either try to control things or people in order to avoid their worst fears from happening. Other people retreat from life as a way of dealing with crippling fears.

No doubt you have heard the saying that the letters in FEAR can represent 'false evidence (or expectations) appearing real.' For instance, if a child fails an important exam, he can believe this is evidence that *he* is a failure and his life is doomed. So, thereafter, he fears failing. Unfortunately, people don't often see the difference between failing and being judged as a failure and have even taken their lives because of this unhealthy fear.

Fear and abuse

After working with many people who have been sexually abused, I realised how traumatised they are and how ever present is the fear of being abused again. They also often doubt themselves, believing it may somehow have been their fault and that they are bad and dirty. They have felt powerless as though part of them was dead in a dark space (many have wished they were dead!) and feel vulnerable. Again, as these memories are gently revealed, we invite Truth to be revealed. In every case, people experience a Light and Presence and can hear Truth. The memory remains, but the associated fear and trauma dissolves. They are left feeling safe, secure and comforted. After Tilly was released in this way, her life changed profoundly. She met a beautiful man who respects her and provides for her: a totally different experience from her previous relationship. It is ironic, but true that unless our fears are resolved, people who trigger those fears often fill those 'spaces' in our lives.

Fear and disasters
In Scripture, Job says *that which he feared* came about. Fears besieged him and Job suffered terribly. He lost *everything* in his life, until he came before God and finally stopped asking 'why' and chose to trust him despite not understanding. After this decision to trust, everything was restored to him in abundance. I now realise many of my deep-seated fears caused much of my suffering as well, but as I have dealt with them, my life has also been changed for the better in just about every way. The effect has flowed over to my children and other family and friends. I'm grateful because my fears have caused me to discover the Source of peace deep within me and have stopped disasters reoccurring. Life is as it should have been in the beginning now, peaceful for most of my family. In fact, my husband said today how much he loves his life, which was so different to how he used to feel.

Religious fears
These types of fears occur when there is an unhealthy bondage to tradition, images, icons or men's precepts. I used to worry when I was a child about so many little things. My mind felt completely occupied by the fear of doing something wrong, especially in relation to religion. I often felt in my teenaged years that I would go crazy trying to figure out what was right and what was wrong, all based on the fear of doing something wrong. You can see how the unconscious memory of believing I was wrong and experiencing rejection, judgement and

abandonment were so deeply influencing my life.

I wasn't aware of a loving God, but only a stern, judging God who was going to punish me if I didn't get it right. I might go to hell! I was terrified! I believed I had to earn God's love by being good. My auntie had said be good and rewarded me when I was three years old. I remembered feeling loved and then knowing what I had to do to feel loved again. This inadvertently set me up with the *fear of getting anything wrong.*

Demonic fears
Most people these days don't want to admit that demons exist. I understand how they feel, but I have witnessed some breathtaking releases and healings when people have been prayed for in situations where it is apparent there is a negative force greater than the human element. Demonic fears exist when we are literally controlled and tormented by all kind of fears that trap and enslave us.

In a book titled *Left to Tell* I believe the author experienced demonic fear. She experienced tormenting and accusing thoughts that would not leave her alone. She was in the midst of horrific circumstances and had seen murder in people's eyes that surrounded the house in which she was trapped. Her way of combating these voices that accused and tormented her was to pray. She said that the act of praying changed her focus, lifting her above the terrifying circumstances and she experienced peace. But the moment she focused on the situation outside where people were being murdered, she felt the terror again.

Fear of people
This is when we are frightened of peoples' reproach. Sometimes this happens because we seek the approval of others as we may doubt our own worth and value, often believing the lie that we are not good enough or similar lies. We can then be controlled and manipulated by

them which only ensnares us further.

When I don't know why I have been experiencing fears of being judged, criticised and condemned, I always ask the Divine Counsellor if I have done something to open the door to being bombarded in this way. Then I have been made aware that I have been judging, criticising and condemning others. Now I know the truth that what I do to others will be done to me.

Effects of fears on our bodies
Fear can lead us to feel uptight, uneasy, hysterical, full of dread, terrorised and fearful to the point of being frozen. The physical effects of fear can also be felt as panic attacks. Our teeth can chatter and our body may shake. Phobias can also result. Fortunately, I, and others, have experienced being released from these effects of fear when they experience Light, Truth and Presence.

I now see my body as a wonderful instrument to alert me to fears created by worry and certain situations. My body becomes tense and aches and pains develop. My right shoulder becomes knotted up when I take on responsibilities out of fear. When feeling frightened of being judged or corrected, my legs and hips would ache. I discovered it was as a result of bracing myself, tensing my legs and locking my hips ready to defend myself.

How fear and body pain can be released
Although there are many reasons why we experience pain in our bodies, and there are many ways of dealing with it, I discovered *a great deal of body pain can be a result of what is going on in our minds* in the present as well as triggering off similar deep-seated fears from the past. The Healing Meditation in Chapter 16 has released many of these fears and associated pain.

Oppression can create fear and pain. There have been other occasions, for no apparent reason, where I have suddenly experienced overwhelming fear and physical pain. On one such occasion I was driving the car feeling just fine, but suddenly I had this awful experience. (Later on, I realised this was a true case of oppression, not depression.) Darkness, fear and terror surrounded me. The only thing I could do was to begin *calling out the name of Jesus over and over again.* After 20 minutes, all the darkness, fear and pain dissolved as quickly as it had occurred. Extraordinary! This rarely occurs now thank goodness.

Sometimes you don't understand your fear and pain. Earlier on in my journey, when filled with fear and pain, I would simply go somewhere quiet, become still and wait, often up to an hour or more, until everything melted away and I was left in the Presence and at peace. At those times, I had no idea what caused the fear and pain; however, the transformation never ceased to amaze me. I was left feeling very grateful.

Using the power of the Word—the Truth—to dissolve fears
I remember standing before John one day who had, in the past, the power to terrify me. I had often gone home after seeing him in an emotional mess. I didn't realise it then, but I would often arrive *fearing the worst* as he had often been pleasant in the beginning, but he could suddenly switch into a threatening personality.

One day a profound change occurred just as I could feel John's personality changing for the worse. As I was conscious of fear beginning to rise up in me, I remembered that someone had said to speak the Word, as God and his presence and power would become present and help. So silently I said, 'Greater is he within me than he that is within the world.' I was stunned to see the immediate change. John became like a lamb before me. I actually experienced the power of the Word and his Presence and Power dissolving that terrifying situation.

The words 'fear not' are mentioned 365 times in the Bible. We can *claim the truth* of these strong, yet tender words in Isaiah 43:1-2 even before we feel them. They tell us not to fear as we have been redeemed, called by name and that God will be with us and, even if the circumstances seem overwhelming, we will not be hurt. Try reflecting on these rich and powerful words.

Many people who have been taken back into unresolved, frightening memories have believed that God wasn't there for them at the time. However, through the Healing Meditation when they come to experience his Presence, they realise he was always with them; they just couldn't see him (fear creates a veil of darkness over people's minds). Thankfully, Light and Peace replaces the darkness and fear.

Circumstances that can cause trauma and shock

Abuse
When we are abused, we can become frozen and traumatised. I have seen many people whose whole lives have been dramatically affected as a result of a particular moment of physical or emotional abuse. This can happen anywhere: at home, school, work and in religious organisations. Sexual abuse usually has a tremendous impact on the individual's self-worth. Some have shared with us that they believe they are dirty and doubt their worth and value. They have been left wondering if it was their fault that they were abused and that maybe they could have done something. That is what a young girl shared with me before she experienced Truth and absolute Peace.

Unresolved, these experiences influence relationships as these people justifiably guard and protect themselves. People can't get close to them. Phobias can also develop. One person for example never felt clean and was constantly scrubbing and washing herself. In the memory of abuse, she believed she was dirty until she too experienced release in the Presence of Light and Truth.

Accidents

At a healing seminar, we were told about a man who remembered an accident when he had fallen off a bus backwards. He was traumatised emotionally and his back was damaged. As he was prayed for, he encountered the healing grace of God emotionally and spiritually, but his body was left twisted as it was at the time of the accident. But as the person ministering to him commanded, in the name of Jesus, for his body to come in line with the healing received in his emotions and spirit, his body twisted back to how he was before the accident! His whole being was healed!

Operations

As we led Sue through a Healing Meditation, she became aware of a time when she was being operated on. She remembered becoming semi-conscious during the operation and feeling completely powerless and traumatised as they proceeded to operate. She was unable to speak. Then as Sue observed herself in this memory, we asked the Spirit to reveal where he was at this time. She then saw herself on the operating table again, but now bathed in Light and at Peace. As all the trauma and associated feelings dissolved, she was left with the memory but no associated pain. As always, it was a privilege to see this life-changing experience.

Another example of trauma occurred when one of my children was taken to hospital because of a dislocated elbow. I had no idea this experience had damaged her in this way until she was an adult and had to go to hospital again. She was terrified. As I invited her to face her fear under the guidance of the Divine Counsellor, the memory of the incident surfaced when she had dislocated her elbow. She could see herself in her mind's eye as a young child with four medical staff holding her down to give her an injection, but she couldn't see me at that moment. She said in this memory she had felt helpless and terrified and believed she was going to die. As she identified with Jesus, I asked him to show her the truth. As she encountered Jesus in this traumatic memory, she felt a great release. She has remained completely free of any terror when revisiting hospital. Again, this shows when we resolve our past, the present changes. Thank God!

Death

It can be such a shock when someone dies suddenly. There is normal grief, but some people experience an overwhelming grief that they cannot move through.

Leslie came to me seeking help as she felt stuck in her grief. Her family had encouraged her to move on as her husband had died many years earlier, but she still found herself crying at all sorts of times. She realised that she hadn't had time to grieve when it occurred because of all the responsibilities she was left with. As she became present to the feelings of being shattered, alone and terrified, we asked for the Spirit of Unconditional Love to reveal his presence. As she encountered Light in this memory, Peace flooded her being. A few weeks later, she realised what a shift there had been as she no longer had any grief to deal with and no further tears. She now felt a Presence and Peace.

When my father died, I went into shock. I felt very alone and devastated. A few days before I was going to speak at his funeral, I turned to God and asked him for help, as I also felt totally helpless. At that moment of asking, I felt as though a Presence reached down from the sky and touched me. A Peace beyond understanding flowed through my whole being. I wasn't alone and knew I could go on.

Wars
I am sure you are aware of the many people who are still suffering from traumatic stress and shock experienced during war. Although I have not worked with anyone who has returned from war suffering traumatic stress and shock, I have seen people who have suffered from their own personal 'war' wherever that may have occurred: at home, school, work, etc. As you will read throughout this book, they have been released from traumatic stress and shock and thus I believe this is possible for all those who suffer in this way.

Other occasions when we can experience trauma and shock
There are so many other occasions when we can experience trauma and shock. The list is long, and includes: divorce or separation, redundancy or retrenchment, relocation and even violent horror viewed on TV, the movies, the internet or played in games. Dabbling with the occult can also open the door to experiencing trauma and shock.

My experience of being released from trauma, shock and terror
One of my experiences of being released from the influence of trauma, shock and terror occurred some time ago. I share the story in depth as you may relate to some area in your life where you feel overwhelmed by feelings, yet it doesn't seem rational.

On this particular evening my husband and I were having coffee after dinner with a member of my family. During a conversation about my husband having to work the following morning, tears began rolling down my cheeks. I couldn't stop them. I was overwhelmed by the emotions that began surfacing, particularly of feeling sad, powerless and very alone. (I later realised hearing that my husband had to work again had triggered off much deeper unresolved experiences of being left alone and abandoned. At that point in our lives, he worked six days a week and the phone was also ringing frequently even on his day off.) I couldn't understand then what was happening so how could I begin to share with those present? What I had felt seemed ridiculously over the top.

I decided to quietly remove myself from the room to try and regain my composure. I had intended to go to the bathroom, but what followed amazed me. I passed the bathroom door and kept walking, right through the house and out the front door without saying goodbye to anyone. Tears continued to cascade down my face as I began walking home (about a 30 minute walk in high heels!) I cried from the depth of my heart all the way home and stayed awake for hours calling out to God to help me as I didn't have a clue then what was going on inside me.

Spiritual direction opened the doors to understanding. During the session, I remembered the dimly lit room on the Saturday night and the emotions I experienced. Then a deeper memory surfaced where I sensed I was alone in my mother's womb which was a dark frightening place. I could feel a sense of panic and terror in this memory. I then felt I went into shock and felt traumatised as the memory unfolded. I felt suffocated and like I was about to die. The terror in this memory was unbearable.

Then, in my mind's eye, I saw an image of a baby floating down a river in a cradle made of straw. As this straw cradle came to rest against an embankment, there was a crowd of people. They lifted me out of the water and I was passed over their heads. There was a sense that I was being passed to a king. I didn't know if that was good or bad, but I did know I was vulnerable and powerless. Then I saw an image of Jesus, as seen in the picture of the Divine Mercy, carrying this baby. I realised then that he was the King! At this moment of encounter, I felt an extraordinary peace envelope me and all the negative emotions disappeared. A few minutes later, I had the sense of being back in the womb. I felt safe and knew I was no longer alone. The darkness had been replaced by Light and I felt only Peace and Presence. I could now breathe easily.

I went to visit my mum a few days later and asked her what life was like when she was carrying me in her womb and if anything had happened. (I didn't tell her what I had experienced earlier during the Spiritual Direction session.) She said the circumstances she was in were horrific when she was pregnant with me and she didn't know how she was going to survive. But she said there was a particular incident that occurred where she went into shock. She felt traumatised, numb and frozen and felt completely abandoned and alone as a result.

I then realised the feelings and beliefs mum had experienced have been the same as I had often felt. No wonder my emotions seemed over the top at times! Through this conversation, I became aware that I had absorbed my mother feelings and beliefs, not knowing they did not belong to me. To survive, a part of my memory had disconnected, which often happens in trauma. This was symbolised by the images of me as a baby floating down a river of sadness.

I have never felt alone or ever been triggered off with those overwhelming emotions described since this amazing release. Instead I just 'know' I'm never alone as I am usually aware of Peace and Presence with me and now feel safe and secure. What a contrast to how I used to feel!

How I now see fears, trauma and shock
As a result of all the transformations I and other people have experienced, no matter how fearful or traumatic the circumstances that occur now, I see them as an opportunity to encounter Peace and Presence. My experience now is that Perfect Love does cast out fears and terror and releases trauma. Would you be open to joining me in accepting this life-giving perspective on this subject? If so, read on as

we journey together.

9

Finding Your 'True' Self Versus Roles and Masks

Frances is typical of many people trying to find acceptance. The only problem is she is not presenting her 'true' self to people. Deep down she believes she is not good enough and is hiding her anger and resentment. She wears a mask when she is in front of people. They probably think she's 'got it all together' as she appears confident and in control. This couldn't be further from the truth. Wearing this mask and staying in control was exhausting. There were many moments, particularly when alone, that she felt depressed. She said that she felt lost and disillusioned. During a Healing Meditation, she felt safe to let go of protecting and guarding herself. She realised then that there was a part of her that had believed for a very long time that she was not good enough. She said she would never tell others she felt this way for fear of rejection so she always put the mask of being capable on. As she experienced Light and Presence, this belief just dissolved. She then knew without doubt that she was loved unconditionally just as she was and peace flowed. She found her true self. She was encouraged to practise remaining in this Presence and Truth.

Foundation for our true self
When you read the following truth about our authentic identity according to our Creator, it may be hard to accept, as you may have

felt the opposite for a good portion of your life. However, I now know people from any background can come to know and experience these truths in the Presence—once the barriers are removed. Then we can *accept* the truth about our authentic identity: that we are created in the image and likeness of Perfect Love—despite what has happened or what we have believed! Another truth is that we are chosen, adopted and heirs to his Kingdom. As a real relationship is developed between ourselves and Unconditional Love, we just know we don't deserve what we receive, but realise it is a free gift, just as a loving parent gives gifts to his child. Trying to personally establish our identity, worth or value through *what we do* is no longer needed. When people come to 'know' this truth deep within their minds and heart, it releases them from the stress and tension of striving to 'do' something to 'get somewhere' to 'be acknowledged' as someone of value.

   I have discovered that when we come to know the truth of who we are in the Light we may, after this experience, have to change some bad habits and patterns that have developed over the years. For instance, instead of blaming and judging others, Frances had to ask for forgiveness, let things go and begin to look for the good in other people. If we don't, our bad habits can separate us yet again from Truth and Unconditional Love.

Dissolving the barriers
The following are some of the barriers many people have had, but during Healing Meditations they have thankfully dissolved away to reveal their true selves:
- roles and masks we create to survive
- negative reactions and actions
- negative emotions
- negative beliefs

Roles and masks we create

The first resistance or barrier to finding our authentic self can be the roles and masks we create. The most common roles people develop are being super responsible for everyone and everything, guarding, protecting and controlling. Some masks that we create can be becoming a joker, victim, martyr or saviour to mention just a few. These ways of 'being' are usually developed to cope or survive in life and cover up insecurities and the lies we've believed about ourselves or life. As we become aware of these roles and masks, we need to be gentle, grateful, understanding and respectful of these aspects of our personality. Each aspect has done the best they knew how to cope, not knowing what else to do in most cases.

The only safe and gentle way I believe to discover if we have a barrier in this regard is to ask the Divine Counsellor to make us aware of any roles or masks that we have developed. We then need to acknowledge these aspects of our personality and thank them for what they have tried to accomplish. I often ask people if it has been hard or easy to operate in these roles and masks. People always say it's hard, and in fact exhausting. I then invite them to listen to the One who can make life lighter and easier. Ironically many of these role parts of us want to know what they have to 'do' then as they always have had to be 'in action' in one way or another. I suggest that what they 'do' is listen to the greatest Helper of all who is also Wisdom!

As a result of Joan believing she was inadequate, guilty and responsible as a child, she developed the roles of being the one to be responsible to make everything right in her life and the lives of others. She felt she had to protect herself and her children and be there to save them when they were in trouble. She couldn't bear to feel the pain she felt as a child of being inadequate and being blamed for being guilty and responsible for everything that went wrong. She found that everyone relied upon her to do everything! She had become the source and centre of other people's universe (sometimes called a saviour role).

Joan thought this was her 'authentic' self until she buckled under. She was then willing to allow the Divine Counsellor to reveal what she actually believed about herself and how she was coping. As she let go of these roles, and the other barriers of unforgiveness, resentment and bitterness, she listened to her Creator's truth. Then she experienced a Presence and every negative belief and feeling dissolved. The exhaustion that resulted from trying to make herself 'good enough' dissolved!

I always ask the Divine Counsellor to reveal any other actions or reactions that are creating barriers. I recommend letting go of and renouncing what you have said or done that has created a barrier and if necessary ask for forgiveness.

Negative actions and reactions
Although there are many more actions and reactions that act as barriers to being our true self, these are some of the most common:
- judgements and condemnations of self, others and God
- hatred, revenge and jealousy
- decisions/inner vows such as 'I will never trust anyone'
- death wishes or not wanting to be here

Negative emotions
Negative emotions are often buried because they are too painful or embarrassing to acknowledge or people suppress them not knowing how to deal with them constructively when they surface. Common negative emotions are: anger, fear, confusion, resentment, powerlessness, sadness, hatred, murder and revenge.

I recommend asking the Divine Counsellor to reveal every feeling (you may just have a sense of them). Take time to allow them to rise up in you and then check how strong the emotions are from zero to ten to understand their intensity. Ten would be the strongest feeling. Then ask the Divine Counsellor to reveal the beliefs causing these emotions.

Negative beliefs

The foundation and root barrier of many negative emotions and roles are our beliefs (lies) about us or the circumstance or trauma. The most common beliefs (lies) are: not being good enough, being responsible for everything, being bad, unworthy, alone, abandoned and dirty. To encounter the real truth, tell the Divine Counsellor what you believe and ask him how true this belief is from his perspective. If there is no further barrier, you will experience Truth and your belief (lie) will dissolve along with every negative emotion. This is an awesome experience and happens because our Creator reveals the truth in the innermost recesses of our souls. This brings gentle, yet profound transformation and we discover our true and authentic selves in the Light and Presence.

Getting to know your 'whole' self ... body, mind, heart and spirit

You will gain further knowledge about yourself through a suitable mentor, spiritual director or life-giving group. I am not sure that I would have gone from surviving to thriving if I hadn't had a supportive team around me. I had to learn about myself and how to take care of all parts of me, becoming balanced: physically, mentally, emotionally and spiritually.

Spiritually: our human spirit

As we grow spiritually, we begin to really connect to our true selves and develop authentic relationships. As I grew spiritually, I began to 'see' people and situations differently, including myself. My life began to open in a different direction and I began to feel fully alive. Many adventures followed as a result of growing in this way. This I know is possible for anyone seeking Truth.

And yet developing this aspect of myself was difficult at first. I had to learn how to become still and that seemed a huge task as I always felt I had a pitch fork in my back that never allowed me to stop. I felt I had to always be 'doing' something (a learned behaviour I later discovered). However, I began with making a *decision* to pray 10 minutes a day, even though I almost felt I had to chain myself into a chair! Learning to take time out like this felt like I wasn't '*doing* anything,' but I knew I had to give this way a try because I was desperate for change. Little by little, my time alone: talking, praying, listening and learning to be still began to bear fruit in my life. One day, I entered a place when I felt I was in a cloud. There was perfect stillness, peace and a Presence. I was concerned later that I hadn't prayed. What was this experience … what was happening?

A book came my way shortly after this experience called *The Cloud of Unknowing*, which explained what had happened to me and reassured me that I needed no words when I was in the Presence for my words and my prayers had served their purpose. This was to be at one with the Presence. It was an extraordinary experience. There was nothing I had to *do*—no effort other than to take this time aside to *be still*. Now I seek to practise being in the Presence, which is like always being with a Divine Friend, in the moments of every day, as well as taking time to be still. I usually come away from these times, particularly when I have soaked in the Presence for an hour or more, totally revived, pain-free and feeling like I have taken a long draught from the fountain of life. I have felt so full of joy at times I wanted to visit someone to share this experience.

I need to share though that in the very beginning of taking time to connect to my Creator, I found it difficult not to fill the time praying for and focusing upon all the people who were struggling. Instead of feeling full of life, I'd leave this time feeling burdened. I later sensed these instructions in my spirit: 'I will tell you who to pray for and when' which *released me from being responsible* for everyone having battles. Later on, I was shown in my mind's eye how I was blocking God's healing grace by standing in between him and these struggling people. I was told to step out of the middle, stand beside him, focus on him and thank him for helping them. It took some practise to do this, but I was left feeling lighter and grateful even before I saw the result. In most cases, this was the most fruitful way to help struggling people. I was then able to *be still and know that he was God.*

There were times when I just knew I needed to pray for others and time and time again I saw a power beyond me take over. One such time was when Josephine left our home one evening and drove away distraught and suicidal. She was so upset that I was very concerned that she could have an accident in the car. We had felt totally powerless in our own strength to help her being unable to reach her in any way. However, I then remembered *we are never powerless if we pray*, so I asked my friend who was with me to turn to the great Helper of all through prayer. We prayed and meditated on the powerful Rosary, praying ever so slowly with all our heart. Within ten minutes, Josephine returned and had totally changed. Her eyes had gone from being filled with blackness to their normal blue colour. She looked at us, burst into tears, and fell into our arms. Then she apologised for causing any concern. She was calm, like the calm after a storm. The oppression had lifted!

Another time, a lady rang in distress, struggling with what was happening in her house. She said some invisible presence in the house was moving furniture and pulling the families' hair and they felt frightened and powerless. I suggested they seek the help of a priest. She said she'd tried, but had been given no help. I wasn't keen on visiting her place, but as she believed after prayer that I was to help, I said I would pray for the situation. *I asked the Spirit of Wisdom what I should pray for and how should I pray?* (I always recommend asking the Wisdom in this way). I immediately had a sense of a lost soul so I began to pray for this soul. When I rang this person a few weeks later, she said there was no longer any interference of any kind. I was astounded, grateful and again felt humbled at the power of the God to bring peace in this family's battle.

Physically: body

Our body is a gift. I believe it is created in the image and likeness of our Creator, although I did wonder when I was younger why he couldn't have made a better job of me! Seriously, I felt rather unattractive when I was younger. Of course, that was from my critical perspective. Now I look at photos of myself when I was younger and see that I wasn't unattractive at all!

It is vital that we gain our Creator's perspective of our body. Then we will realise how important it is to look after the *gift of our bodies* with appropriate sleep, healthy food, exercise and fun. I have frequently seen people become physically exhausted, even to the burnout stage (which certainly applied to me), as a result of not being conscious of what they were doing to their bodies, which can lead to depression. In fact, pushing oneself too hard can lead us to abusing our bodies through drugs and alcohol. I have slowly learned over the years how to look after my body. I now realise our children often copy what we do. What sort of example are you to others, and how do you care for the gift of your body? Chapter 12 on Healing Body Pain may also be helpful in regaining balance in this area.

Mentally: mind

It's vital to take time to read material that will inspire, relax and bring life mentally, especially the Word of God, inviting the Spirit to bring it alive to you as I had to do. Become present to your thoughts and entertain only life-giving thoughts. Constructively deal with any negative thoughts or memories as suggested in the Healing Meditation chapter until your mind experiences Peace.

I have been shown a simple meditation that usually transforms my often scattered mind into stillness. The great news is that I don't have to do this in my own strength. I become the observer as I invite the Spirit of Peace to help me become aware of the state of my mind. My mind may be scattered or dark. I accept what is revealed and then invite the Spirit of Peace into my mind. I observe what happens as the Spirit reveals, heals and stills my mind. Creativity, clarity and inspiration often occur effortlessly after this simple meditation. Are you aware of what state your mind is in most of the time? Is it at peace or scattered? Chapter 4—Transforming Life by Transforming Thoughts and Beliefs!—deals with this area of our being in greater detail.

Emotionally: heart
Allow yourself to feel from the heart. This will allow you to remain connected to yourself. Whether it is negative or positive, your heart speaks. Listen to it and then listen to the One who created it, allowing Love to touch, heal and fill your heart. After a lot of heartache over the years, I know the wisdom of allowing Unconditional Love to be the first Source of love in my life. From this oneness and connectedness, my heart feels protected, safe and secure and I no longer have unrealistic expectations for others to fulfil me emotionally. From this place, I have been able to develop healthy, unconditional loving relationships that are undemanding. Do you feel connected to what is going on in your heart most of the time? Chapter 18 on the Power of Love Languages may help you understand what

touches your heart and the heart of others.

Enjoy getting to know your true self with the help of Unconditional Love.

10

How Being 'Right' Can Be 'Radically Wrong'

I used to be focused on and concerned with doing the 'right' thing in every area of my life. This proved to be a radically wrong way of living as I lived with inner tension and experienced little peace. As a result, life was hard and I often felt I couldn't be real about my feelings. *I had been operating from a foundation of fear of being judged and rejected.* After much soul searching and a Healing Meditation ministry, I discovered the cause.

  A memory of when I was a child was revealed where I believed I was somehow 'wrong.' The tension and pain associated with the belief in this memory was intense! Then I understood why I had tried so hard to do the 'right' thing most of my life. It was out of my unconscious need to make myself 'right' and avoid the intense pain associated with being 'wrong.' After experiencing the Presence and Truth in this memory, all the tension and pain dissolved. There was a new ease and peace deep within me. I *knew* then I wasn't *wrong* as a person, but that I could *do wrong* things through my words, thoughts and actions. I no longer had the pressure of always having to justify, protect or defend myself. I felt secure and unconditionally loved as a result of encountering the Truth. I now use my mistakes as an opportunity to learn and when necessary apologise.

  Are you fearful of being wrong or getting things wrong like I was?

How would that make you feel about your worth and value? These questions help you to listen to yourself and the Spirit of Truth. Perhaps you have people in your life who try to make everything 'right' in the lives of their children or have to be 'right' when having a discussion. Please be gentle but honest with them until they experience the truth about their worth and value. If they are open, share this article with them. It may help them.

The results of needing to be 'right'

When we *need* to be 'right' all the time, we often *justify*, *defend* or *judge* ourselves or else *attack* others as I did. We are usually *supersensitive* and *easily offended* about what others say to us, especially when they point out that we have done something 'wrong.' We also tend to procrastinate because we are fearful that we may not get things 'right' and then we could be judged. Tension and physical pain is often our companion, just as it was for a young lady who rang me the other day feeling very depressed.

This young women, who I will call Julie, said her body was aching all over. She said she felt lifeless and had been 'out of sorts' and 'off centre' for some time. According to Julie, *nothing* was going 'right' in her life. As I listened to her, she shared how she had tried so hard to 'get things right' at work, but never felt she measured up. She became aware how frustrated she was and wanted to give up. Living was all too hard. She realised how judgmental she was towards herself whenever she couldn't get things in her life 'right.'

After listening to her, I told her that if she wanted to experience change, she would need to be willing to forgive herself and let go of all her judgments towards herself and others. She said she would do that there and then. In only a few moments, she realised how free and light she felt, and that all the pain in her body had dissolved. This was the wonderful result that occurred after asking the Divine Counsellor to reveal to her the root of her pain during our chat. I was grateful and so was Julie.

When we try to be 'right' all the time, we can find it *difficult to apologise* because this would acknowledge that we have been 'wrong.' Our focus is usually on ourselves as we try to defend and protect ourselves, as we don't want anyone to see that we could be 'wrong.' Conflict in relationships can often be experienced as a result. It is an exhausting way to live and we lack inner security and a healthy self-worth, as this is attached to being 'right' or doing things 'perfectly.' This often leads to feeling trapped, largely because of our *unrealistic expectations of ourselves.*

We can also become *self-righteousness,* believing we know the truth about everything and that others are always 'wrong.' Being critical and judgmental of others makes us feel even better about ourselves so we enjoy it when others are 'wrong.' In a perverse way, it feeds the belief that we are 'right.' *This attitude leaves little room for patience, tolerance and other people's opinions and our hearts become closed and hardened as a result.*

'All deeds are right in the sight of the doer, but the Lord weighs the heart' it says in Proverbs 21:2. So it is what comes from our heart that is important. And in Romans 9:30-32 it says clearly that righteous does not come from what we do, our works, but from a basis of faith. When people experience the Truth and Unconditional Love, all the effort of trying to 'make oneself right' through what they do dissolves. What a difference this makes to their life and to those around them.

How to experience freedom
The first thing I did to experience real freedom was to invite the Divine Counsellor to reveal any ways in which I was acting that was

damaging my relationships. This is a gentle and safe way to become free, as we can be very harsh and critical of ourselves (and others). It did, however, take me three years in the beginning of this journey to have the courage to ask this question. When I became conscious and convicted of the areas in which I needed to change, it was always in the Presence of Love. I never felt any condemnation, just awareness, like a light bulb moment. Then I would simply ask for forgiveness and learn from the experience. My relationships blossomed as a result.

After I became aware that I was not wrong *as a person* and never had been, but become aware that my *actions could be wrong*, there was no need to defend or justify my actions if I made mistakes. I began to 'see' with a new perspective that life was offering opportunities through which I could learn and grow. I know that I have flaws, but I also know that Unconditional Love lives within me ready to forgive me and teach me.

It's now safe to try new things and learn from everything without worrying if it is 'right' or 'perfect.' I now feel secure enough to be open and honest with others and listen to their perspectives, accepting that what they think or say may differ to what I think. This stops most arguments and develops respect by allowing everyone to have a view without making them 'wrong' and me 'right.' And thankfully I no longer judged and condemn myself when I 'got it wrong' and no longer fear other people's judgements or rejection when I don't 'get it right.' It's now easy to say *sorry* when I have hurt others, even if I don't understand why they are upset, as I can be genuinely sorry that they are hurting. What a difference these changes have made in my life.

I believe anyone's life can change for the better if they ask the question of Unconditional Love: 'Do I have to be "right" or "get things right" to feel ok about my worth and value?' If the answer is yes, you then can ask for the power of your Creator within you to enable you to change any negative ways of being, and your relationships usually change for the better as a result.

I have just been reading a book by Richard Rohr called *Everything Belongs*. Some of the things he says have struck a chord within my heart. He said the wonderful thing he has discovered is that we come to know God not by 'doing it right' but more from 'doing it wrong.' Our wounds and mistakes become the very things that lead us to experience mercy, grace, love and transformation. This certainly has been the experience of hundreds and hundreds of people who have come to us at Agape Encounter, the organisation I have worked in, seeking real freedom. The great news too is that life becomes easier as we know we are loved despite our imperfections and are then able to love others despite their imperfections.

It says in Matthew 25:37 that those who will be judged righteous at the end of time are those who fed the hungry, gave the thirsty a drink, welcomed the stranger, clothed the naked, took care of the sick and visited those in prison. So it is the difference we can make in another person's life that matters. Isn't this the way the world can be changed for the better? When you look back on your life, what do you think people would most value about you? Do you think they would care if you 'were right' or 'got things' right? Nope. So, let's make a meaningful difference in other people's lives every day, even if it is smile or a random act of kindness. This will release the tension and dissolve the need to 'be right' or 'get things right,' as our focus will be on making a difference in people's lives. Now that's what I call doing the right thing!

11

The Power of Words

Are you aware that words have a powerful influence to either build or destroy people? You may think this is a bit of an overstatement, but take time for a moment to remember a time when someone said something positive about you. How did you feel? Uplifted, encouraged and maybe inspired, right? Alternatively, think of an incident when someone judged or criticised you. How did you feel? Some people have said to me that they felt devastated and wanted to curl up into a hole. So words definitely have power!

The power of negative words

As a teenager, I made myself a large check skirt in heavy material that I thought was stunning. As I wore the skirt proudly for the first time, a close relative said, 'You shouldn't wear such large prints because you're a big girl.' The reality at the time was that I was quite slim as I was modelling. However, these words influenced my perception of myself for years! No matter how slim I actually was, I felt big and became critical of myself and self-conscious. This just goes to show how susceptible I was at that time and also how words can damage us. My focus and worth and value then was on how good I looked. I believed then that if I looked good I would be liked and accepted. I am sure many young people may relate to what I have said, and that you are aware some people suffer with anorexia or bulimia which may have occurred because of their distorted perception of themselves and their need to belong and be accepted.

I can now see clearly and am happy with myself just the way I am—thank God! In fact, when I look back at photos of myself at that point in my life, I realise how deceived I was. I said to my husband, 'I actually looked okay then.' He said 'of course you did!' This may not seem important, but just think about all the young teenagers that have either heard negative comments made about their appearance, or make negative comments about themselves after comparing themselves with movie stars in teenage magazines. I wonder if they have made these people their role models. It is interesting that there are now more overweight young women than ever before. I wonder if many of them have given up the battle to look 'slim' because it's all too hard to 'live up' to the image of these models and movie stars. If only they were open to gaining Truth's perspective from within them, they would be able to 'see' they were loved and acceptable anyway. Then they could relax, accept and respect themselves and enjoy life. Other people's words would no longer influence them either. The truth is stronger than lies!

It's amazing how many people I have assisted whose lives have been shattered and influenced by negative words spoken to them or about them. It is because people *believe* these words to be true. If only they had known to take these words straight to their Creator, the Spirit of Truth, and ask for his perspective and *believe* his freeing truth, they would have avoided all the heartache and pain that was created by the destructive words. Then their lives would have taken a different direction.

The power of *slanderous words* can taint a person's character, as people can begin to wonder if those words could be true about them. I have been slandered a number of times and have experienced the influence of those words. In one particular case, I heard from other people what was being said about me. It took some time to work through my feelings at such an injustice and I began wondering if I was at fault. Yet when I asked God to show me the truth, nothing was shown to me. The person rang me six months later and apologised. She said she hadn't resolved her feelings with her mother and had instead taken her anger out on me as I was an authority figure in a group at that time. She even asked if she could be my friend! What a turnaround. Unfortunately, doubt about a person's character is placed in the minds of others through slander even when what is said is not true.

I have found it very common to hear people speaking negatively about themselves. This is a sample of a few words I have heard: I'm too fat, too skinny, ugly, hopeless, useless, stupid, a misfit and not good enough. Negative self talk opens the door to *attract criticism and judgment like a magnet* from others. This is one of the laws of life that say as you judge so shall you be judged. It's ironic how we get upset when others judge us, but we are often judging ourselves very harshly. Please be aware of your self-talk.

How to deal with negative words
It is very important for us to constructively express and not suppress any negative words so we don't get depressed. I recommend that we express these negative words in one of the following ways before unloading them on others or ourselves, creating even more harm. Write or speak out these negative words and negative feelings *on your own,* expressing everything you would like to say about a situation or person who has hurt you. We then allow ourselves full expression of having a voice. This also helps us to empty our minds of these words

and feelings which makes space to allow other perspectives.

After you do that, using the Three Perspectives Exercise in our mind's eye helps us gain even greater release, insight and clarity and it dissolves any negative words we might want to project on others in reality. Invite the Spirit of Truth to bring the person/people you are having trouble with into your mind, and look into their eyes as you express every feeling and belief you have. Then ask the Spirit what this person would say back to you. Listen to these people whilst looking into their eyes. The third perspective is that of the Spirit of Truth. Ask for any further insight. People who have done this exercise are usually amazed at what is revealed and in many cases all negative feelings dissolve and compassion replaces anger and resentment.

The Healing Meditation in Chapter 16 will help you gain further release from any negative words you have experienced that still influence you—or any negative words you would still like to speak to others!

When others around us don't want to take responsibility for the negative words they are speaking, what I do is silently pray that their eyes be unveiled and ears be unplugged so they become aware of what they are saying and the negative effect it is having. Sometimes repeating the words they have spoken back to them such as, 'So you think Richard is useless?' can make them stop and become aware of what they have said. We also need to be careful that we don't react to their negative words by calling them names!

When others begin to use abusive words, we should tell them that we will listen to them after they have calmed down. We shouldn't allow ourselves to be dumped on. It does no one any good. In this way, we are setting healthy boundaries and respecting ourselves. If necessary, we need to walk away from angry, abusive people.

The power of life-giving words
As I am writing this, my husband came in to show me a text message he had received. It was from a past employee he had not seen for years. This lady had seen him walking on the pavement as she drove past. Her message lifted him up as he read her kind words about him. It also bought a smile to my face as I read the delightful message about him. How simple it is to make a difference with our life-giving words. Find every opportunity you can to affirm, encourage and build up others.

I find delight in giving sincere, affirming and encouraging words to others about their gifts, talents, the way they look or their attitude. After I do this, I see people's faces light up. Many say to me, 'You've made my day!' If everyone spoke a kind word at least three times a day, what a difference it could mean not only to others but also to themselves. Try it for one day and see the results.

Creating the life you want by your words
As I have shared, our words create or destroy. During Healing Meditations, many people have shared how they had wished they were dead. Others have become aware that they have said to certain people: 'I wish you were dead.' These words bring a curse on our lives and a part of us can feel dead as a result. After people let go of these words, and experience the words revealed by Truth in the painful memories, Peace and Light flood this area of their mind. They are then open to changing their words and ways. What I suggest as they leave is to begin to accept life as it is, and when life is tough ask Wisdom, 'How would you have me see the situation and what would you have me do to make a difference?' I also suggest they become aware of how their life will change for the better particularly as they continue to listen to life-giving words from the Spirit of Truth within them and share life-giving words to others.

A powerful exercise using words to change our life is to *create and read affirmations* in these areas. Ask Wisdom to help you create each affirmation, as he knows what is best for your life. *Speak these words out aloud several times a day* as words repeated tend to become what we believe.

If you discover you often speak negative words, then try *speaking out life-giving words* that are the opposite of the negative words. In other words, *say what you want, not what you don't want*. I have heard many people say, 'Please God, don't let Johnny have an accident.' They are actually speaking about an accident. Instead they could say, 'Please God, keep Johnny safe' which is what they really want. I hear overweight people who want to be slimmer constantly talking about how 'fat' they are. Other people who aren't doing well at work, but want to be successful have spoken about how hopeless they are. If we keep speaking negatively, our words will continue to create and affect our lives in a negative way.

While we may need to acknowledge negative thoughts or words that come into our minds, we can say the opposite to these thought. For instance, when I think I can't do something, I will then start saying: 'I can do all things in Christ who strengthens me.' I actually feel better even as I speak these words. When you feel like saying: 'I hate life because it so hard' what if you acknowledged these words but then began to replace them with: 'I accept life and with Wisdom's help it will get lighter and easier.' Remember your life was never meant to be hard and heavy but light and easy when *yoked* with your Creator. That means of course every burden would be shared, and you would have to listen to his wise instructions if you wanted to travel, yoked together in harmony. This direction will of course always bring real life to you and your situations.

Another small example of the power of *changing negative words* is when Lewis became aware of frequently saying: 'I'm so tired.' Although he knew he should acknowledge this reality, he said he wanted to feel different so he began saying: 'I'm in need of refreshment!' Even hearing these words made us both laugh. He even seemed lighter and freer as he said these words. Can you 'feel' the difference in the words? What negative words could you transform into positive words? Change what you say and you will change what you get.

My husband and I shared some time ago how we both felt so heavy when we awakened in the morning that it was hard to get out of bed. I simply acknowledged this fact and asked in a prayer that this heaviness be lifted off us. I still don't know what it was, but it dissolved!

The bottom line is we don't have to live life alone in our own strength and can *use our words to ask for help when weak.* The Word was God, so God is in his words and when you speak out his word, Peace, Presence and Power are manifested! It says in Scripture if we abide in God and his words abide in us, we shall ask what we will and it shall be done for us. Are you aware of what words abide in you? If they are negative, they will be blocking your path to life. I lacked awareness at first, but I asked for this gift so I could take responsibility for what I was saying, as I realised my words either justify me or condemn me. Would you be willing to do the same?

Speak your truth in love
I know there have been many times I haven't been honest with others when they ask me what I wanted. I have often said 'yes' when in reality I wanted to say 'no.' I've not been truthful but have been people pleasing to avoid feeling bad by upsetting them. I didn't realise that people can usually tell when you are not speaking your truth. I now see that I was also betraying and trapping myself by not speaking my truth. It is better to be authentic, speaking your truth in love. You are

then respecting yourself and other people will usually develop respect for you as well. The truth is powerful!

May your thoughts lead to words that are life-giving and powerfully creative.

12

Healing of Body Pain

Although most of us react to bodily pain by taking a tablet or going to the doctor, I wonder what you might discover if the next time you have body pain you just ask the Divine Physician to reveal the source of your pain. The Healing Meditation in Chapter 16 shows you step by step how you can discover the cause of the pain and it may dissolve as in Tristan's case. However, please seek the help of a doctor if necessary.

Tristan became aware that she repeatedly became sick after she was angry and had been dwelling on and acting out of her hurt. She was fed up and ready to allow the Divine Physician to make her aware of the cause. She became aware of a memory when she felt alone and no one had taken notice of her. She realised that although getting sick made her feel powerless and angry that she also got attention from people and no longer felt alone. This double-edged pattern was repeating itself in her life. Encountering the Truth in this memory made her realise she was and never had been left alone as she could sense a Presence. She then let go of any decision she had made to use sickness to gain attention. This broke the repeated cycle of illness in Tristan's life. She rarely feels alone, even when on her own, and she began learning how to use anger constructively.

I experienced release from arthritis after dealing constructively with my buried negative emotions. Another lady was thoroughly frustrated after asking for healing prayer and receiving no relief. The person ministering to her asked if she needed to forgive anyone. She said 'no,' however, the next day she returned for more healing prayer and said she realised she had been angry and resentful for years with a member of her family. The moment she forgave this person and received forgiveness, she felt a release. Later on, she discovered her arthritis had disappeared!

Another young lady was considering an operation because of excruciating back pain. During a Healing Meditation session, she allowed the Divine Counsellor to drift her into the body pain and the source of that pain (our body cells retain memory. For further information read *The Biology of Belief* by Bruce Lipton). A memory came to her of when she had a bad fall. She knew she was injured, but everyone told her she would be all right and ignored her pain. A few days later, they discovered her arm was broken. She then realised she had *made a decision* to *become responsible* to help people who were hurting. It was revealed that this decision was causing heaviness and pressure on her back as a result of too much responsibility for too many people throughout her life. As she renounced this decision and forgave those who didn't believe her, she experienced a Presence and felt a deep peace in the knowledge she wasn't alone and a weight literally lifted off her back. She then became aware of the pain slowly moving down from her head, through her spine and out through the extremities of her body. The pain completely disappeared and an operation was not required. Taking on roles of responsibility and saving other people in our own strength on top of our own unresolved pain usually ends up causing exhaustion, burn out and body pain.

So our past experiences, feelings, beliefs, reactions and decisions can cause 'dis-ease' and pain in our body. Our bodies do indeed try to speak to us and can lead us to self-understanding and healing. Now, thankfully, we know that it is possible for our bodies to be healed.

The influences of feelings and beliefs

I was to discover that we could even absorb other people's negative feelings, beliefs and trauma, even as early as being in the womb, and retain these throughout life unless they are resolved. Because I have experienced such a powerful release from a traumatic experience in the womb, as mentioned in this book, I know how the associated physical pain can be released.

A Nobel laureate and world-leading expert on the workings of memory, Eric Kandel, says that the brain cells involved in memory are constantly and subtly interacting with tiny physical and chemical changes accompanying every experience. So, an event happens and it leaves a trace in our head and thus the next time a fleeting component of that experience comes to our attention it can bring back what we felt in the previous experience. That's why we often over-react to certain situations; we are not only experiencing what's happening in the present, but past memories are also being felt.

Our body reacts to what we think, believe and feel. Anxiety and worry come from the 'dis-ease' in our thoughts and beliefs which Eric Kandel says releases tiny physical and chemical changes, which can often create disease in our body. Worry destroys and anxiety produces tension which many of us know produces pain. Fear is devastating to the physical well-being of the body and unresolved anger can poison our system. Thus I believe it is vitally important, if we wish to have a healthy body, mind, heart and spirit, to become aware of how we are acting or reacting, thinking and feeling when we begin to feel any physical or emotional pain. It is there to gain our attention before we crash. The book Molecules of Emotions by scientist Candace B. Pert

PhD also has profound information showing how emotions influence the health of our cells, in fact our whole being.

An example in my life of how my emotions were influencing my body was when I became aware I was developing arthritis in my hands. I asked Wisdom to show me what was causing this stiffness and pain. The thought that came to me then was just one word, 'resentments.' My first thought then was, 'I'm not resentful!' But within a few days I became aware that I was riddled with resentments toward other people. Slowly, I began to deal with my feelings towards each person and forgave them. My arthritis disappeared completely.

Eloise had experienced traumas from an early age, which had left her with deep fears of being judged. After a number of hours of allowing the painful emotions and beliefs to surface during the Healing Meditation, she felt released mentally and emotionally. However, cancer was detected sometime later. Eloise realised she needed to also let go of self-judgement and self-loathing. She sailed gently through this difficult time, as she had connected with Peace and Presence within. Her physical health has now caught up with her emotional healing and she is very well.

Joe's skin complaint disappeared as he changed, becoming more peaceful instead of anxious. Another person began loving, instead of hating and resisting, the small cancerous lump in her bowel. When she was operated on to remove the growth, they could no longer find it! If you ask the Divine Physician to reveal the root cause of any physical problem you may have, be alert and aware of what is revealed to you. If you need to let go of any blockages and obstacles from the past, which you can read about in Chapter 5, do so to allow yourself to continue on your journey to wellness.

Healing our bodies naturally
We can help heal our bodies through healthy eating, rest and exercise, as well as dealing honestly with our feelings, thoughts and beliefs. Exhaustion, which is common these days, unfortunately can open the door to depression. Other common blockages that have prevented people from caring for their bodies, or even abusing them, are unrealistic expectations, self-criticism, self-rejection and judgement. Many people have said this way of acting has made them feel they are under a heavy weight, but as they let go of these blockages, their bodies feel light and they feel free! I wonder what you think about your body and if you feel heavy? Do you help or hinder yourself and your body through the ways mentioned?

Healing and forgiveness
It is vitally important to remember that if we want to be healed of all of our diseases, we need to acknowledge if we need to be forgiven or to forgive others. Over a six-week period in my life, I felt prickles and unease all around my body. It wasn't until people told me that I was being slandered by Jenny that I realised what was causing these physical reactions. After asking Wisdom what I should do to put a stop to this damaging situation, I knew I was to ask Jenny if she could forgive me for whatever hurt she felt I had caused. Despite not understanding, I did what I believed Wisdom was telling me to do. As the slander stopped, the prickly feelings over my body ceased and my body felt peace flow through it. It didn't matter who was right or wrong, Wisdom showed me what to do to stop my physical pain. Six months later, Jenny apologised as she realised she had been projecting her unresolved anger with her mother over to me.

    I suggest that for the next few days you take note each time you are emotionally upset and become aware of all your feelings, thoughts and reactions and any unforgiveness! Be especially aware of what you feel in your *body*. Often when I become aware of how I am feeling, I realise that my body is full of tension, which of course restricts the blood supply to my body, causing physical pain. So let your body pain become an opportunity for healing and freedom.

Divine healing—beyond human understanding
After seeing the ultrasound that had been taken of Johnathan's shoulder, his doctor told him the only way the tendon could be healed was by an operation. However, before he had the operation, he went to a Catholic charismatic healing mass where he received prayer for healing. During this mass, he actually felt the tendon being healed and became aware shortly thereafter that he had full movement in his shoulder again. To confirm this had actually happened, Johnathan had a second ultrasound that showed the tendon had grown back and was completely healed! The doctors couldn't understand how it had happened, as from their experience it wasn't possible. Some 10 years later, his shoulder is still feeling fine.

Mark 7:32-37 tells of Jesus healing a man who was deaf and could barely speak. The people who had begged Jesus to lay hands on this man were amazed. Nothing is impossible for God, our Creator!

All were healed and evil spirits were driven out
We are told in the Word of God that 'Jesus drove out the evil spirits with a word and healed all who were sick.' We are cautioned not to lean on our own understanding so I suggest when praying for other people that you ask 'what should I pray for' and then 'how should I pray for the circumstances' so you are working with the mind of Christ: Wisdom. I have personally seen people experience mental and emotional release instantly when I have prayed asking Jesus to release them. I never cease to be amazed at the relief available to those who are being tormented.

Renew your strength
I have been exhausted, burnt out in fact, suffering all sorts of pain throughout my body. I could have become depressed and despaired, but I remembered the promise in Isaiah 40:31: '... those who wait for the Lord shall renew their strength, they shall mount up with wings like eagles, they shall run and not be weary, they shall walk and not faint.' I didn't know if this was true or not, but I made a decision to begin waiting upon my Creator. This started at five to ten minutes and grew into an hour and at times two hours. I remember saying to God one time that I wasn't going to move until he did something with me. As I waited before God expressing my feelings, praying and then becoming silent, I experienced complete physical, mental and emotional renewal. All it takes is a decision and perseverance. Try waiting on the One who can renew you and see what happens!

How to stay young and strong
I believe we were meant to stay young and strong as mentioned in Psalm 103. I recommend allowing these words to soak deep into your soul. Just imagine if we read this every day, believed it and began thanking God for bringing what it says into our lives. Then wouldn't we begin to feel younger and stronger, no matter what age?

I remember coming home from the worst day possible at work. The atmosphere in the office was sickening. I felt dejected and low, but remembered where to turn for help and who to share my feelings with. I also remembered to thank God for being there for me and surrendered *every* situation to him. As I began to praise him, despite everything, I felt an overwhelming sense of joy flow through my whole being. I wondered if it was a foretaste of heaven as I felt literally transformed. I felt young and strong, instead of depressed, dejected, frustrated and weak. I invite you to do what I did when you feel down in one way or another and see the results. It will transform you and you too can stay young and strong despite your circumstances. Although I was meant to stay in this office for five years, it was reduced to two years only. I learnt a lot during that time that was beneficial.

Life and healing for our flesh

How powerful is the promise in Proverbs 4:20-23: 'My child, be attentive to my words; incline your ears to my sayings. Do not let them escape from your sight, keep them within your heart. *For they are life to those who find them, and healing to all their flesh. Keep your heart with all vigilance, for from it flow the springs of life.*' Although at one stage in my life, I felt the Word of God was boring, I discovered after making time to ponder, and even memorise, certain significant passages, the words began to come alive and feel as rich as honey running through me.

Fountain of life

Listen to these profound words: 'The mouth of the righteous is a *fountain of life.*' What about these words: '*Death and life are in the power of the tongue,* and those who love it will eat its fruit.' Are you aware of what you say and the difference you can make, bringing either life or death emotionally or physically?

After I spoke to John out of my anger and rage, he withdrew. He later shared that he felt my words were like a blow torch on him. You can imagine the destruction he felt, even though I felt justified at the time. Thank God I now know when I need to say sorry and take responsibility for resolving my anger constructively before speaking to others. I want to bring life not death.

A cheerful heart is good medicine

When I read these words from Proverbs 17:22 they speak to me: '*a cheerful heart is a good medicine, but a downcast spirit dries up the bones.*' On reflection, I realised I became bone weary as a result of being downcast (resentful, angry, and unhappy) and then trying hard in my own strength to 'fix' all the things I saw that were wrong. I even ended up with osteoporosis so *these words became a physical reality in my life*. I had to learn to accept things as they were, ask for the Helper of all helpers to take over and begin being thankful. This changed my focus. I developed balance in my life and began to have more time to enjoy life and look after my body. I believe these words were a wakeup call to point me in the right direction before my body collapsed. Do you ever get 'bone weary' like I did? I like the thought that a cheerful heart is good medicine for us all.

A daily check up

If we don't get our car checked out and tuned up at the garage it won't work at its best. The same applies to us. Before you even get out bed and begin your day, I recommend you get tuned in and tuned up. Perform a daily check-up so you remain connected and aware of how every part of you is feeling. I find asking the Divine Counsellor to reveal how I feel in my body, mind, heart and spirit helpful. I acknowledge how each area feels and then ask him to breathe his Life into these areas of my being and guide my day with his wisdom. My husband is often amazed when I jump out of bed full of energy, not long after telling him how tired I felt when I woke—and sometimes so am I! However, it's because I had just finished this powerful, refreshing, connecting meditation.

Will you give this meditation a try first thing in the morning and see the difference it makes?

Section 2

PRESENCE

13

Discover What You 'Really' Want

It has been freeing to discover that the reason I wanted or needed something, or someone, was ultimately because I believed (wrongly!) that I would then feel good, secure, happy, peaceful or fulfilled. I was *hooked* on wanting to feel good, not realising that it was the reason I was on an emotional rollercoaster ride as I never got what I really wanted. I am grateful now that the disappointments and emotional pain I suffered served as a wakeup call to discover the truth, which is that I was to find fulfilment and all I ever needed within me, in the Presence of the one who created me. When I am in his Presence, nothing else matters. I feel I have everything I really wanted but had been seeking elsewhere.

What do you want right now?
One of the most important questions I ask when someone seeks my help is what they want as a result of our time together. One young woman said she wanted her husband to see things as she saw them. I then asked if that occurred how would she feel? She said she would feel at peace. *So she really wanted peace.* She came to a place of peace and clarity through the Healing Meditation, despite not knowing what her husband would be like when she returned home. She was delighted

to discover that her husband was happy to listen to her when she returned. So as she changed so did her situation!

So let's discover what you want and how you would *feel* if that occurred. If you wrote a list of what you wanted now, what would it contain? If you wrote beside these 'wants' how you would feel if you obtained them, then you can understand what you ultimately want! For instance, when I thought about what I wanted at this point in my life it would to finish editing *Peace, Presence & Power*—which is a compilation of 11 years of seminar material sold in booklets over this time—a daunting task for me. I then believed I would feel at peace and could relax. So I realised I was relying on the book to be completed before I could be at peace. Of course, this is the very subject I share about; however, I knew how to get back to the Source of peace, which is really what this book is all about.

I simply asked Wisdom how he wanted me to see this whole process of editing the book. I was then shown that what I had been doing was similar to running a marathon and I was nearing the end ... that's why it seemed so hard! I then sensed he didn't want me to push myself, but rather go gently with it all. Now I am at peace as I proceed with this work. I further saw that this task could be a joy as it is a way of sharing what can change people's lives as it has mine, which has been my heart's desire. I remember the pain of being lost and not knowing how to get myself out of the pit I often felt I was in.

When we want someone or something to happen before we are at peace, we are restless and dissatisfied and often put pressure on others to fulfil our needs. I wanted my husband to change, even though he often said, 'I never want to change you! But you make me feel as though I am not good enough.' When I heard this comment, I became aware that *I* needed to change.

I hear children wanting and almost pleading for more sweets, toys or having friends over to play, but it doesn't satisfy them for long. I also hear teenagers wanting to be prettier, slimmer, and richer or to have a boyfriend. I see them expressing their frustration and unhappiness when they don't get what they want, just as I used to.

Other people want success, to be acknowledged, to belong, whilst others want their emotional or physical pain to disappear to experience peace. The lists go on and on. If only they knew how discover lasting satisfaction and true peace.

When we get what we want how do we feel?
When I received what I wanted, I often felt happy or delighted … but only for a brief time. Then there would always be something else I wanted! The same feeling applies to children, teenagers or for that matter anyone who feels they lack something and want something to make them feel happy or at peace.

How do we feel when we *don't* get what we want?
When some children don't get what they want, they become upset, angry, miserable, unhappy and rebellious. I remember feeling like this as an adult! Depression can result if we stay stuck on this crazy merry-go-round focused on what we want, believing it is the source of our happiness. This can lead to addictions of all types. I know of one particular lady who just adored her husband who eventually left her for another woman. When he left, she fell into a deep hole, became ill and disappeared into dementia. I felt so sorry for her and gathered that she'd believed her happiness was in a happy marriage. Having lost what she was clinging to left her with it seems nothing.

The consequences of reacting negatively when we don't get what we want.
When we continue to react negatively, we have in a sense entered a

trap, a bit like a spider's web, leaving us feeling powerless, frustrated, resentful, angry and eventually bitter. We have become controlled by what we believe we *need* to make us happy or at peace. So what could be good about negative consequences? They are meant to be a wakeup call to tell us we are believing a lie and are going in the wrong direction. I heard someone say that a sign of insanity is when we keep doing the same thing and keep hoping for a different outcome.

Creating space for what you 'really' want
I discovered that I needed to *let go* of what I thought I wanted and needed as it was only creating the opposite of what I wanted: stress. Although I had believed I would be alone and unhappy if I let go, the opposite was true. I discovered the Presence within me and a Peace I had never experienced before as I faced my deepest fears and was empowered to take responsibility for my life. As I asked for forgiveness and forgave others, I began to feel lighter and freer and could 'feel' the new space where Peace resided within me. I got what I really wanted deep within myself and my outer life began to reflect it. I knew never again to expect anything or anyone to be the source of my peace and happiness. Can you imagine how freeing that is for them as well, to be released from the heavy burden of being someone's everything? No wonder my relationships changed for the better!

Discovering what you 'really' want within yourself
I continued to experience an even deeper peace, security and fullness of being which was not dependent on anything or anyone as I committed time daily to be still and persevere. I became more centred and at home within myself with a 'knowing' I was never alone for the first time in my life. It was like being beside restful waters where I was refreshed and energised. Even though it felt like I was walking in a dark valley from time to time and being challenged, I was able to

remember that the Presence was deep within me. So I would walk in blind faith calling upon my Shepherd to lead me back onto the path of life. Everything continued to change for the better. Psalm 23 was becoming more of a reality in my life—a promise which is given to us all if we want it.

14

Discover True Treasure

My Treasure bought displeasure!
Reflecting on what had I treasured most in the past, I was reminded of a time when work was my treasure. I felt important dressing up and going to a modern office in the city and being able to use my gifts and talents. I loved being acknowledged and rewarded by my employer. Everything revolved around work. It was my main focus and I directed all my energies to it. I was consumed with the work of being a personnel consultant in a well-known city consultancy. It was highly competitive and I had opportunities all the time to prove how successful I could be at this work. However, I now realise that my motivation was to be noticed and valued.

Although what I treasured then gave me pleasure, it didn't give my husband any pleasure. Apparently, I would often wake him up in the middle of the night, as I would sit up in bed and begin to interview people in my sleep. My conversations with friends or family, I later discovered, were often focused on me and my work. I often became exhausted as I was running on adrenalin. Eventually, I had to resign at the request of my husband. The Managing Director came to see me shortly after, inviting me to stay on, enticing me with promises and other alternatives. I was tempted but knew to refuse the offer. I had begun to 'see' that what I treasured wasn't really bringing long-term satisfaction. I only felt noticed and valued when I was doing well—it was conditional.

True and lasting treasure
As the shine wore off what I thought was of value, I began to realise there was an emptiness within me and I was restless. I knew something was missing from my life, but I couldn't put my finger on what that was. After calling out to God for help, I was invited by a very gentle woman to a charismatic prayer group of all things. Up until I met her, I didn't trust this type of group, unsure if they were unbalanced. However, during my time with this group, I invited the Holy Spirit to come into my life and change me. What a journey of discovery ensued! My life began to change and I saw other people's lives being changed for the better. But some months later, it seemed like all hell let loose in my life. Only now do I realise I was beginning to face many of my deep seated fears, and was also learning to change the manner in which I responded to these fears.

During one of the many Healing Meditation sessions I experienced, a memory came to me in my mind's eye. I saw darkness and felt terrified. I felt lost, alone and believed I was worthless. When the person facilitating this session asked for the Truth to be revealed, I began to see Light and then sensed Jesus coming into the memory. I then heard I was his precious child. I felt safe and valued like never before. The whole experience left me filled with Presence and Peace. I felt like I had discovered *lasting treasure deep within me* when I had felt undeserving and at my worst. The words I had heard about Jesus being called *the pearl of great price* became a reality in my heart. I just 'knew' he loved me despite what I had believed and had paid the price for all the wrong I had done.

I understood after this experience why I had been so driven at work to be acknowledged and valued. Deep down I had felt worthless. I had even been thinking of opening my own personnel company before this transformation, but the change within me had moved the very foundations of my beliefs and life so much that I only wanted to listen to and respond to the Source of this encounter. After changing my focus, I made time daily to wait upon this Presence, learning to really pray (coming as I was) and to wait and listen in the stillness.

After three months, I strongly sensed the words within me 'I want you in my employment,' but didn't know what that meant. Yet. On reflection, I see how gently, step by step I was being made suitable for my new work. This process included taking responsibility for my actions, saying sorry and generally beginning to change bad habits. What had been coming out of my mouth when I was upset had revealed a lot of supressed pain that continued to hurt others. I needed to learn how to deal with my anger and hurt constructively. The words I had read that said a good person brings good things out of good treasure in his or her heart, or the reverse, were speaking to me.

Developing an intimate relationship by spending time, waiting upon the Presence (my new employer) became my priority. I wanted to listen and respond to any new directions. Doors began to open and I was invited to leadership roles in different areas and became involved in many groups over time. There were many times when I felt tested in my faith, often wondering what had happened to that wonderful experience I had when I discovered and experienced the precious treasure, Presence and Peace. I know now I was being taught to persevere and walk in faith and not just by feelings. I later learned how to use these feelings to lead me and others back into the Presence and Peace.

Discovering your treasure

So *who* or *what* is the source of your treasure? Is it your work, money or family? Does this treasure take all of your focus and energy? Does it bring you peace, joy, love and balance? I now know why we are instructed to first seek our happiness in the One who is Wisdom and knows how to bring good from everything. We are then protected from being disappointed, used or abused. Only recently another film star took his life. He appeared to have what many people would treasure: money and fame, but despite this the dark times he experienced eventually overwhelmed him.

What if you allowed the difficult times to be opportunities of discovery to unearth true and lasting treasure within yourself? You may come to *know* the truth that you are one of God's treasures. Who treasures you like that now?

15

Discovering the Loving, Powerful Presence Within

As I refer to the Presence throughout this book, it is important to spend some time sharing how I and other people have discovered, through experience, the loving powerful Presence within that has changed our lives. Although you will read many names that refer to the Presence, I encourage you to accept the name you relate to best at this point in your life.

How the Presence has been experienced
Many people have discovered during the Healing Meditation the Presence is revealed as Light which dissolves the darkness and pain in unresolved memories. Others have experience the Presence as a gentle breeze as did a very close friend of mine who wasn't at all religious. After she experienced the Presence in a gentle breeze that surrounded her, she began an amazing journey of discovery and healing. She wrote a book called *The Breeze* sharing her extraordinary journey to transformation which has inspired and encouraged others. Her pen name is Felix.

Others who come from a religious background often sense in their mind's eye an image of Jesus or angels Other people hear life-giving Words that dissolve their negative beliefs as they gain clarity and experience Truth.

I have experienced the Presence as just that. A realization there is a powerful person present in pure Light. At other times there have been images given to me in my mind's eye, but there is a *knowing* in these experiences that the Presence is the gentle yet Supreme Being, my Creator and God. I also refer to him as Friend because that is how my relationship has developed over many years. I realised that we are called his friend as well if we do what he commands. The word 'command' sounds hard, and even controlling, but for me it is like a loving parent protecting and guiding their children for their own good. How beautiful is the commandment he gives us to love him with all our heart, mind and soul and then love our neighbours as we love ourselves. This means, of course, that we have almost a duty to love ourselves so we can extend that same love to others.

Many people have experienced the Presence as an Advocate and Defence Attorney. I remember one such time when I had gone to visit my elderly parish priest to thank him for something he had done. I was welcomed by the lady caring for him and was taken to see him. I didn't get the chance to thank him as he erupted in rage the moment he saw me, abusing me for interrupting his breakfast. He stood up and ushered me out of the house—still screaming. I returned to my car feeling numb, in complete shock. After catching my breath, I asked for Wisdom's perspective to explain what had gone on. I heard nothing, but instead felt a Presence and Peace literally envelope me. All the numbness and shock dissolved. I felt secure and safe as I had an Advocate defending me. What had occurred no longer affected me. I knew to leave the situation in my Advocate's hands until directed otherwise.

The very next day I was in church for a service for our school children. This same priest stopped, looked at me and loudly made some comment about the previous day's incident in front of everyone and then moved on quickly to begin the service. It sounded like he was trying to justify his behaviour, again blaming me! I was again astonished. He was totally unapproachable as you may gather, and certainly not open to hearing my perspective.

Then in a third encounter with this priest, when I needed keys to conduct a meeting for the school, he again yelled down the phone. I was furious this time, with a righteous anger, and firmly told him not to bother helping, that although I had a very sick child I would somehow find another person to give me a key to the school. He became very quiet and lowered his voice inviting me to get the key I needed from him. He was very docile when I arrived and gently handed me the key. This time I was given an opportunity to speak. I learnt there is a time to speak and a time not to speak. Justice will always be done in the end.

If you do not relate to the language I have mentioned, or find what I have said hard to accept, but you're seeking Truth, you may feel comfortable asking the Spirit of Truth to help. Some people have told me they don't believe there is a God. When I have asked them what they believe in, they say they don't know. I have then asked if they believe in Love and they always say, 'Yes!' So, in their case, I suggest they allow the Spirit of Love to guide them.

Asking the Presence to take over!
I discovered that the Presence was waiting for me to ask for his help, even to the point of saying 'take over.' When I have asked this, I have been amazed at what I have said and done. It has usually been the opposite of what I was about to do, or say, which on reflection would only have destroyed relationships. I am constantly being taught from these experiences, especially when I ask explicitly, 'What can I learn from this particular experience?' I wonder what you would experience

if you said 'take over' to the Presence who knows what is best. Why not try it?

Life becomes easier and lighter
For many years, prior to asking for help, my husband and I often felt almost too exhausted to get out of bed. In fact, it felt like we could fall through the bed! I went through burnout twice and my husband was stressed from working long hours. Over time though, we asked Wisdom, the Presence, to guide us and slowly as we asked for help, listened and responded, every area of our lives became easier and lighter.

Will you ask the Spirit to lighten your load and make life easier with his help and presence showing you a new way to live? You have nothing to lose and *everything* to gain.

Qualities of the Presence
Some of qualities of the Presence that I and many others have experienced in painful situations or traumatic memories are mercy, forgiveness, gentleness, light, truth and unconditional love. We learned that he has all the treasures of wisdom and knowledge. This reminds me of once seeing a treasure chest in my mind's eyes when meditating one day and knew I was invited to take from it what I needed. So I asked for the quality of his *gentleness* to flow through me. I then began thanking him daily for three weeks for releasing his gentleness through me. Then on one particularly day numerous people told me how gentle I was. I was astounded as all I had done was to ask and thank. I didn't 'try' to be gentle in my own effort; it was given as a gift from the treasure chest of his qualities. We are told that we are God's treasured possession, but I couldn't relate to these words until I began to experience Truth in many memories. What if you began asking and thanking for the quality you want to flow through you? I wonder what might happen after a few weeks.

A barrier to experiencing the Presence—our distorted perception
One of the barriers that used to exist in my relationship with God was my distorted perception of him through damaged relationships and abusive experiences with authority figures, particularly in religious institutions. How can people have a relationship when there is little trust left and they guard themselves? People have often asked me, 'Where was God when I was being abused?' But rather than answer them I invite them into a Healing Meditation where they can hear the answer to their question themselves. They become conscious that the Presence suffered with them. They also see they didn't know to ask for help then. However, at that moment of encountering the Presence and Truth, all the pain of the abuse dissolves and their dignity is restored. In this case the Presence is experienced as the Just Judge and Defence Attorney.

Beliefs, terror, trauma and shock act as barriers to the Presence
I wonder if you *believe,* as many others have, that you aren't good enough and don't deserve to receive good things? The way to dissolve this barrier is to ask Wisdom for his perspective and truth and listen.
I wonder if there's also a voice in your head saying, 'I've tried that and it doesn't work. Nothing ever changes!' The bottom line is, if you believe nothing will change, it never will. That belief occurs when we have tried in our strength to fix situations and failed. I suggest that you ask the Presence to be your Helper and invite his Wisdom to guide everything and see what happens.

Joan's experience is the perfect example of what I am saying. She came seeking help as she had tried everything she knew to help herself, yet she still felt alone, empty, and powerless. So I invited the Divine Counsellor to make her aware of the first time she had felt powerless, believing she couldn't do anything.

As she waited, she became aware of darkness in her mind's eye. We began to listen to that 'part' of her memory in the darkness. This 'part' of her felt alone, vulnerable, unprotected, frozen and totally powerless. It was a scary place.

She then became aware of a door in the darkness. I asked if this 'part' of her would like someone to help her. After some encouragement, she said yes. As I invited Unconditional Love to reveal his Presence, the door in this dark place began opening and she could see Light coming through the door until it flooded the whole area. The darkness disappeared and all the negative feelings and beliefs no longer felt relevant!

She was left feeling free, warm, protected and empowered in the Presence and Light. She then became aware of the relevant traumatic memory when this darkness had entered her mind as a child. However, the memory now was just a memory without the trauma and pain. It felt completely different. It is awesome to witness such transformation.

This dark unconscious part of people's memories that surfaces during a Healing Meditation is commonly experienced as many people have experienced terror, shock or trauma. When any similar experiences happen in the present, this triggers all of the feelings, beliefs and pain experienced from the past.

Many of us become aware that the Presence had always been present with these qualities, but we weren't present to his Presence! We couldn't 'see' or experience them because of the darkness that acted like a veil and barrier over our eyes. After these were removed, we came to *know* that nothing can really separate us from his love: not hardship, distress, persecution or famine, neither death nor life, nor angels, nor rulers, nor things present, nor things to come, nor powers, nor height, nor depth, nor anything else in all creation. That's beyond price.

Promises given by the Presence … my Divine Friend
These words have become a reality now in many people's lives who used to experience the very opposite. They and I know them to be true, so enjoy reading them and hopefully you too will experience what they say. The promises given by the Presence are to:
- always look after you – Isaiah 49:5-16
- love and enable you to love – 1 John 4:19
- provide for you – 2 Corinthians 9:8
- adopt you as his child – Psalms 27:10
- give refuge and help – Psalms 118:6
- strengthen you – 11Tim. 4:17
- give life abundantly – John 10:10
- protect and defend you – Exodus 15:1,2
- give you your heart's desires – Psalms 37:3,4
- bring *all* things to good – Romans 8:28
- battle for us and bring victory – 1 Cor.15:57
- comfort – 11 Corinthians 1:3-4
- restore – Psalm 23:3
- deliver you – Deuteronomy 4:37
- establish you – Psalms 7:9
- free and save you – Isaiah 25:9
- never forget you – Isaiah 49:15-19
- never change – Malachi 3:6
- give us wisdom – James 1:5

Lovingly corrected
Just as a true friend does, in an honest relationship, the Spirit also lovingly corrects us for our own good. You can even ask him to show you anything in your life or attitude that needs to be changed (as I did). Within hours of asking this question, I was gently made aware of what

needed to be changed without any sense of being judged. It greatly benefited my relationships. Remember that all he desires is to build us up, not destroy us.

A solid, secure foundation

In the Presence, as we feel complete, safe and secure, we don't have to prove anything! The Truth really sets us free. Knowing this provides a solid foundation in our mind from which to use our natural gifts and talents in life and to learn from our failures. On the other hand, if you don't have this foundation you can be driven and controlled believing something or someone will make you secure.

Jim was controlled by his deep insecurities. He came from a very poor family and decided when he was young man that he would not be without money when he grew up. He believed he'd then feel secure and happy. This belief controlled him all his life. He drank heavily to relax and became a workaholic. This destroyed his family, separating him from the woman he loved. His children loved him, but were frightened and insecure because they never knew how he would act.

Before he died of old age, he lost almost all the money he had worked so hard for on a few investments that turned sour. One day I visited him in hospital. He was very frail, but yet peaceful. He said to me that he had come to the realisation that he knew nothing. (This man had always been very much in control believing he knew what was best). I replied that I thought that was the beginning of wisdom. He had begun to reflect on his life and as a result softened and changed for the better. I believe he gained Wisdom, and wherever Wisdom is so is the Presence.

Sensing myself, the created within the Creator, as one!

I had a profound experience of encountering the Presence one day. In my mind, I could see a large outline full of light. I then saw a smaller outline of myself within this Presence. It was the little created me within the Creator and his presence. The words that came to me were: 'Remain in me and I will remain in you.' Again I felt totally secure, loved, peaceful and content.

So when I re-read the profound, life-giving truth that we are created in his image and likeness, I just knew in my heart this was true. In his Presence, I believe we all had *everything* we ever needed. So what separates us from his Love and why do we suffer so many fears, rejections and trials?

The moment we enter the world into our mother's womb, we begin being influenced, often negatively, absorbing what she felt and thought and the environment surrounding our birth. Then we often began interpreting, believing and reacting as a result of these experiences. We become *blind* to the truth—and it separates us from the Presence and the Truth. That is where the Healing Meditation has made an extraordinary difference as people are reunited with the Presence and can accept this profound, life-changing truth.

Abiding with the Presence

Practising the Presence of God, a small book sharing Brother Lawrence's experience, is a clear example of how simply we can come to abide in Unconditional Love and Presence. Brother Lawrence, a simple 16th Century monk, said he had tried to change himself but gave up and decided instead to acknowledge his flaws, say sorry and develop the habit of loving God in the moments of each day, doing every little task for the love of God. He said it took time and perseverance to develop this habit, but once established he found himself filled with joy which continued on for over 40 years. Even the task he was given of washing dishes, something he had previously hated, became an opportunity to talk or sing to God. He realised what was good about washing the dishes is that his mind was free of mental responsibilities. In fact, he was so filled with joy that he would often be seen dancing and singing as he washed the dishes! Many people ended up coming to him for the answers to their problems. He would just ask God for the solution, tell the people and witness the amazing results.

What a wonderful example of how to abide with the Presence, who for me is the greatest Friend one can have. This occurs like any friendship as I spend time developing a simple, loving, open, honest relationship with him, coming as I am. As I am learning to develop the habit of practising the presence of God, *learning to abide* in the Presence, I find myself chatting about certain situations and asking for his perspective. Answers often come effortlessly and there are times I only have to think about what I need or want and they come to me ... amazing! But I am not attached to this need or want being fulfilled for my peace or happiness, as now there is a greater trust, after all my experiences, that 'all is well' and somehow Unconditional Love, the Presence, is working things to good.

Does the Presence leave us?

There have be plenty of times when the Presence seems to have disappeared and left me alone, but on reflection I realise I had been focusing elsewhere or an unresolved dark area of my memory had been triggered by some upsetting situation in the present. Many people over the years have discovered they too have felt alone and abandoned, but during the Healing Meditation they discover this wasn't true. In fact, one young man who felt left alone and terrified discovered, after the trauma, fears and darkness in his mind had dissolved, that he was being held in the palm of a hand. I asked if he wanted to know whose hand it was. After he said yes, his eyes opened and with amazement said, 'He said his name was Jesus.' He also said this experience felt better than taking drugs!

When talking about his carving of David, Michelangelo said David was always there; he just chipped away all that was not David until he was exposed. So that's just what occurs during the Healing Meditation as *everything that is not from the Creator* is chipped away until we can 'see' the freeing truth about ourselves and come to know that he never left us and that he never will.

After Lenny's healing experience, she saw an image of a person who had a bench full of chipped, broken vases. She saw him mending the vases, gently and slowly. But there was a bench to the side where the broken vases had been left untouched. When Lenny asked what would happen to these vases, the person mending the vases said he couldn't put them back together because they weren't ready.

So the question is, are you ready? Are you tired of being broken? If so, ask the Divine Counsellor to make you aware of the blockages and obstacles so he can gently chip away to reveal Truth, Light, Peace and Presence. He's waiting.

What helps us to discover and maintain this Presence?

Belief: You may have heard the words that *'All things can be done for the one who believes.'* But what do we believe, and where do we develop our beliefs? I have discovered that many beliefs are lies.
I didn't like the things that were being done to me, and in my life, and often felt powerless. So I began seeking and asking for the truth to be revealed to me. That led me to join a group where I was gently encouraged to invite the Spirit of Truth to guide me. Not long after that the words written in the Bible began to come alive for me. I read that they held the Truth, but at first I couldn't believe many of the words as they felt contrary to what I had believed. Over many years, this changed as I experienced the reality of these truths deep within my mind and heart. I believed and then experienced Truth, Peace and

Presence, releasing many lies. And pain.

Our *beliefs* will bring emotional and physical pain if they are lies, and if our *beliefs* are the Truth, they will release Peace and Presence.

Faith: means the *assurance of things hoped for,* the *conviction of things not seen.* I believe *faith comes from believing.* People have shared with me that they have put their faith in someone only to later be let down or betrayed. They believed that person would make them happy and would never leave them. Or they have believed if they invest all their time and money in education for their children that they have the best chance of being successful. Although this can occur, in many cases children fail their parent's expectations and can't live up to the faith they place in them. The only safe place I have discovered after hearing so many sad stories is to have faith only in the Spirit of Truth and Wisdom—the Presence.

I had to learn that faith is just like a muscle; it needs to be exercised so it can become strong enough to move mountains. We have been told in the Word of God that we only need *faith the size of a mustard seed and it will still move mountains.* I have seen mountains being moved in many lives now, including mine, and I want everyone to know what is possible. You don't have to be concerned about not having faith but rather *ask for the gift of faith or for your faith to grow* in the One who wants to supply all your needs.

Be aware though that doubt kills faith, opens the door to torment and prevents mountains being moved in our lives. Some people have had the most wonderful breakthroughs and experienced transformations in their minds, but within hours have doubted what happened. Then instead of Peace, anxiety and fears begin to enter that area of their minds again and they begin sinking into the quicksand of discouragement. Although Peter walked on water towards Jesus, he changed his focus and began to become fearful and sank! I remember when I doubted and had little faith and I especially remember the consequences. I used to feel hopeless and helpless and was tossed around like I was in a storm. I had to learn not to 'lean on my own understanding' but rather lean into and trust Wisdom's perspective.

Grace: I love the fact that *grace is unmerited favour* from the Presence. It is the *source of faith* and it is *all-abundant and all-sufficient*. Frankly, I needed all the *unmerited favours* that were possible when I felt I couldn't cope. When I had to begin reading through and editing this book for the last time, I needed grace, as I struggled with having to revisit all I had written over the years. So I asked for grace. The next day I experienced Peace that replaced the struggle as I began to edit the book for the last time. It is the most peaceful I have ever felt since I began writing. What a blessing and a joy and what a change to how I first felt.

So you can ask for grace whenever you are in need and see what happens. My favourite song is Amazing Grace as I relate to the words and realise the grace I was given over the years. I even began singing them to my children as they went to sleep and now on occasions sing it to my grandchildren.

Endurance: When I was going through some very tough times, I would repeat these words, clinging to them even though I *didn't feel any joy*! I liked the possibility of *becoming complete, lacking in nothing:'Whenever I face trials of any kind I consider it nothing but joy because I know that the testing of my faith produces endurance, and let endurance have its full effect, so that I may be mature and complete, lacking in nothing.'*

Now I have a deeper understanding of how I can become complete, lacking in nothing, and it's usually through enduring trials. It has often been when I am weakest that I often encounter the Presence and when this occurs, I feel complete. It is because *he* is complete, lacking nothing and I experience this in him, his Presence, and through him, his grace and truth. I am so very grateful.

How making a decision to be still changed everything
It was when I *made a decision* to stop being super busy that every area of my life began to change for the better. Tracey's life also changed when she decided to be still in the Presence of God. Six months prior to this change, she had approached me at a church service sharing how her life was still in turmoil, even after years of people praying for her and trying to help her. As I listened to her, I silently asked Wisdom what I should say. What came to my mind was for her to commit an hour a day to *be still in the Presence of God*. I said he bought order out of my chaos so he can do the same for you.

Six months after making this suggestion to Tracey, I saw her in church again. She ran over to me smiling from ear to ear and excitedly told me that it was *after making a decision to be still* each day for one hour, as I suggested, that every area that had been in turmoil had changed for the better. She didn't quite understand how all this occurred as she often fell asleep in this hour of being still. She was overjoyed and I was delighted.

What if you *made a decision to be still* each day? I wonder what would happen in your life. Hopefully, like me, you will come to *know who the Presence is for you,* and become aware of how this relationship can bring Peace, changing *everything* for the better.

16

The Healing Meditation—
A Step-by-Step Guide to Peace

This Healing Meditation has been developed from years of experience and has become one of the most wonderful, gentle ways for many people, including me, to experience Peace, Presence and Power. You will read the many stories throughout this book which show you when this has occurred and the benefits. This step-by-step guide can now help you experience the same freeing and healing benefits, including helping you become present to yourself, others and the Presence who created you which usually transforms relationships and lives.

One of the greatest blocks to Peace and Presence is unresolved negative feelings and beliefs. Once I had no idea how to resolve these when difficult situations occurred. I was unaware that I was often experiencing the combined influence of both the negative emotions and beliefs from the present situation, as well as similar unresolved situations from the past. I had often been left overwhelmed and isolated when this occurred, not knowing how to constructively deal with myself, let alone others.

The information I share comes from dealing with my own life as well as assisting others with an extraordinary team of facilitators over many years. The results have been amazing! What is truly wonderful, especially to a society that admires strength, is that people have these experiences in their weakest, most vulnerable times. Healing has been experienced in childhood memories even as early as being in the womb and released and restored people in mind, heart, spirit and body. The topics I have covered in seminars over the years, many of which are in this book, have come about as a result of people not being aware of the power they had to change their lives. So they go hand in hand with this meditation, as they offer many other practical guidelines and tools to bring about change for the better. Please use this meditation only when you find yourself off-centre, stressed or having some reoccurring painful situation presenting in your life.

The Healing Meditation Step-by-Step Guide

1. *Preparation*
    - Make time for yourself and find a quiet place where nothing can disturb you.
    - Ask the Divine Counsellor—or use what terminology you relate to such as Unconditional Love, Presence, Truth, Holy Spirit—to reveal only what is appropriate and guide you through the whole process. Do not try to do this in your own strength as our minds can be very deceptive!
    - Become an observer of what is revealed.
    - Acknowledge and accept what comes up in your mind or body. Do not try to understand or work out what is happening—understanding comes later! Avoid asking why!
    - You can write down what you sense, feel or hear – it may help.

2. *Identify what needs to be resolved.*
    To begin the Healing Meditation, ask the Divine Counsellor to

reveal where you are at now as a result of your life. Wait, watch, observe and accept what is revealed in your mind's eye. (You may see a recent situation, a memory, blankness or darkness or just experience pain in your body. Remember that our body cells have memory).

3. *Emotions/Feelings*

Ask the Divine Counsellor to make you aware of what you sense or feel in what is revealed. Acknowledge and accept all the feelings that are relevant. (There may feelings of fear, terror, anger, rage, resentment, confusion, disappointment, frustration, powerlessness, sadness, doubt, numbness, hatred, revenge, shame or judgement of self or others).

4. *Thoughts/Beliefs*

Ask the Divine Counsellor what you are thinking and believing as a result of those feelings. Acknowledge and accept what comes to you. (Beliefs may be: 'I can't do anything; I'm not good enough; I am bad/dirty, nothing, worthless, hopeless; It's hopeless; It will never change; It's my fault; I'm responsible; I'm not wanted; I'm alone, abandoned; No one cares; I'm a misfit, useless, ugly; I don't deserve to be loved' and more!

5. *Listen to the freeing Truth.*

Hold up your *strongest belief* from above, and then ask the Divine Counsellor if it is true from his perspective. Be still, wait, sense and listen. Acknowledge and accept what is revealed. (You may hear words, sense Light, Presence, angels, Jesus or just experience a change for the better. The Spirit reveals himself and his truth in many ways.) Hopefully, you will now experience peace and freedom.

If there is a little *doubt* about what you have experienced, then let it go, renounce it, and again ask for Truth to be revealed again.

If anger still remains in what is revealed, the following exercise can help.

6. **The Three-Way Perspective Exercise: resolving anger, hurt and conflict**

Ask the Divine Counsellor, if it is appropriate, to bring into your mind those people with whom you still have unresolved anger, hurt and conflict.

- *Your Perspective.* As these people come into your mind's eye, *look them in the eyes* and tell them how you have been left feeling as a person as a result of what they did or didn't do. Be totally honest.

  If necessary, and *only for the motive of resolution*, ask the Holy Spirit what you would like to do to this person. For instance, you may feel like shaking them up, hitting them or yelling at them. This allows anger or rage to be vented without hurting them in real life. After expressing and emptying your feelings, it should make space for you to gain their perspective.

- *The Other Person's perspective.* Then ask the Divine Counsellor what the person would say back to you. *Look into their eyes and listen to them.* More often than not, anger turns to compassion as you 'see' the person with different eyes.

- *The Divine Counsellor's perspective.* Then ask the Divine Counsellor if there is anything else he needs to reveal to you.

You have then been given three perspectives: your perspective, other people's perspectives and the Divine Counsellor's perspective (the true version).

I have found I can now use this with great results in everyday situations when I am struggling with someone or have felt angry or upset. I just excuse myself from the gathering and deal with myself. Then I can return with peace and calm, instead of allowing my feelings to fester.

If you are unable to come to experience Peace, Presence and Power by using this process, ask the Divine Counsellor what the blockage or obstacle is and listen. Chapter 5 on Blockages and Obstacles may offer further help. Deal with whatever is revealed as suggested and see what happens.

Experiencing Peace, Presence and Power
When you have encountered the Truth, Peace will replace your negative feelings, beliefs and trauma. When you return to the situation or memory, blankness or darkness in your mind, you will see the memory without the pain. There is usually only Light and Presence and the darkness has dissolved. You should feel a greater sense of connectedness with yourself and the Presence. The pain in your body should also disappear unless there is another cause. Give thanks after this experience and ask for the grace to be aware of the subsequent changes in your life.

If this Healing Meditation or the Three Way Exercise hasn't helped you, please seek help from a trusted professional counsellor. Find someone who is genuine and makes a difference in your life to share your journey. Take responsibility for your actions and your life and see the difference it makes.

17

True and Lasting Happiness

As I share with you what I have discovered, my hope is that you will become aware of the many *healthy* ways we can experience happiness. The word 'happy' is defined in the *Oxford Dictionary* as 'feelings of, or showing pleasure and contentment.' I understand now why may people get hooked on 'things' or 'people' as this makes them feel pleasure and contentment, but does this really provide them with *lasting* happiness? I used to rely on 'things' to look forward to: some holiday, dinner or outing to make me feel happy. The only problem was I *relied* on these things for my happiness which left me feeling flat. I was on an unpleasant rollercoaster ride until I discovered the Source of true happiness, despite what was going on in my life.

Other people seek their happiness in human achievements, relationships, wealth, notoriety, science, technology, art or nature. But these 'things' are always changing so it isn't long before they are left feeling empty and dissatisfied. They are all to be enjoyed, explored and used as gifts but not to be *relied upon* as the foundation for lasting happiness.

A young man in a TV program called *Man vs. Wild* shared in an article how he adored his father who taught him to sail and climb. He said it wasn't that he loved being cold and scared up a rock-face, but that he loved being close to his dad, and those times provided this opportunity. His father died in 2001. He went on to say how he thinks he has been trying to recreate that same feeling of intimacy on his expeditions ever since. The intimacy with his father gave him pleasure and contentment which made him happy. This was then the driving force behind his life's dangerous works.

Discovering your perspective about happiness

By answering the following questions, you will become aware of what you believe about happiness and what you *rely* upon to be happy. Writing the answers can be helpful.

- *What do you believe to be true about happiness?*

- *What makes you happy? For example: 'I'm happy when ...'*

- *How do you feel when you don't have what you believe makes you happy?*

Making space for a new perspective on true happiness

To make *space* for a *new perspective* on the Source of true happiness, I suggest you place all you have written into an imaginary basket. Then by letting go of the basket, all that you *expected* would bring you happiness can be released. This should create space to experience what is left and how you feel in this new space. You may feel at peace in this new space, or you may feel empty, as though there is a void in you. This emptiness can be filled up with the Presence, the Source of true happiness. This experience provides everything within people that they have ever desired. As they listen to and apply Wisdom's instructions, their life begins to be transformed. True happiness is deeply moral and spiritual and is really human fulfilment.

Judy came over to me at church today. She was anything but happy having felt teary and overwhelmed for weeks. She wanted some help. As I led her through the Healing Meditation, she discovered a part of her memory that was dark where she felt *unhappy*, alone, trapped and unable to do anything. She believed she didn't belong and didn't like herself. She also realised she had taken on the role of being responsible to make things better which hadn't worked. This role only left her feeling heavy and overwhelmed.

After letting go of self-rejection, thus removing a blockage, she was willing to listen to the Spirit of Truth. She then saw Light, experienced a Presence and realised she wasn't alone. When we checked to see if the negative feelings and beliefs were the same, she realised they were no longer relevant. She said she could hardly believe the extraordinary change she now felt in her whole being. She looked happy and felt as light as a feather. She was amazed and absolutely delighted.

I remember seeing an image in my mind that spoke to me about this journey to happiness. I saw a road going up to the top of the mountain, with people slowly walking along it. I also saw people stray off the path and begin to slide down in the slippery sand that was on the side of the road. Some were being helped whilst others were stuck and not willing to be helped. As people came to the top of the mountain there was a glorious Light and a sense of real freedom, joy and peace. There was a *knowing* that everything would be lighter and easier from this point onwards. This revelation simply conveyed that it may take time and perseverance to change some bad habits and patterns, but thankfully we can do it with Wisdom's help.

In case you can't break through to experiencing the Presence within yourself, Chapter 5 shares what causes many people to be stuck and unable to experience true happiness within may assist you.

The source of happiness
A young man, who I will call Tony, came for help one day as he was feeling really unhappy. As I assisted him to find the truth, he experienced a Light and Presence. When I asked if he wanted to know the name of this Presence, he said yes. He then said he heard the name 'Jesus.' So the Presence became a person with whom he could develop a relationship. He said this experience was far better than the drugs he had taken in the past. He said there was no darkness or terror left in the memory, only Light, Presence and Peace. At that moment, his whole being reflected peace, security, contentment and true happiness. Previously, drugs had given him pleasure that did the absolute opposite in his life. Tony discovered the Source of lasting happiness.

I remember reading in Scripture earlier in this journey that if I sought my happiness in God, *he would give me my heart's desire* and all these other *things* would be added into my life. This appealed to me then, but it was necessary for me also to begin to find out who was giving me this instruction before I could begin trusting. Although people had talked to me about God, I didn't *know* him nor had I experienced him. Thankfully, as the blockages in me were removed, I began to experience a deep and true, abiding happiness particularly when I spent time being still in his presence. I began to experience him as a Comforter, Helper and Divine Counsellor and that made me very happy.

Many years later as I near the completion of writing this book, I realise how those words I clung to have become a reality in my life. I have not only found a deep place of peace and happiness with the Presence within, but my life and relationships has been transformed. I am thankful beyond words for the grace I was given to persevere through unhappy, challenging and dark times by the One who I discovered is always there to help me. To discover, experience and know this truth is almost beyond description.

Wouldn't you feel *truly happy* if you came to know you were not alone, but that the Presence, and all that he is and has, was available within you?

A simple way to discover *true happiness* despite where you are at!
When I wanted to find peace and true happiness, after many years of often *pretending to be happy*, I decided to be *honest* about how I really felt and what I thought. The reality was that I didn't feel happy all the time. but I learned over the years how to return to this state of being, despite my circumstances.

One such example occurred after having a very difficult day at work with aggressive, rude individuals. I felt every other feeling but happy as I drove home. So I began sharing with my Comforter how I honestly felt. I then began praising and thanking him for being there to listen to me, for being able to hand the situation to him, and for him to bring good out of it somehow. As I continued to praise him, an exquisite joy began to well up in me and every negative feeling and thought dissolved. I thought 'this must be a foretaste of heaven.' I was *truly happy,* despite my circumstances. It was extraordinary. I had been encouraged to praise in all circumstances as a result of reading a powerful book called from *Prison to Praise*.

Practical tips to discover and maintain *true happiness*
Did you know that there are more than a hundred universities in the United States at present that offer courses on happiness? *Time magazine* published some research on happiness conducted by one of these universities and the results may surprise you. Although the first response made by many people was 'money' or 'fame' when asked, 'What makes you happy?' upon deeper reflection they realised that happiness is found in having a *positive approach to life and in good relationships with other people.*

The following suggestions should move you along on the path to discover and maintain happiness:

- Be *gentle and kind to yourself* and others instead of having unrealistic expectations and *care for your body* as it is a gift!
- *Discover something in life that can brings you joy* through such simple things as walking, gardening, dancing, friends and nature. When I dance I feel fully alive so I dance twice a week!
- Develop a positive approach to life, but also be 'real' about your feelings and deal with them constructively.
- *Give wisely and generously and practice random acts of kindness.* Discover how deliciously good it is to be a generous person. Research confirms that giving to others is the number one way to get a 'happy hit'! This confirms that it is in giving that we receive! A University of British Columbia study went as far as saying that not giving makes us sick so begin to think of all the ways you can give, without expecting anything in return, other than the happy hit!
- Nurture healthy, authentic relationships with others.
- Listen to other people's perspective.
- *Let go of past offences and forgive frequently* so you can be free of the heavy baggage from the past. See Chapter 27 on How to 'Really' Forgive.
- Be *open to learn* and look for the good that can come from everything.
- Look for the good qualities in people, ourselves, and situations.
- Be thankful at least five times a day.
- Learn from the Beatitudes in Scripture that show us how 'to be' and what 'attitudes' to adopt so we experience blessings and true happiness (I recommend reading the easy to understand, inspiring commentary in Matthew 5 of the Christian Community Bible, Saint Paul's Publications).

- Seek the Creator of lasting happiness, the Presence, before seeking it through the people and things he created. I once read that the accumulation of things is the seat of all discontentment.
- *Give up being responsible to make other people happy.* A lady at a luncheon was asked the question, 'Does your husband make you happy?' to which she replied, 'No.' She then went on to say: 'I'm responsible for my own happiness!'
- Use the Healing Meditation in Chapter 16 when you feel unhappy and have unresolved, painful memories. It will help you become centred and at peace.
- Be still. I love repeating these words from Psalm 16 frequently: '*You show me the path of life. In your Presence there is fullness of joy; in your right hand are pleasures forevermore.*' They change my focus and I know that as I speak these words they begin to create this reality in my life. Making a commitment daily to become still in the Presence is vital to maintaining lasting happiness.

Would you be willing to adopt and apply just one of the suggestions I have made here? It will, I believe, lead you onto the path to *true and lasting happiness*.

18

The Power of Love Languages

I wonder if you think that you already understand other people's love language. That's what I thought when I saw the book *The Five Love Languages* by Gary Chapman, but I was curious so I checked it out anyway. As I began to read, I realised there was much to learn on this subject. I was encouraged by the stories of the stunning turnaround in relationships he described. Although I *thought* I knew my husband's language of love, I was keen to discover if what I thought was right!

Discovering another person's love language
Although I share an example from my marriage, I believe you can apply this information to any relationship. As I wanted to discover my husband's primary love language, I chose an appropriate time then asked him the question: 'When do you feel most loved in our relationship?' I was surprised by his answer, as it was entirely different to what I had believed. In fact, I thought 'we've know each other for 45 years and I never knew when he most felt loved by me!' He said it was when I remembered to complete certain tasks that he had asked to me do. I thought about how often I had put off doing these seemingly insignificant tasks, thinking 'one day I'll get around to them. When I asked him: 'How do you feel when I *don't* do the things you asked me

to do,' he said 'not important and neglected'. What an 'aha' moment for me!

When I asked him if he had any idea what my love language was, he said: 'Yes. Words of affirmation, physical touch and quality time.' He knew me well. But then I asked him if he knew which one was the most important. He said: 'I think it's quality time.' I think he realised this fact as I had often talked about spending more quality time together. I said that when we didn't have this quality time, I wondered if he cared about me and if I was important in his life. He then said, 'For the first time I now realise how you feel when I neglect doing what is important to you.' It was a moment I will treasure, as we both realised how important it was to listen and respond to each other's love language. Now we knew how to love each other in the way we each understand love.

Who is it in your life that you'd like a better and richer relationship? I recommend you treat this as an opportunity to gather valuable information. However, make sure you have resolved any conflicting issues *before* discovering each other's love language!

These are the steps that I took to discover my husband's love language, which helped build a good relationship into an even better relationship:

o Choose an appropriate time and ask the other person if they are open to discovering what is important to each other, i.e. each other's love language.
o Give them an example if necessary from the information on different types of love languages. Then if they are willing to have the discussion, continue with the following questions:
o When is it that *you* most feel cared for and loved in our relationship? Also ask what they feel when you *don't* care in this way.
o

- Ask them if they want to discover when *you* feel cared for and loved in the relationship. Share what you feel when they *don't* care in this way.
- Ask them if they are willing to use this information to strengthen the relationship. Even if they don't want to participate, you can still choose to love them in the way they identify being loved. Usually this softens their attitude and you will benefit in the long run.

The benefits

I realise now that to *really love another person* it is vital to take an interest in learning about what is *important to them*, rather than just assuming you know (as I had done). One of the benefits both people will experience is learning how to communicate effectively, which is shared in greater detail in the chapter on How to Develop Healthy Relationships. The lifeline to love, I discovered, is effective communication.

Although you may not identify with the other person's love language, as it is often the opposite of your love language, treat this as an opportunity to *choose* to love the other person in the way *they* understand love. By doing this you are loving unconditionally and will benefit in more ways than you can imagine, as we reap what we sow. It helps to ask God for his capacity to love the other person unconditionally. Try it and see.

As a result of being *aware* of each other's love language, my husband and I have noticed how we feel even closer than we had been. By being open and willing to talk about what mattered to each other developed further trust. When you sincerely apply this knowledge, your relationship will change for the better.

As I read the book on this subject, I began to ask my friends if they knew what their partner's love language was. Most said that they had never thought of asking and certainly didn't realise that it could make a difference. Many of the relationships Gary shared in his book on love languages had deteriorated and lost the spark of love. In some cases, there appeared to be no hope for revival of love, but all of the relationships turned around as each person was willing to discover the other person's love language and respond to this knowledge.

The different types of love language

Words of Affirmation
What people say, their words, have had a profound influence in my life. So words of affirmation are very important to me. I realise now how everything that comes out of our mouth either builds or destroys, despite what we think. It is another law of life!

Unfortunately, many of us criticise one another and complain about what the other person hasn't done. We focus on their flaws and failings instead of their good points. I certainly have been guilty of acting this way so I began to ask Wisdom to make me aware of the people's good points and show me how to genuinely affirm them.

When you discover words are a primary love language of your spouse or friend, then make sure you develop a habit of finding every opportunity to speak sincere words of affirmation even if you are not used to doing so. I find people's faces light up with one sentence of praise or encouragement. When I think of something good about another person, I now tell them ... even in the supermarket! Many people look surprised but often say, 'You have made my day!' What a different nation we could be if they enjoyed affirming one another instead of thinking it's funny to 'knock' each other through words.

Quality Time
Quality time for me is when someone genuinely *wants* to spend time with me, is present to me and open to listening to my opinion—even

if they don't agree. I remember my children saying to me, 'Mum, you're not listening.' They were right. I was often too busy and preoccupied with other things. But when I took the time to really listen and spend quality time with them, it made all the difference to them. You could see it on their little faces. They felt loved. When quality time is important to someone, it also helps to find out *how* this person would like to spend quality time together. Don't presume you know!

Receiving Gifts

As a result of observing my friend, I thought that her primary love language was possibly giving gifts. I noticed how she loved giving gifts to people for all sorts of reasons. What made me also believe this could be her primary love language was her expression of genuine gratitude after I had given her a small parcel of little gifts and flowers. She said how much they had meant to her as she recovered from her operation. As a matter of fact, she talked about how much it had meant to her for weeks! So *observe* what is meaningful to others. Gifts don't need to be expensive, as it is often the thought that someone cares behind the gift that is most important. I remember thinking how much I appreciated a child bringing in a flower from the garden or my husband thinking to buy flowers for me. I also notice when someone has taken time to beautifully wrap a gift or send a card of appreciation.

Acts of Service

Acts of service include a wide range of activities, including tidying the house, paying accounts, cooking or helping with the children, but the important key is that you discover what types of acts of service are meaningful to those you care about. These acts must always be done from a foundation of love, *not* resentment, guilt or fear. Remember also that *requests* may give direction to a love language, but *demands stop the flow of love.*

Physical Touch
I have read articles where babies who have been in orphanages in war zones have died because they have been deprived of physical touch. We all need to receive a kind and sincere touch that is appropriate, but it's especially important to those whose love language is in the physical realm. Even the warmth of a loving animal can make all the difference to people who feel lonely. I am aware of the constraints today, and the need for wisdom in regard to physical touch, so please be respectful and wise.

When it is appropriate to hug someone, I silently ask for God's unconditional love to flow through me to the other person. Many people, including my children, have commented on how special my hugs feel. It has melted down barriers between people and has been very healing. I remember when I first discovered the power of a genuine, present hug when I was going through a very stressful period in my life. A lady I knew from a prayer group arrived unexpectedly at my house. As I opened the door, she took one look at me and then gave me the warmest, most understanding, present hug I had every received! She didn't need to say anything. I felt her understanding and compassion. I was not alone in this struggle. She left me feeling re-energised and able to go on!

What if you silently asked for Unconditional Love to flow through you the next time you gave a person a hug and became *present* to them as well? This is how my husband and I now usually hug one another. Words are not necessary, as you can feel the love. We used to be thinking or talking about other things whilst we briefly connected in a hug. We weren't present at all to one another, but present to the 'things' on our minds. That can be felt too.

These are only some of the ways I have discovered people relate to being loved. May you enjoy the journey of discovery and enjoy richer relationships as a result.

19

Becoming Free To Be Me!

Do you feel free to be yourself at all times? I certainly didn't! I often felt like I had to tippy-toe around people, and that I couldn't be honest about how I was feeling. After asking the Divine Counsellor 'what prevents me from being free to be me?' I began to become aware of many things that blocked me.

Blockages and obstacles to freedom
The things that stop most of us from feeling free to be ourselves, which certainly applied to me, are fears of all kinds and doubts. These come from our life experiences and the meaning we put to them. During a Healing Meditation, some of these memories have been shown as an image of being trapped in a dark cage. This part of us in the cage could see a door, but it was locked. In many cases, some of us have felt that this part of us didn't want to leave the cage because of the fear of being hurt yet again. The cage in a strange way acted as protection, despite also conveying the feeling of being confined and trapped.

In my experience, as I listened to this part of my memory, I discovered that I was frightened of being judged. I felt trapped, insecure and alone and believed that I deserved to be in this place as I believed what had happened in the memory was my fault. It took some time listening to and waiting with this part of me (my memory) in the cage. Eventually, this part of me was willing to listen to the Truth. Then a Light appeared at the doorway. There was a knowing at that moment that whatever had happened wasn't my fault. The fear of judgement dissolved and I felt I could breathe easily again. It then felt safe to go towards the door of the cage. I was then invited to step outside into the Light. As I did this in this memory, I felt *totally free to be me*. It was as though I was still myself, yet merged with the Light. It was a place of total security, all I had to do was be ... me!

Different types of fears

The most common fears are of rejection or judgement by others. One way to try to avoid experiencing any of these feelings is to retreat from people and/or situations, which closes us down to some extent. Some people become people pleasers and end up being controlled by other people's needs and wants. They lose their right then to speak their truth and suppress their true voice. Many other people are driven in all they do, never being able to rest and just be themselves, striving to prove their personal worth and value through what they do or achieve.

This story about John is an example of being driven. He shared with me how he heard that at the Awards Night for his company he was placed with others who had been excellent at selling. He said he was ashamed when this happened because he believed he had not earned the right to be considered for the award as he had not done enough. (Mind you, he worked six days a week!) He said that the products were just there for him to sell. He wanted no-one to know about this outside of work because he felt like a fraud and believed that *he wasn't good enough*.

It appeared, from my perspective, that he had unrealistic *expectations* of himself, setting unreachable goals that would prove in the end what he believed about himself: that he wasn't good enough. He was a like a greyhound in a race, running to get the prize, the rabbit on the boom. As you know though, the greyhound never gets the rabbit; it's always out of his reach. What I have discovered is that if you believe that you are not good enough (which is a lie from your Creator's perspective) no amount of trying to prove your worth will satisfy you. Many people unfortunately are unaware that they are living life based on a lie. On the other hand, I have seen many other people who are ready and open to listen to Truth's perspective. They then feel safe to have a voice, speak their truth, follow their dreams and be their authentic self.

I can remember as a child being frightened to speak up and say what I thought and felt, not only because I would be judged, but because of fear of upsetting other members of my family. I hated the thought of being the one creating tension. My deepest fear was that my family would fall apart if I added to the tension that already existed. I would then be alone in a place of devastation. So I became a people pleaser. I had no freedom to be me when acting from this fear. Thankfully this dissolved as I experienced Truth and Presence in a Healing Meditation.

Roles and Masks

As I mentioned previously, one of the roles I took on was making everything 'right' in people's lives … a little like being a saviour or caretaker. This way of 'being' was exhausting and not possible to maintain in my own strength. In fact, it eventually led to burnout. Another one of my masks was that of having it all together, being like a Superwoman. I gave the impression to others that there was no stress in my life, which was a lie. I often felt like a dried up old prune! There were, of course, many times where I just enjoyed life, until my mask went up and my roles took over which prevented me from being me. I later discovered people hated me being their caretaker!

I was subtly controlling others out of fear as well. This was another role! The roles and masks I created were not only for my survival but to make life how I wanted it to be—safe, peaceful and ordered. In fact, this way of acting only created more chaos and barriers between others and myself. My Creator— who I later experienced, had been waiting for me to stop, listen and discover that he was the Source of safety, peace and order. I didn't realise this though for a long time.

Doubts

Doubts occur when we don't feel secure about who we are. When we are insecure, we wobble all over the place with no firm foundation. Thoughts of making the wrong decision, saying the wrong thing, or acting in the wrong way could make us feel open to judgment or rejection.

Janine always doubted when it came to making decisions or if she had conflict with others. She often rang me and was being literally tormented by the fear of getting it wrong in some way. She frequently procrastinated. What if she made the wrong decision? What if she was the one at fault? When she rang asking for help, I would always ask her how she would feel if she did the wrong thing. She said she would feel bad. I asked the Spirit of Truth to reveal if there was any time in her past where she believed she was bad. Then she remembered an incident as a child when someone close to her had been told to leave the house and she felt it was her fault. I asked her to listen to the Spirit's perspective. She sensed a Presence and heard in her mind that it was not her fault. I asked if she still felt bad in the memory. She said she didn't feel bad at all anymore, but in fact felt at peace and secure. There was no sense of being judged in this Presence, only of being loved unconditionally.

She realised that every time she had faced a situation where she had to make a decision, or in any situations involving conflict, that the fear of being blamed and feeling bad was triggered from this earlier memory. It was like a mountain of fear had been removed from her whole being. If we listen to Truth and believe, and don't doubt, mountains really can be removed in our lives.

Trauma

Experiences where we have been traumatised can leave us feeling frozen and feeling totally alone and helpless. It can be through accidents or abuse. (This is dealt with in greater detail in Chapter 8 on how fears and trauma can dissolve.) After these experiences, we are changed, as part of us is no longer free but frozen. The tendency is to withdraw from life and spend a lot of energy protecting and guarding against any further traumas.

When Josephine found out she had been betrayed, she went into shock. After that experience, she put up her guard to the person who had betrayed her, her husband. They continued living together but their relationship changed. Josephine felt like some part of her had died. There were many other incidents of betrayal later on in their relationship. Later on she was released from being frozen and everyone remarked on the change in her.

Dealing with trauma is a process. The first step is to face your fears or any disturbing situation that prevents you from being free to be yourself. Ask and allow the Divine Counsellor and Advocate, the one who wants to stand up for you, to give you the grace to face whatever lies, roles, decisions or trauma that stand in your way, which may be stored in your conscious, subconscious or unconscious mind. Gently acknowledge this and then let go of these ways of being.

Let go of the following:
- any decisions that entrap you and stop the flow of life and freedom;
- expectations you have had that you were relying on for your freedom;

- judgement, rejection, hatred, resentment, condemnation and revenge;
- unhealthy roles you have taken on; and
- blaming and complaining.

How to remain free

What if the tension returns? Let's face it, life can be a challenge sometimes so you may slip into old patterns. The key is to be awake, aware and alert to what you are thinking/believing and how you are acting. Is this way of being leading you down the path where you are free to be your authentic self, despite what happens? Ask yourself, 'What if I did face my fear. What would I feel and believe about myself or life?' Then ask if there are any barriers you have set up that need to be acknowledged and let go of so you can make space for the Source of truth and freedom.

Spend time focusing on and being aware of the presence of Unconditional Love daily, thus developing a real relationship. You will begin to reflect the qualities of the One with whom you spend time with. Other people will notice the change in you.

Always ask for the Spirit of Truth to reveal his perspective when you begin to lose your sense of freedom to be your true self. Ask also what good you can learn from the experience.

What to some people is experienced as loss in their life can actually be an opportunity to access a deeper, broader sense of the true self who is already content and has a sense of total abundance. This is who you are in the presence of Light, the one who created you. Keep your identity tied to this level of deep inner contentment and draw life from the deeper abundance.

Why settle for a scarcity model for life believing such thoughts as: 'I'm not good enough'? This mentality only robs people of freedom to be their true selves. In a content and abundant space and place, you are overwhelmed by more than enough-ness. What feels like a loss is actually the loss of the false self. That which is not true is dismantled and crumbles away and the 'true self' remains—as we were in the beginning!

I eventually came to a place where *whenever* I was centred and in the Presence of my Creator, my safe home within, I felt free to be me in the presence of anyone.

20

How 'Really' Listening Melts Hearts

When I saw the list of comments on what prevents authentic listening, I identified with every one of them as I had often experienced people acting this way with me. I remembered thinking, 'What's the point of sharing with this person as they're not interested in listening. I might as well be talking to a brick wall!' I often backed away from the relationships as a result. On reflection, I also realised I had also been guilty of acting this way! I wonder what you have experienced and if you relate to the following list?

What prevents authentic listening?

Distraction	Attention is on our own thinking, needs and wants
Assumptions	Assuming you know where the conversation is headed
Judgements	Making judgements on other people's thoughts and actions. Most people can *sense* when they are being judged and may stop sharing.
Interrupting	Not allowing people to finish speaking
Controlling	Interrupting and steering the conversation where you want it to go!

Authentic listening

Authentic listening is when we genuinely listen with our full attention: body, mind, heart and spirit. It's when we allow time and space to hear not only the words spoken, but what is being said *behind* the words that we are fully present to the person speaking.

When speaking with Jessica over the phone recently, I could *sense* her agitation. Just by asking her some gentle questions, she began to share how her friend hadn't been to see her whilst she was recovering from an operation. I said, 'Do you feel she doesn't care about you?' She said, 'Yes.' I also discovered she believed I didn't care! I gently responded by saying I was really sorry. Jessica's voice softened and the agitation in her voice disappeared. I asked if she would like to meet for a chat over a coffee. She said she would really like that. Without authentic listening, a rift in our relationship could easily have developed.

Listening to yourself

I realise in hindsight how I used to want others to 'really' listen to me, but then became aware I wasn't taking time to listen to myself—a little unfair don't you think, expecting others to do for and to us what we don't do for ourselves!

So one particular day I listened to my inner voice as I was driving to present a seminar. I became aware of how irritable I felt without really knowing why. So I asked the irritable part of me, 'What's wrong?' As I listened to what I was feeling and believing, I realised there were two parts of me present. One part was asking myself the question and listening (the observer) and another part was 'irritable.' The irritable part felt resentful and frightened because I had accepted the invitation to do the seminar, whilst the other part of me wanted to present the seminar. I was divided in myself! As you probably know, 'a house divided against itself will fall.' So thank goodness I listened to the irritable part of me and was able to release all of the negative feelings and beliefs just by listening to my weaker, struggling self. The seminar was a success by the way and I was able to enjoy the whole day.

Do you 'really' listen to your feelings and beliefs without judgement when you feel out of sorts? If not, will you give it a go? This is taking responsibility for your feelings and beliefs and using them constructively. It's a positive and healthy way to reconnect.

I spoke to Jennifer the other day. She is going through a massive change in her life. She felt like she was losing her memory and felt frightened and alone. She wanted help so after gently leading her through the Healing Meditation she became aware of a part of her memory that was black. After listening to all the feelings and beliefs in this memory, she realised she disliked this part of her and hadn't wanted to listen to this 'weaker' part. As she apologised to this part of her memory, she was willing to listen to the Spirit of Truth and then experienced Light in this memory. She then felt connected and lighter. Whenever we dislike, reject, judge or hate ourselves, it creates division within ourselves and feelings of heaviness and darkness can enter this part of our memory.

How to listen to quiet/shy people
There are times when we are with people who rarely speak, so how do we listen to and connect with these people? Give them an opportunity to speak and be listened to without judgement. I found asking questions helps them to have a voice, but sometimes just allowing the quietness between you and a quiet person can provide a space for them to speak. I used to fill the space with my words, as I felt awkward with the lack of conversation. Then I learned to be quiet for some time and it worked. I found the quiet individual, given

the space, will often speak. This can make a real difference to quiet, shy people to have a voice and be listened to.

Do we listen to people who never stop talking?
I do not believe that we should keep listening to others who never draw breath and who constantly talk about themselves. Nor do I believe we should listen to loud, aggressive people. They can really disturb us, and should be listened to only when they are calm, or when they are willing to become present. There is usually no conversation or relationship possible in these situations. So choose who you wish to listen to wisely. You can inform these people that you are happy to listen, when they feel calmer.

Listening to the One who created you and the Universe
Over the years, I have learned to trust what I sense or hear in my heart and spirit as I ask for guidance or perspective from the Spirit of Truth. I find it always agrees with the words of wisdom in Scripture. When I first began this journey, I would ask Wisdom to repeat what I had heard or else take the words away from my mind. As my relationship developed and I spent time in communicating and listening, I began to 'know' what was authentically from Wisdom and what was just me!

Some people have placed too much emphasis on what they think they have heard from Wisdom without testing the thoughts or words they get and their life has gone off track. Other people have gone to God only to get what they want. There is no relationship there, nor are they willing to listen to his wisdom and instructions. They then can become disappointed and disillusioned and give up on God, because he *hasn't listened to their request.* (God always listens to his children. However, sometimes the answer though is no.) The point is though, without listening, there isn't a genuine relationship; it is just a one way conversation!

Some practical tips on how to be an authentic listener
- *Silently ask for the grace to listen* with the ears, heart and mind of Unconditional Love.
- *Look at the person when they speak* and gently turn your body toward them to indicate you are willing to listen and be present to what they have to share.
- *Listen without interrupting* except when you need to clarify something they are saying such as, 'Did you say…?' When you interrupt others, it can say to them, 'What I have to say is more important than listening to you.'
- *Be aware of what the person is really saying*; their body language can be different to what they are saying. For instance, I have heard people say to me, 'I'm fine' when in fact they actually look fed up, insecure, neurotic or emotional.
- *Stay calm*, particularly if the person is upset or their conversation triggers some emotions within you (Deal with your feelings later.)
- *Be aware of your non-verbal reactions.* The person will be aware if you are making judgments by the way you look and if you are not genuinely interested. Avoid yawning, looking at your watch or over the person's shoulder as it can send a message to them that you are bored! If you ARE genuinely bored, politely excuse yourself.
- *Empathize with the person when appropriate* i.e. identify yourself mentally with the person and understand their feelings. Feed back to them what you believe they said so they know they have been heard. Once the person knows you have *heard* their point of view, ask if they would like your perspective.
- *Be aware of any key words* that come to your mind or a sense

of how they may feel as you listen. Only after they have finished sharing, use this knowledge in the form of questions, if appropriate. For instance: 'Did you feel betrayed (blamed, abandoned, sad or angry)?' Many hearts have been melted as a result of someone being in touch with the feelings of others, whether they be right or wrong.

- *Only if it seems appropriate,* ask the person who is sharing with you what they have been left *believing*. You can do this by asking questions, such as, 'What did that leave you believing about yourself?' or 'Did you believe somehow you were not good enough?' Accept what they say and then *ask if they are open to listening to the Spirit of Truth and his perspective*? If they say yes, just wait with them in silence. Then silently ask for Truth to be revealed. Many people have sensed or heard words in their mind that have been life changing.
- *Respect the person's boundaries!* They will indicate by their words or body language when you have gone too far in trying to listen to, understand or help them.

Be encouraged even when you fail to authentically listen

We all make mistakes and becoming an authentic listener takes time and practice. Remember that life is a journey where we can continue learning and growing. We are like children in this amazing universe. When we fail to listen to others, our Creator or ourselves, just say sorry! In most cases, I have discovered sincerely apologising usually strengthens relationships and people are generally very forgiving and all guilt dissolves.

21

How to Develop Healthy Relationships

As I wanted to develop healthy relationships, I made a commitment to learning how this could happen. Although many of my relationships were okay, there were others that needed a lot of work. Thankfully I realised the only person I could work on and change first in these relationships was me. I never felt powerless after I *accepted this fact* and was willing to apply what I learned. It's been extraordinary on reflection how other people have changed as a result of the changes within me.

What I share is not easy to apply at times, but it's well worth doing what you have to do *to get the results you want*. Are you ready for a change—that I hope you will see as an adventure—which will help you develop healthy relationships and even enrich the ones that are working well?

Being open and honest about relationships
Looking back over my life, I realised I couldn't bear to face the truth that some of my relationships weren't healthy ones. I didn't know how to be open and honest about how I really felt. I used to tell people I was *fine* when they asked, when in actual fact I often felt *fed up, insecure, nervous* and *emotional*. I didn't know it then, but on

reflection I was a *people pleaser* trying to earn my right to their friendship. Had I known to ask myself the question 'What if I didn't please people or do what they want, how would I feel?' the answer would have revealed a deep fear of being left alone, separated and of no value.

As a result of ignoring and suppressing my true feelings and thoughts, they would build up in me and at times explode unexpectedly. One person close to me shared that they had felt crushed when I did this. I then realised I was doing to others *what had been done to me*! So the journey of learning to deal with my deeper insecurities and fears began as well as learning how to express my feelings and thoughts *appropriately*.

A time to speak
So often, out of my need, I would approach the person I wanted to speak when it was inappropriate. For instance, I used to talk to my children while they were watching TV, or try to talk to my husband when he was reading the paper or running out the door. This led to resentment, anger, frustration and arguments. I needed to become aware and respectful of other people's space.

It's *common courtesy,* of course, to let people know you have a need to talk to them, *agreeing upon a suitable time* to do so. This then develops respect and usually you become respected as a result. When people feel respected, they are usually willing to listen to what you want to say. This sounds so obvious, but I can't tell you the number of times I used to interrupt people in the middle of what they were saying or doing, immediately launching into what I wanted them to hear. I definitely lacked awareness as I was living in my own world, wanting my needs to be addressed first and foremost. I wonder if you relate to what I am sharing?

A way to speak
If you approach others when you feel angry, resentful or bitter, you will usually attract the same from the other person which is disastrous to a relationship. I know this from many painful experiences. The other person knows instinctively what is on your heart. They can *feel the vibes, the tension within you,* through the sharp edge or sarcastic tone in your voice. I can remember many dinner parties where I would throw little verbal darts at my husband, out of resentment for something he had or had not done. Of course he had no idea what was going on in most cases, but it built a wall between us and killed any warmth and love at the time. Love cannot exist in the same place as resentment. I was still blaming and judging instead of resolving the issues I was resentful about by making an appropriate time to talk about them.

After a Marriage Encounter weekend, our relationship began to change because we had been *equipped with some tools on how to communicate effectively.* These tools helped us to connect to what was going on in ourselves and communicate this effectively with each other. In fact, the night we came home two of our children were arguing and we were able to show them how to listen to one another and how to share their feelings without judgement. They were both amazed at what they heard from each other and were reconciled as a result.

Be aware of your body language
Did you know that non-verbal communication is even more powerful than verbal? Standing with our arms crossed tightly almost shouts something like, 'I'm making a stand here and I'm going to get my point across.' There is no point in communicating when someone has this attitude.

Have you ever seen hate in another person's eyes or sensed

judgement from their expression? Well, other people will see this in you too. People will not have an open attitude or heart to what you want to say if this is your approach. A wall usually goes up for protection and they will avoid you or attack you before you even say a word! Have you ever experienced this in your relationships?

The most effective and productive way to speak is always from a heart that is clear of negative emotions and wants the best for yourself and the other person. Speak your truth in love in other words. Our approach should be one that makes the other person feel they are important and that we want to listen to them and discuss any situation needing to be resolved. The tone of our voice should be gentle and non-threatening and our eyes should be focussed on them, not moving all over the place (especially your watch!)

The "I" word
In expressing our feelings and thoughts, it is important to use the 'I' word and avoid the 'you' word which may make the other person feel like they will be judged or blamed. For instance, when one of the members of my family leaves dishes undone, clothes hanging around and generally does not respect the space we all have to share, I would say something like, 'When the dirty dishes are left undone and clothes left all around the house, I feel angry, frustrated and not respected. I want to find a solution so that our relationship will not be affected because of this situation. What do you suggest?'

When children don't respond to any approach, then it's perhaps time to listen to what's going on with them or set healthy boundaries. However, I have found that when children are misbehaving, it has been helpful on occasions to say quietly and patiently: 'I'm not sure that what is happening here is helping us.' This statement has made them stop and think. Then I ask: 'What can you do that would be helpful?' This gives them a chance to act in a better way.

The power of asking questions

Questions are brilliant because they allow the other person we are communicating with to have a voice. We get to hear them. When there is conflict, it calms the whole situation down as we ask questions and listen to the other person's perspective. We're not just talking 'at' the other person, telling them what we think, or what *we* want them to think! Again, this develops respect and they may then listen with an open heart to our perspective.

As a result of asking questions, we may also gain insights and hear a possible solution we hadn't thought of. Situations are often not as we think they are. We all 'see' things through the eyes of our past experiences, which are usually different. This type of dialogue contributes to an atmosphere of safety where both people can become open and honest and allow each other to have their own point of view. Otherwise, we can give the impression that we know best and we're always right.

If we want to help, or offer the other person our suggestion, first ask, 'Would you like me to help you or suggest some possible solutions?' Either way, be respectful of their answer. When I asked my teenage children this question after they had shared about some situation, for two years they always said 'I just want you to listen'. Sometime after this period, they began to ask for my opinion. Respect had been developed.

Many people, I have discovered, feel they have no voice so let's make a difference by asking questions and listening to their answers which are often very creative and revealing.

Listen to others

When you know another person may be struggling with what you have done or said, make a time to discuss the issue. Listen to them thoroughly and try to understand their point of view. Do not interrupt or try to defend yourself before they have finished. Hear them out. If you can do this, give yourself a pat on the back; you're building a healthy relationship! People will know if you care by the way in which you listen. Be aware of your body language when listening. When a child wants your attention, listen to them straight away unless it's inappropriate, in which case let the child know you will listen to them shortly. Always give them a time and honour it! This obviously applies to everyone.

Let your words be like gifts
Remember to affirm and build one another up with what you say. When you think something pleasant about others, tell them. These words are like little gifts. Let those people you care about know you want to spend time with them and make (and keep) plans to do so.

Qualities required for developing healthy relationships
You will require certain qualities to develop healthy relationships. If you lack a certain quality then do what I have done, simply ask the One who has every quality within you, to release this quality through you and see what happens.

Quite a few years ago, I remember feeling as though I was very loud and aggressive. I loved gentleness in others and desired this quality. The thought came to me that 'if God lives within me, then all his gentleness must be within me too,' so I asked him to release his gentleness into me. For the next three weeks, I thanked him daily for releasing his gentleness. A few weeks later many people began remarking how gentle I was. I was amazed as all I had done was ask for this quality and then I received it!

Some other qualities I needed and asked for over the years to develop healthy relationships have been patience, understanding, unconditional love, forgiveness (in abundance!), openness, wisdom, truth and courage. Would you be open to asking for a quality you desire and then see what happens?

Do you have a healthy relationship with yourself?
It has taken time and perseverance to come to know myself, accept my strengths and weaknesses and learn to be encouraging and gentle with myself. Most people I have assisted have had a problem with their self-worth. Many have judged, hated and rejected themselves as a result of their negative experiences in the world and the beliefs developed from these experiences. But I have seen these people acknowledge their feelings and beliefs and open themselves to hearing and experiencing Light and Truth which has transformed how they have seen themselves. It is truly an awesome way to care for oneself.

I wonder how you treat yourself? We usually end up treating others as we treat ourselves. For your sake, and the sake of developing healthy relationships, I hope you can be gentle with yourself, as you and I are like little children in this universe hopefully still learning from everything.

My hope is that you come to know we have been made in the image and likeness of Unconditional Love and perfection so allow him to show you how he sees you!

Becoming present to yourself and the power of your Creator
To become *present* to where I am, as well as *present* and connected to the power of my Creator, I often do the following simple body, mind, heart and spirit meditation, particularly when I need to become centred. It is also a great way to begin the day, otherwise I can be all over the place.

As I see the Spirit as the Divine Counsellor, I always ask for his help which brings real power for change and an effortlessness to the following simple meditation.

Body, mind, heart and spirit reconnecting meditation
I ask the Spirit to give me a *sense* of what my **mind** is like as a result of my life. I frequently sense it is darting all over the place. As I ask the Spirit to gently come into my mind, I observe what happens. My mind usually becomes settled and peaceful.

I then ask the Spirit to give me a sense of what my **heart** is like. I wait and may sense that it is broken, dark, light or a bit dead for instance. Again as I ask the Spirit to blow the breath of his love into my heart, I usually observe my heart becoming more whole as a result. Then I focus on my **body.** I ask the Spirit to give me a sense of where my body is at. Often I observe a painful or tense area. As I ask the Spirit to bring his life and healing into my body, I observe what he does and the resulting changes.

I then ask the Spirit to make me aware of what my human **spirit** is like. I often am given a sense of it being grey, flat, lifeless or sometimes light and alive. I again ask the Holy Spirit to breathe his life into my human spirit. It is truly wonderful to observe the changes. This is really tuning into yourself so you can care for every part of you. I believe that we can be in touch with the Presence, the Spirit, only to the degree that we are in touch with our own selves.

What is your relationship like with others?
Do you have healthy relationships with others or do you struggle with them? Resolving negative thoughts and feelings about other people is imperative for healthy relationships. We usually attract from others how we are being so this should encourage you to quickly deal with all negative feelings.

I have found the following exercise invaluable in resolving my negative feelings towards others and also gaining a healthy perspective:

Three Way Perspective Exercise
Ask the Spirit of Truth to bring into your mind's eye the people that you are struggling with. Tell these people how you have been left feeling as a result of what they have or have not done, as though they were really present, until you are empty. You can do this silently or out aloud. Then ask the Spirit of Truth to reveal how these people respond. Listen to them and watch their expression. Then ask the Spirit if he would like to say anything. This is listening to yourself, others and then the Spirit of Truth.

I recommend asking the Spirit of Unconditional Love to be present in you in all your relationships asking for his mind, eyes and heart. I know this works as it totally changed the way I saw a particular lady I had found difficult to tolerate. I now see her with compassion.

What is your relationship with God like?
Many people relate to God as they relate to their earthly father or other authority figures in their lives. If these relationships have been unhealthy, then our perception of God can be negatively influenced.
Painful experiences with those who are supposed to represent God in religious organisations can especially distort our image of God. An elderly man shared how he used to be very involved with his local church until the minister of the church was unjustly treated and then sacked by the board of administrators. He said the inappropriate behaviour of those involved disgusted him and he never went back to church again. I wonder if he had gone to God and expressed his feelings and thoughts, then listened to his perspective, if the outcome would have been different. These unfortunate incidents can get in the way of letting us develop a healthy, honest relationship with God.

When people have expressed their anger and negative feelings in unfair situations using the Three Way Perspective Exercise, they have then been able to hear God's perspective. What a difference this has made in relationships, especially with God as they experience his presence, peace, compassion and justice.

There have been many times in the past though when I *haven't* experienced God and his presence, but I have clung to the words that it is by *grace* that I am saved through *faith*, which is the substance of things *not* seen, the evidence of things *to come*. And the evidence of his power to bring *all* things to good has come in my life, when I don't doubt.

Many people have told me that they feel God has abandoned them. However, when we discover the memory where they experienced abandonment and the blockages are removed, these people then become aware of Presence and Light. As a result of this experience they realise that *they were never abandoned.* They just didn't experience his presence and were unaware that they could ask him for help. So be mindful whenever you feel lost, alone or abandoned that some incident you are experiencing in the present may be triggering an unresolved memory.

I encourage you to persevere until you have discovered the truth about God and develop an open, honest, healthy relationship. The section in Chapter 15 on Discover the Loving, Powerful Presence Within may help in this regard.

22

Relationships with Healthy Boundaries

If you don't set healthy boundaries in your relationships, especially with children, you more than likely won't have healthy relationships. Resentment and a lack of respect is often felt when boundaries are violated. So I recommend that you make a decision to *learn how to set healthy boundaries* and see the difference it makes in your relationships. It should be a win/win situation for everybody.

Being calm, centred and consistent

Never enter a discussion where boundaries have not been respected when you are not calm, centred and clear about what you hope the outcome will be. Entering a discussion whilst angry will only make the other person step back and be less receptive to what you have to say. Deal with your anger first and then approach the other person at an appropriate time.

I recently watched the *Dog Whisperer* DVDs where the main character, Cesar Millan, shares how he rehabilitates dogs and trains people when certain situations are out of control and there is a lack of clarity and boundaries. I felt like I was being trained as I watched the episodes! He knows how to set healthy boundaries with the dogs because in his heart he knows *without doubt* that it will bring peace and security to the dog he is rehabilitating.

The Dog Whisperer is calm, centred, consistent and confident in dealing with the animals and owners, I repeat, there is no doubt in his mind that what he is doing is the very best for all concerned. He genuinely wants a good result for everyone. The transformation that occurs in the dogs when they are being rehabilitated by the Dog Whisperer is profound. The dogs tune into his calm but firm instructions as he sets healthy boundaries. When the owner copies the Dog Whisperer's actions, the dog also responds to them, unless they doubt what they are doing and become frightened thus losing their calm, centred posture. When this occurs, the dog usually reflects what is going on in their owner.

I applied what I had learned with a young child who cried every time I said 'no' to him. From a quiet, calm, centred place, doing what I believed to be the best for us both, I gently but firmly put him in his room, saying that I loved him, but to stay in his room until he calmed down and was willing to have a chat. It worked a treat, and I felt our relationship benefited as I was consistent with my reaction to his meltdowns after being told 'no' to something he wanted. It was a lot better than being frustrated at the child and getting angry which would leave me feeling bad for being out of control myself.

Setting appropriate time boundaries

When my husband worked long hours, six days a week, I became concerned not only for his health, but also for the health of our relationship so I approached him at an appropriate time and asked if he would be open to discuss this issue. I believed we both needed to hear each other and somehow find a way to set healthy work boundaries for the good of our relationship. It was a delicate subject to discuss as he ran his own business and was very responsible.

Although at first he didn't understand the importance of spending quality time, he finally said, 'Let's get the diary and make a date!' We made time at first to chat over a coffee. These times of catching up developed into a night away every few months. He benefited by being refreshed and our relationship was nurtured. It was time out from work and fun spending time together in different places. After having a night away at a friend's beach house, we both began to dream about having our own holiday shack, so we could have more quality time as a family. Ten years later, our dream became a reality as he decided to sell his business. He would become an employee again which would free up his time.

Now our quality time together has developed into every second weekend away at our beach home that backs onto a scenic reserve which is only four minutes away from a beautiful beach in a little country village. Thank goodness I made a time to have a chat about setting some work boundaries!

Agreements and consequences

There is a wonderful book called *Horse Sense for People* by Monty Roberts, the Horse Whisperer, who fostered 47 children, some of whom were very difficult. He says he remains as a friend to the children who come to stay at his ranch even when they don't honour the agreement they had made together to do their chores. He would thank them in these cases for honouring the agreed upon *consequences* when this occurred. In one instance, a young boy was supposed to make sure his horse always had water. He forgot and their agreement was that he would have to fill the horse's water tub with a cup. It took a long time, but he learned the lesson and never again forgot to make sure his horse had water. The consequences helped him become responsible.

If you and I don't experience the consequences of our actions, and allow others to do the same, we may never grow into responsible, happy adults. Everything we do and say has consequences. I believe that if we sow blessings, we will reap blessings. Likewise, if we sow anger, we will reap anger and if we sow judgements, we will reap judgement. One of the most common mistakes I have seen people make is that of judging themselves. They then attract and reap judgement from others. We do need to judge what we and other people *do,* but then learn from our mistakes.

When one of my teenage children was brought to the front door by the police, my husband could see that the child was terrified. In his wisdom, he could see that he had already suffered the consequences of his action and led him inside. The young teenager was very sorry, yet grateful as a result of his father's way of dealing with the situation. A greater respect grew between them. The situation never occurred again. This child is now growing into a responsible young adult.

What do you do when others do something wrong? Avoid yelling at them, heaping further judgement on them when they already know they have made a mistake. This destroys your relationship and you may end up being judged one day for doing something similar. We should pursue peace with everyone as much as possible to avoid resentment and bitterness developing. Choose to build confidence within them by your firm, gentle, respectful stance and allow them to suffer the consequences. Remember not to rescue others, as they need to learn the consequences of their actions and grow in wisdom. This is short-term pain for long-term gain!

No boundaries = chaos!
I know when I *didn't* set boundaries with my children, they became insecure and I felt inadequate. I was so frightened of upsetting them as I would then feel bad. I know a number of people who have done the same. I doubted my own gut instinct so often that I would often give in to them. I now realise it was my distorted belief that I would be a *bad* mother that undermined my confidence to set healthy boundaries.

This led to times when things got out of control and I would yell at the children. Then of course I felt like a *bad* mother for my inappropriate behaviour. That which I feared came about!

I discovered through a Healing Meditation that these feelings and beliefs of being *bad* had begun when I was a very young child. I became aware then that I was always trying to avoid feeling bad! After I experienced Truth and Peace in this memory, setting boundaries became easier. I was now operating from a solid foundation of truth and could *see clearly* that setting boundaries was healthy for the children and myself. My children have now, after many years, become secure, responsible individuals. Thank God for the chaos that caused me to become conscious of how I needed to change. How effectively do you set healthy boundaries? Is there order or chaos in your relationships?

Listen to and accept no when appropriate
When people say *no* to you for whatever reason, do you listen to them? Perhaps they are trying to set boundaries. You may make the other person feel inadequate as a result of appearing to know what is best for them. Maybe they need to learn for themselves. If you ignore their wishes, they may feel you are trying to control them and respond with anger and resentment.

When my husband used to say *no* to me when I wanted something, I used to try to get him to change his mind. He shared later how he felt I was trying to manipulate and control him to get my own way. Of course he was right! If he gave into my request, I could see his body slump in defeat. I wasn't respecting his wishes and although I got what I wanted, it certainly didn't bring us closer in our relationship. Of course my children learned to do the same, until *I* changed.

We need to respect other peoples' free will and 'allow' them to have an opinion. You may need to grieve the loss of control, but you'll end up feeling sad rather than bad. If you're left feeling frustrated that they won't listen or change, then change yourself by dealing with your own feelings, thoughts and beliefs and ask for Wisdom's perspective. Peace will come.

When fear threatens to overwhelm you from setting healthy boundaries

I remember a time when I visited a very close relative whom I was very frightened of because I never knew if he was going to be charming or abusive. When I went to visit him one day, I remember feeling so frightened of what might happen that I would pray all the way to his house.

When I arrived this day he was fine, but suddenly as we were chatting I could sense him beginning to change in front of my eyes. I could feel fear rise up inside me, but remembered at that moment to call for God's help. I silently said, 'Greater are you within me than he that is in the world.' I was stunned to see an *instant* change in him. He became like a lamb before me: calm, quiet and unthreatening. I realise all the fear I had experienced had dissolved as well. It was an awesome reminder of being able to call upon God's presence at any time using his word to overcome fear. *He in fact stepped in and powerfully set the boundary* in this case.

Some fears and false beliefs about setting boundaries
- Belief: I'll hurt others if I set boundaries. Truth: You hurt them (and yourself) more if you don't.
- But they've done so much for me. (You are responding from guilt.)
- Boundaries are permanent. (They change as we grow.)
- Setting boundaries is selfish. (Love others as you love yourself.)
- If I set limits, I might not be loved. (Seek love from the One

who is Unconditional Love within you.)
- It might break down relationships. (Breakdowns can become breakthroughs!)

Do you feel free in your relationships or is there fear, resentment or chaos? I know establishing appropriate boundaries, for the good of all, brings freedom, peace and builds healthy relationships.

Section 3

POWER

23

Powerfully Resolving Conflicts

Conflict stoppers!
Here are a few ways that I have found to be very helpful in either working through or stopping conflict.

Asking questions brings clarity and takes the attention off you!
If you ask questions of the person who is looking for an argument or is upset, this should draw further conversation from them. Also, the focus turns to them and off you. You may also gain further understanding about the situation from their point of view. The other person can often become calmer as they are listened to. Tell them you are willing to agree to disagree, and ask them if they will do the same.

Asking *Wisdom* questions like, 'What can *I* do that could be constructive in this situation?' or 'What good could come from this situation?' will open *you* to some constructive, creative ideas. Listen to what comes to your mind and apply it to the situation and see the results.

Mirroring what people say to you
Repeating back to people what they are saying to you, particularly if it is judgemental, gives them a chance to hear what they have said. For

instance, if someone says 'You're hopeless,' I just say, 'I see ... so you think I'm hopeless!' This can quite often stop them for a second—and maybe altogether! It works well in many cases when people are not open to a constructive conversation.

The other advantage of repeating back to another person what you *think* they have said may bring clarity as we can all *misunderstand or misinterpret* what other people are saying. I recently had someone explode in anger and rage as I was sharing my thoughts. When they calmed down, I asked them what they *thought* I had said. It was totally different to what I was actually saying, as they hadn't let me finish my sentence. This changed the other person's perspective and bought peace. This whole situation could have been avoided if the person had repeated to me what he *thought* I was saying before exploding!

A powerful on the spot conflict stopper
Dealing with someone who was being rude to me in a meeting provided me with an on the spot conflict stopper. Ideally, I always want to respond from a centred and balanced perspective in any potential conflict situation. When this situation arose, I was aware of anger rising up in me so I knew I had to take a few moments out and leave the room. Otherwise, I would have responded out of anger.

In just a couple of minutes, I was able to come to a place of peace and gain another perspective by using the Three Way Perspective Exercise I described earlier. I asked for guidance from my Helper for the exercise and I definitely needed a lot of help! This is how the exercise went. I brought Jo into my mind's eye, then looked at him and expressed my feelings of resentment and anger as he had treated me like dirt, and was having fun kicking me around like a piece of dirt! I also expressed my anger by telling him how I could quite easily kick him in the shins! I immediately noticed how much better I felt. That was my perspective. It was time to gain Jo's. So I asked my Helper what Jo would say in response. In my mind, I could see him hanging his head in shame. He looked like a lost, awkward little boy. I realised he was just trying to get attention—the wrong way! I felt compassion for him at that moment and was able to forgive him. I sensed he was sorry. When I asked for my Helper's perspective on the whole situation, I entered into a place of peace.

As a result of using this way to resolve my feelings, I was able to re-enter the room at peace with compassion in my heart. I looked at Jo and then told him how I felt and what I could have done to him a few minutes ago as a result of his actions. He laughed sheepishly. As I was coming from a place of peace, I could see Jo didn't feel threatened by what I said. He then genuinely said sorry. We were able to move on with the meeting in a place of reconciliation and peace.

Letting go of destructive relationships that are in frequent conflict
When situations and relationships *frequently* have conflict that hasn't been able to be resolved, even after seeking professional help, then it may be time to let go of the relationship. If you continue to remain in destructive situations, allowing others to verbally abuse you, you are *allowing* that bad behaviour to continue. Then you can become a victim. Be honest about how the relationship leaves you feeling.

When people have been abusive to me in certain situations, I discovered they are usually not willing to hear what I have to say so there is no point in continuing talking or being in their presence. So I distance myself from them until they have calmed down. Then, in some cases, they are willing to listen to my perspective.

Avoid making an abusive person feel *wrong* in conflict as this will inflame and enrage them. Accept the other person's perspective, even if you don't agree, as everyone is entitled to a perspective. However, let them know you see things differently.

I have heard of people who want to let go of destructive relationships where there is constant conflict, but have felt trapped for a number of reasons. Sometimes their partner has threatened them with dire consequences if they leave, or else they have been frightened to be left alone not knowing how to cope financially. In these cases I suggest people seek a professional relationship counsellor to help them deal with all the issues until resolved.

When you withdraw from a destructive relationship it makes space to develop meaningful, authentic relationships, particularly when you discover your true worth and value in the eyes of your Creator.

How conflicts can be constructive
Learning about oneself and how to change for the better!
I used to freeze up with fear when conflict began. I remember trying to stop an argument between two members of my family, getting in between them, trying to get them to see each other's point of view. This only caused more conflict. The person I defended didn't feel any better, and in fact turned on me in anger for getting involved when I hadn't been invited to help! Then the other person left the house saying that there was no place in the family for him. I was left feeling confused, not knowing what to do next. Nothing was resolved and in fact everyone felt worse as a result of me trying to end the conflict!

This taught me to avoid triangles in a relationship as it usually bought further conflict. Rather, I learned to stand back and pray for those involved in conflict, instead of getting in the middle trying to save them both! I also dealt with the triggers to do with conflict: unresolved fearful memories.

Being set free from the deep-seated fears of conflict
As I dealt with memories that held unresolved fears and conflict, I came to experience Presence, Peace and Power. These memories were

flooded with Light where I felt secure, safe and supported. This made all the difference in future conflict situations as there were no underlying, unresolved fears of conflict to be triggered off.

I remember one particular day, after I had been released from the underlying fear of conflict, I heard two family members begin raising their voices in anger. I realised I would have usually run in to help resolve their conflict, but remembered to instead turn to the One who released me from my fear of conflict. I ask him to help them resolve their conflict, as it sounded like they were murdering each other verbally! As I waited, the voices became calmer, and I returned to the room to discover that the whole conflict episode was very constructive. I later found out that as the person emotionally shared about some hurt that had been bottled up within them, the other had listened, acknowledging the hurt they had caused. These two people went on to develop a very healthy, open, honest and loving relationship! If I had interfered, I could have prevented them hearing each other and stopped their reconciliation.

Express your feelings
I now know that all feelings must be expressed or we can become depressed. Everyone must have a voice and also the right to be heard respectfully. However, there are times when people won't listen to us, no matter how we approach them. Fortunately, we can turn to the One within us who is always present to us who, I have discovered, will listen to every feeling we have.

If at home, I go to my favourite place to express all my feelings and thoughts in relation to any conflict. I let it all out until I am empty. Then I wait until peace is restored within me. When I first began to go to the Divine Counsellor in this way, it seemed to take ages to come to a place of peace. I can remember saying one day, 'I'm not moving until you do something with me!' Other people express their feelings through writing or painting. Whatever you do, never suppress or deny your feelings. Otherwise these unexpressed feelings and thoughts can *explode in any conflict situation and get out of control.*

The other advantage of expressing all feelings and thoughts in this ways is that our bodies can be released from suffering. A member of my family used to suffer from psoriasis until he began expressing his feelings. Then all his psoriasis disappeared.

If there is unresolved conflict within a group or organisation that you work with, and you have done all you know how to resolve this conflict, then go to a senior person you can trust and *express your concerns* asking for their wisdom and help

Anger in conflict
Resolving our anger is imperative as unresolved anger in conflicts can easily get out of control and destroy others either verbally or physically. Unresolved anger can also turn into rage and hatred in conflict. It is all right to hate what people do, but not to hate them. We need to stop the cycle of hatred and anger by resolving it. Remember we also attract what is deep within us!

Anger consumes an enormous amount of our energy so let it be used constructively. Anger just means you are hurting so listen to your feelings and thoughts, become present to yourself and ask for Unconditional Love's perspective.

Assisting people who feel angry because of an injustice done to them has often been difficult as they seem stuck in their anger. When I mention Unconditional Love is also called the Defence Attorney they feel safe to allow him to help them. They often need someone who will not judge them but listen to and defend them in their anger.

When appropriate, particularly when people have unjustly been abused, I invite people to join their anger with Jesus' anger. I remind them that he was angry when he saw his temple being destroyed and that he sees them as the living temple of God.

How do you respond to conflicts?
It's important to answer these questions so you become aware of how you are responding to any conflict in your life.
Do you ...
- fight or retaliate verbally and/or physically (which is destructive)?
- retreat, withdrawing within, giving people the silent treatment?
- resolve your feelings and thoughts and seek resolution in conflicts?

I encourage you to try some of the ways I have found empowering and see the results!

As I applied all I have shared with you, many of my relationships that used to be full of conflict have developed into healthy, respectful relationships. However, having done all I could, I was willing to discontinue destructive relationships where the person continued to blame, judge, condemn and verbally abuse me. In one instance when I moved away from Jean who was talking destructively about me to many people, I heard later she had begun to judge and blame others. Jean later apologised and has now developed a healthy respect for me. In fact, Jean has even asked for help with some conflict in her family!

Allow yourself space and time to heal
It is important to allow yourself time and space from the person with whom you have had conflict. I remember one time when I had to do this with Lena, as I felt like I had a gaping hole within me that was bleeding. Like any wound, it took time to heal.

I know how it feels to be verbally abused. It was as though I had a sign on my forehead saying, 'I'm wrong! I'm responsible!' Of course this caused a lot of conflict not only with them but also within me. I didn't understand consciously why this was happening over and over again. *Allowing time to listen to my feelings and beliefs* was crucial to experiencing healing in many childhood memories that were often been triggered off where I had felt blamed and judged in conflicts. I was then able to deal with conflict powerfully and constructively

Consequences of conflict, resolved and unresolved
Unresolved conflict can be divisive. We become disconnected and separated from ourselves, others and our Creator. We usually feel sorry for ourselves so we become a victim or become self-righteous and hard of heart. Unresolved conflict can leave hatred, revenge, judgements, unforgiveness and even murder in our hearts. Those who have shared this with me have felt trapped, heavy, almost dead, alone and powerless.

Resolving conflict on the other hand will lead to greater unity and harmony with oneself, others and God. We are willing to see conflicts as *opportunities for personal growth,* rather than blaming and complaining. As we gain Wisdom's perspective, we 'see' people with the same mercy and compassion as we have experienced. People have shared how light, secure, and free they feel after they have resolved their conflict. It is then safe to be responsible and accountable for our actions or inactions as we have experienced Unconditional Love and Mercy. Energy and life begins to flow.

Looking at the consequences of not resolving conflict as opposed to resolving conflict constructively spurs me on to always doing my best to *use conflict as opportunities to build and not destroy relationships!* What about you?

24

The Power in Acknowledging, Allowing and Asking to Receive

I realised the power that flows from *acknowledging, allowing* and *asking* only after many years of denying, resisting and struggling to find solutions in my own strength. I finally learned to stop, become present, let go of control, acknowledge and accept my fears and weaknesses, asking Wisdom to take over.

I had to *acknowledge* I couldn't make my daughter well with all the natural methods I believed in. I *allowed* myself to face my worst fear—that she could die—and that I needed to surrender her to the One who created her, *asking* for his will to be done. The moment I did this all the fear and tension within me drained away. I then *received* a peace beyond my understanding. I felt a Presence in this place of utter peace, a vision of her dancing in the daisies, and instructions to *no longer talk* about her illness. There was no longer any resistance in me, as a result of this experience, to using medication that could cause terrible side effects. The peace I felt flowed over to everyone and her health recovered to the point of her becoming a personal trainer.

I had to *acknowledge* that I felt abandoned as a result of my husband working six days a week. Up until this point I had pretended all was well! Then I *received* healing and peace in a childhood memory where I had felt abandoned. Within two weeks, I also *received* news from my husband that he had decided to sell his business, enabling him to have more time with the family. This experience powerful changed me, my relationship and my family.

I very gradually became aware that I had frequently not accepted myself, others or situations just as they were. I was resisting them and trying to bring change because I felt uncomfortable. Resisting caused tension in my body. I can see myself now, digging my heels in, fists clenched, mouth tight, looking very serious and somewhat righteous! I wasn't accepting or allowing others to have an opinion then. This attitude of mine kept me stuck and going round in endless cycles, leaving me even more frustrated. Thank God I woke up and realised that as I changed, my life would also change for the better.

Janice's situation is another great example of the change that occurs when we have an attitude of acceptance rather than resistance. She shared with me how she was often trying to get her husband to listen to her needs in the marriage. She wanted him to change and be at home more to help with the children. His attitude to this request was to tell her to tough it out as this is what mothers did! You can image how incensed Janice was. She didn't feel he cared about her or the family and was left feeling frustrated and powerless. After fully acknowledging and accepting how she felt, I said there was another way to bring change.

I shared with her that there is often a natural resistance in people when we want something from them, particularly if we begin to complain, beg or demand. This usually irritates people as they feel pressured and controlled. They may then respond by resisting the request and backing away from you and/or the situation. She said this is exactly what her husband was doing. I suggested that she could *accept* her husband's attitude as it was, as she couldn't change him anyway, and recommended that she let go of begging him for help and do the best she could and see what happened.

Janice said that this is what the counsellor had also suggested. In fact, she had tried this approach just the day before. She told her husband that she wasn't going to ask for his help any more, but that she had decided to go forward from this point doing the best she could with or without his help. She also let him know that the door was always open for him to be involved if he chose. He was absolutely dumbfounded and a little lost by what she told him (he obviously was not used to Janice acting this way!) She noticed that after saying this to him, he went into the kitchen and began to get his children breakfast and help them prepare for school. Janice's voice was now calm rather than agitated.

Allowing and Receiving
Acknowledging and allowing *does not mean that we agree* with what is happening. *Please do NOT accept or allow* others to abuse you or take advantage of you but learn rather to set healthy boundaries. With that said, you can see from Janice's experience that she finally accepted that she couldn't change her husband although she didn't agree with his behaviour. She *received* power in a healthy way when she decided to change her approach by respectfully informing him she was now willing to move on in life with or without his help and would no longer struggle to change him. As a result, he chose to change his behaviour.

These suggestions regarding *allowing* may lead you to receiving benefits in one way or another:
- Allow your Creator, who I see as my Divine Helper, to take over when you are stuck and don't know what to do. Acknowledge and allow yourself to be aware of all your

feelings and beliefs and then listen, allowing yourself to receive God's perspective and experience the power of peace that flows as a result. Refer to Chapter 5 on Blockages and Obstacles if you have difficulties in this area.
- Allow other people to have a voice, a choice and a different perspective, perhaps even agreeing to disagree! This takes away the effort and discomfort of struggling with others, trying to convince them of what you believe to be right. You should receive greater respect from others, who are more likely to listen to your perspective.
- Allow time to listen to yourself and your needs, especially the weak, grumpy, cranky parts of yourself. You will receive greater self-knowledge and unconditional love of yourself. This brings release of stress and tension and develops patience, understanding and balance in life.
- Allow others, especially children, to experience the consequences of their actions. They will receive greater awareness and hopefully learn how to take responsibility for their lives.
- Allow regular time to *be still* in the presence of the One who is all powerful. You will receive truth, a deep peace within, clarity and direction for a fulfilling life.

I recommend that you choose one area of your life where you are not accepting and allowing things to be as they are, then apply what I have shared so you can enjoy the benefits of receiving as Janice and I have in our lives. Enjoy this continuing adventure of discovery!

25

The Power of Curses and Blessings!

Some people have said they feel like their lives are cursed as a result of the many things going wrong in their life. They said they felt like a black cat had crossed their path, causing their life to be cursed. They had begun to *believe* they were cursed and unfortunately didn't realise it may be only their *beliefs* and their subsequent *actions* that were causing fears and problems. They have also *believed* they can't do anything to change being cursed. But we have seen that as people's beliefs and actions change, so have their lives. Many people have also been unaware of how *life can become a blessing* rather than a curse. So let's understand what a curse is and its influence and then how blessings can occur in our lives.

What is a curse anyway?
According to the *Oxford dictionary*, it is 'something that causes evil or harm and to wish or invoke evil.' The *Macquarie dictionary* states it is 'the expression of a wish that evil befall another.'

What is the 'something' that causes evil or harm?
I believe it is our negative, misguided beliefs and the subsequent emotions and reactions that cause evil or harm. When we live our life

from faulty thinking, our life can become stinky (so to speak)! Unchecked, this way of living continues to harm us mentally, emotionally and sometimes physically. Living this way is debilitating and if there is no change for the better it can destroy us and others. Life literally then makes us feel cursed.

Janice's life seemed to be cursed as she couldn't bear the emotional pain that she often experienced. The only thought that came to her for relief was that of cutting herself. While I was helping her to resolve this feeling, a memory came back to her of when she was a young child. In this memory, she had been abused. As a result, she believed she was wrong, responsible, dirty and bad. The child in the memory felt angry and trapped in the dark. She hated herself. All of this created unbearable pain. There was no relief it seemed.

However, as Janice faced this incident, listened to the thoughts and feelings of the child in the memory, accepting her as she was, she was then able to listen to her Creator's truth. She then sensed deep within this memory that it wasn't her fault. She also knew she wasn't bad and dirty. The inner tension and negative beliefs dissolved and so did the pain! All she felt was peace in the Presence. She felt surrounded by light in this memory. This of course created a healthy foundation and a new space from which to begin to receive blessings, not more self-inflicted pain.

Many others have shared how they rebelled as a result of their circumstances which only led them to more harm and disaster. They have said if other people believe you're bad, and you don't like yourself, you might as well do whatever you want. If people only knew how to listen to their feelings and beliefs, and let go of the judgements and hatred, they would be able to discover Truth, and experience peace and power within as Janice did. I believe then much of the harm and evil people do to themselves and others would stop and it would have a lasting effect on generations to come.

Another example is exemplified by Josephine's story. As she was led through the Three-Way Perspective Exercise, Josephine became aware of her anger towards an auditorium full of people which she could see in her mind's eye. She said if she expressed how she felt towards them it would be like using a machine gun on all of these people who had hurt her. This anger was released as she expressed all her negative feelings towards all these people and then listened to the Divine Counsellor's perspective. The murderous feelings she had felt towards them all, only minutes earlier, changed to feelings of compassion as she gained clarity. She now saw that these people didn't know what they had done.

Whether you believe in the story of Adam or Eve or not, for me it is a perfect example of what happens when we don't respond to but rather rebel against our Creator's principles and guiding words of wisdom. Adam and Eve, like many of us, believed they knew best and listened to the ultimate liar and thief. Their life became cursed as a result of their disobedience. Everything began to go wrong from that point on. In Adam and Eve's case, they turned on one another and the blame game began, instead of learning from their mistakes, taking responsibility for their own actions and receiving forgiveness and mercy. As a result of the shame they felt, they then hid from their Creator. Separation began from the One who wanted to forgive them and restore them to a life of ease and grace in paradise. Life became very hard as a result of Adam and Eve's choices and decisions and they and their children suffered as a result. And many in the world are still suffering!

Wishing evil is the same as cursing others!
Are you aware that by speaking words like: 'I wish I was dead and 'I hope they suffer and go to hell' actually curse either yourself or another person? When looking back on my life, I realise how wishing

I was dead and hating life only compounded my problems. By my words, I attracted near-death situations to those closest to me through illness, accidents, depression and suicidal tenancies. Death was in my face and life was full of stress. This no longer occurs. We are now blessed abundantly after many years of unravelling our old ways, and we are all learning and applying new ways of thinking and acting.

The road rage and verbal abuse we hear these days only goes to show there are many people who are cursing others—and of course themselves. People can actually sense what we think, which is often referred to as vibes, But when we actually verbalise what we are thinking, our words can either build or destroy others. The tone of our voice, even a glance spiced with hatred, resentment and jealousy can influence others negatively, particularly if they believe what is said. It's so much better if we deal with these negative thoughts and feelings privately before dumping them on other people. Few people want to be in the presence of another when they are cursing, blaming and judging others or themselves for that matter. This can cause separation in relationships.

People, particularly children, believe words that are said to them such as, 'You'll never amount to anything' or 'You're useless!' These words act as a curse, often negatively influencing their entire lives unless they experience Truth in that memory. They can become driven to prove themselves as a result of believing the negative words spoken about their worth and value—or they can go the other way.

Just pause for a moment and ask the Divine Counsellor to show you when you may have heard others or yourself cursing or wishing evil. You can then choose to apologise or forgive yourself or others to release any negative influences. This action opens a new space for blessings.

What does invoking evil mean?
You are probably aware that there are books available to teach people, even children, how to cast love spells, and others spells over others, to get what they want or take revenge. This invokes and calls upon the powers of evil spirits to influence the lives of others negatively. You must sense how wrong this is as we are meant to love and respect one another, not control each other for our own personal satisfaction. People who invoke evil forget the law that says 'as you do to others, so shall it be done to you,' meaning that they will eventually get what they give out.

We can place ourselves under a curse when we believe in and seek to gain knowledge, power or solutions from tarot cards, palm reading, reading star signs, spells, witchcraft or in any other way apart from going to the Creator of the stars and the universe. We need to renounce all this and ask for forgiveness and to be released from ALL that has negatively influenced us and others. Then we must seek the One who has all the knowledge, power and unconditional love that we will ever need.

Having worked in the area of healing for years and listened to many prayers for release from such things as hexes, spells, voodoo, witchcraft and freemasonry, I have seen people being caught up in fear in case they have forgotten to mention some other curse. *Fear* itself then becomes a curse from my perspective. What I suggest now is to prayerfully say the Our Father, the prayer given to us by Jesus, who dealt with all kinds of evil. This prayer asks that we be released from ALL evil ... and Jesus does this for us. I believe this prayer covers every form of curse or evil in any dimension. We have a choice either to invoke the help of the Spirit of Truth, Love and Wisdom, the Source of all Life, or the deceiver, liar and robber, the source of all evil.

How blessings occur
If we think of ourselves as children in creation, surely it makes sense to listen to and obey our Creator's instructions on how to live life so we receive blessings from and through everything. I now understand why he gave us commandments; they are there to guide us and protect us from harm. It's a little like commanding your three-year-old child to stand away from a fast-running stream. These commandments protected me when I was young (out of fear!), but eventually led me to a life of blessings and an authentic relationship with God. We are told in Deuteronomy 28:1 that if we practice and observe all the commandments, God will raise us high above all the nations of the earth and blessings will come on us. There is now little resistance to listening and responding to my Creator because I know and have now experienced the blessings that flow.

In the midst of what were very difficult and challenging times, as I turned my focus to God and praised him for being there and granting his help, I felt lifted up into a place of peace, despite not knowing what was going to happen long-term. It was an extraordinary experience and a real blessing! There are a whole heap of blessings that are promised us. It's worth checking them out.

Let's look at a few other examples where people have responded to God's instructions. After Noah *obeyed* God's instructions, God said he would never again curse the earth by water because of man, even though his heart was set on evil from childhood. Noah and his family were saved from the flood and were taken to safety. That is how I now feel … literally saved from the flood of disasters that kept coming my way many years ago.

After Abram was given instructions to leave his country he *obeyed* God's instructions. God said he would bless those who blessed him and would curse those who cursed him, saying also that in Abram all peoples of the earth would be blessed.

So too Jesus *obeyed* his Father and gave his life up for all men so they would know how unconditionally loved they were, despite messing up! But as you know he rose again—and so can we! God sent his only Son Jesus to take the consequence of our sins (curses) to the cross. Can you imagine sending one of your children to pay the price for the evil others have created so they could be free?

Because Jesus listened and *obeyed*, we can now have the benefit of receiving forgiveness, mercy, unconditional love and true freedom, if we so choose! We just need to acknowledge and accept what we need to let go of and who we need to forgive so there is space to receive blessings.

The Spirit of Unconditional Love will gently make you aware, if you are open, of any areas of your life where you are being cursed, then how to make space for blessings. This is what happened to me. What about you? When you reflect on your life and choices, are they leading to life and blessings rather than disaster?

Helpful hints to receive blessings: the 5 Rs

Realise
- No *corrupt* communication (any words that negatively influence others) should come out of our mouth. Be angry, but don't let it do any harm to anyone. This is often the time we curse ourselves and others. Use the Three-Way Perspective Exercise to resolve your angry feelings and come to peace.
- We are instructed to *bless those who persecute and curse us* (Again, the perspective exercise helps clear the way to bless people). This protects us from being dragged down to the other person's level of behaviour and being cursed as a result.
- Invite the Spirit of Truth to gently *probe our hearts* and reveal anything we do or say that is cursing our lives so blessings can occur.
- We are called to seek our happiness first in the One who

created all things. From this place of oneness, we then feel safe to develop relationships with people without *expecting them* to fulfil our need for happiness.

Repent—Say sorry!

We *all* make mistakes so deal with your feelings and thoughts with the Divine Counsellor's assistance in the Three-Way Perspective Exercise which more often than not will give you a perspective that releases you and others. You can ask for the grace Jesus had on the cross to forgive to flow through you so you don't retain what has happened. This has helped many people who have struggled to forgive. Remember that if you retain other people's offences, it acts like a wall and a block to blessings. Retaining hurt can become a curse, attracting more hurt and often causing bad relationships and ill health.

Renounce

Bad habits, bad ways of living and 'stinky thinking' have to go if we are to make space to receive blessings. Again, I ask for the grace necessary to change, remembering that it is by grace that I am saved through faith. This has helped me enormously to change, especially when I have been ready to explode.

Receive

One of the hardest things for many people I have assisted has been to be open to receive. Some people believe they are not good enough and *don't deserve anything,* which acts as a block to receiving. In these cases, people are invited to hear the Spirit of Truth. Other people don't trust anyone, including God, so they guard and protect themselves. In these cases, we invite the guarding and protecting aspects of people's personalities to step aside so they can at least hear their Creator's perspective. In many cases, people have needed grace or God's angels to be sent to guard them as a form of protection to make them safe enough even to listen! This enables them to experience a breakthrough and are able to receive blessings in many ways.

Restore
We restore ourselves and others by saying sorry and then by asking to be shown the good qualities we and others have and focus on them. If necessary, restore anything you may have borrowed or taken that doesn't belong to you. (This includes money, other people's spouses, etc.) We can also ask our Creator to restore anything that has been robbed from us during our lives in any way. Reading about Job's experience has helped me realise how generous our God is. In fact, he is in the restoration business! He gave him double what he had before!

Generational release
We are all influenced negatively or positively by our families, including the family members who have died. Beliefs, feelings, spiritual influences, actions, patterns and habits are passed on through the generations. Children can often inherit their parents' feelings and fears and don't know they are not their own. Also, children tend to learn from what parents **do** rather than from what they say!

I have often sensed a need for forgiveness for those who have died when assisting others. I have been drawn at special moments to cry for, name and commit unborn children to Jesus, only as they have been brought into my mind. I have found this to be amazing and a real blessing as well as an enormous release.

A wise way to pray for the generations is to ask the Spirit of Wisdom whom to pray for and how to pray. Many people have held a Healing of the Family Tree mass so as to bring release for all who may need this. As we are all connected, this does make way for peace and blessings to flow through the whole family.

Life and death, blessings and curses, have been set before us all. We are invited to choose life so that we and our descendants may live, loving God, listening to his voice and obeying him. This is what I chose, many years ago, and although it has been very painful at times, as I learned to persevere, my life, family, and many other people have been blessed. On reflection, the changes we have experienced have been extraordinary. But I had to choose…what do you choose?

26

Using Anger Powerfully and Constructively

Let's explore the powerful emotion of anger as in today's society it almost seems impossible to avoid. Most people eventually experience anger either in others or in themselves. The day I finally learned how to deal with anger constructively felt empowering. Why? Because I learned to take responsibility for using it constructively, instead of blaming or accusing others as many people do. This, I later discovered, helped establish authentic relationships. So when you encounter anger, apply what I share and see the change that usually occurs. Instead of being frightened of your anger or other people's anger, as I used to be, hopefully you will begin to see these situations as opportunities to practise dealing with this emotion powerfully and constructively.

We hear of anger being expressed through road rage, bullying in schools, homes and workplaces and domestic violence. All around us, people are destructively venting their unresolved anger, rage or revenge. Domestic violence has escalated within society and marriages are breaking down faster than ever. Suppressed anger can also express itself through tension. I have felt this tension; it causes fear and can control situations. People have shared how they feel like they are treading on eggshells and have to be very careful with what they say and even the way they look! However, I know this can all change.

Before we explore anger further it is important to realise some important facts, some of which I have already mentioned in Chapter 2 (Understanding Feelings and Using Them Constructively), but are worth repeating:

- *Anger is the natural emotional response* to a wrong suffered (or perceived wrong suffered). It is a God-given emotion. Jesus was angry when his temple was defiled. When I talk about a perceived wrong, I mean it is what we have interpreted.

- *Anger is an emotion that is neither good nor bad.* It is important to acknowledge anger when it's present and not deny or repress it. I have met many people who are not comfortable at acknowledging their anger. Some people believe they are bad if they are angry, particularly Christians! Then the anger comes up when least expected and is often not expressed constructively. Then they feel really bad!

- *It is what we do with our anger* that can cause harm to others or ourselves by repressing it, or expressing it in a destructive manner. (You will see some examples in the following stories.)

- *Repressing anger* can damage you in either of the following ways:
    - *emotionally* by possibly making you depressed, irritable and frustrated and possibly leaving you with an inability to cope;

- o *physically* by leading to ulcers, high blood pressure, colitis, insomnia and chemical imbalances.

- *Expressing anger* in a destructive manner can ...
  - o destroy relationships and;
  - o leave us feeling guilty, bad or shameful. This can lead onto blaming, judging and criticising either ourselves, others or God.

Justifiable anger
Justifiable anger is appropriate at times. When you have been violated in some way, you are justified in being angry and can use it for good when you learn how to do this constructively.

Jill had been abused by her father and after expressing all her feelings and beliefs, wanted to be released from her anger and forgive but felt she couldn't. The moment I suggested she join her anger with Jesus' anger, she agreed and within minutes shared how free she felt. The anger had left her completely. Peace flooded her whole being.

Jesus is angry when you are violated and abused. You are his creation and the temple of his Holy Spirit. *Jesus was angry and enraged* when he saw the temple being used wrongly, and he expressed his justifiable anger appropriately. But he wants you to let *him* bring justice in the situation, and wants to release you from all the other resulting emotions that you can retain, such as bitterness, resentment, hatred and revenge. If we retain them, they usually bring further destruction upon us.

Jesus was angry at the hardness of heart in the Pharisees when they watched to see if he would cure the man with a withered hand in the synagogue on the Sabbath which according to them was against the law. I love reading this passage of scripture: '... he said to the man who had the withered hand, "Come forward." Then he said to them,

"Is it lawful to do good or to do harm on the Sabbath, to save or to kill?" They were silent. He looked around at them with *anger;* he was grieved at their hardness of heart.' He went on to restore the withered hand despite what they thought showing mercy, compassion and love.

Murderous anger turned to compassion
I was speaking to Sandra over the phone. She was very upset about something Joseph had said. I could feel the tension and anger coming through her voice. After listening to her, I asked if she would like to deal with her anger constructively. She hesitated at first because she felt justified in feeling angry. Although I agreed with her, I asked if she wanted to use her anger to benefit her rather than destroy her.

As she began to deal with her feelings, under the guidance of the Divine Counsellor, she realised the anger was more like rage. I asked her how she would like to physically express this rage to allow it to be released safely. Suddenly she said, 'I'd like to hit him over the head with an axe.' She couldn't believe she was saying such a thing. She was shocked at the strength and power of the feelings of anger, rage and murder. I encouraged her by saying she was venting these feelings now rather than later! (I wonder how many murders could be averted if people only knew how to express these emotions constructively in this way).

Underlying Sandra's rage and murderous feelings were further feelings of frustration, powerlessness and sadness all coming from the beliefs that she couldn't do anything, and that she was being made to feel everything was her fault. She also realised how alone, defenceless, confused and trapped she felt. She then became aware that the root of her anger was the judgment and condemnation that had been projected on her by Joseph, the one who was supposed to love and defend her.

Sandra was then willing to let go of the desire to murder Joseph which made a new space to hear the Divine Counsellor's truth about what she had believed. She heard the words in her mind, 'It's not your fault.' At that moment, every negative emotion and belief melted away. She felt so light (she'd felt so heavy when we started) and free. When we returned to the memory where she had been judged and condemned, it no longer affected her and she no longer felt alone, defenceless and broken. She then saw Joseph in a different light and felt compassion for him. When she returned home, their relationship began to change for the better. I hope you will ask the Divine Counsellor to help you express your feelings and gain his freeing perspective when you next have feelings of anger or rage.

Unresolved, accumulated anger is like a bonfire ready to be ignited!

If anger is left unresolved, it can build within people until the 'last straw' (offence) makes them explode uncontrollably. This last offence can be like putting a match to tinder. This is often when people say and do things they later regret. Although they may have a right to be angry, they haven't resolved the issues as they have happened.

The explosion is usually not about that particular situation, but an accumulation of situations and hurt over a period of time. I remember someone said to me when they experienced this anger and rage, it was like being burnt with a blowtorch. It can literally destroy!

Suppressing anger

Mary, an elderly lady I know well, often told me, 'I never get angry.' However, she eventually came to the realization that she never really felt *anything* anymore. She was *frozen* emotionally. She said she was happy for me to help her 'feel' again. So after I invited the Divine Counsellor to reveal, in her mind's eye, what her heart was like she said, 'It looks like a little hard lump.' She then remembered after crying many times that she *decided* she would never cry again. That decision closed her heart off, burying within it all her unresolved anger and emotions. She said it was her way of surviving when she didn't know what else to do with all her emotions in hopeless situations. She said she felt tired and lifeless much of the time and looked depressed. She had skin complaints and often felt irritable.

Over time, Mary began to open up her heart to me and share how she had often felt trapped, betrayed, powerless and abandoned in her marriage to the point of contemplating suicide, but knew this wasn't an option because of her children. She said she had expressed her anger, even throwing a knife at her husband after he had tormented her, but only cut her own hand. Other times she had tried talking to him, but nothing changed.

One day Mary allowed me to invite the Divine Counsellor to reveal where she was at that point. She saw in her mind's eye that part of her memory was trapped alone in a grey, lifeless void. As I invited the Divine Counsellor to help her, she became aware of a Presence and light which dissolved the grey. She then realised she no longer felt trapped and alone and actually felt *alive*.

Victims of other people's anger
Unfortunately, people who don't know how to take responsibility for their feelings can often dump their anger on innocent people. The victim is usually in shock, not knowing what they have done or why the person is angry with them. The bully it seems can sense who to target, someone for instance who won't or can't retaliate because of age, size or lack of confidence. Have you ever experienced this in your life?

Some adults abuse their innocent children or those under their care. They use their authority to take advantage of those under their control. The anger projected on the innocent ones can damage these peoples' lives forever, unless healed.

John remembered his school days during a Healing Meditation. He said he felt anger, fear, hatred and terror especially when he thought of the priests and brothers who were his teachers. This is what John saw in this memory:

The picture was clear in my mind. I could see myself as a 12-year-old at school, holding my swollen red hands under the running tap and feeling the pain as well as the shame of once again being strapped. This was happening to me once or twice a day, with six or eight straps at a time on each hand. I felt alone and believed that no one cared about me. I believed I was there for their amusement. I remember one of the priests laughing as I got the strap. He really enjoyed seeing me suffer.

I realised then that I wanted to tie them all up back to back and put a hand grenade on their laps then stand back and watch them *suffer. That's how much anger I had suppressed. Then I remember how Jesus suffered for me during his passion, with all the humiliation and everyone laughing at him. I wanted in my heart to forgive them and was about to say the words when Mary, the Mother of God, appeared in my mind's eye. I felt embarrassed to see her, because of what I had just said and what I would like to do to the teachers. But Mary just said, "I don't blame you, I understand how you feel." I was surprised to hear her say that.*

In this memory, Mary took me by the hand and we walked away from the school to a milk bar, where she brought me a vanilla ice-cream. It was delicious, the best I had ever had. I could even smell the vanilla.

I wanted to explain to Mary about the priests at school and why I felt so angry with them because I remembered how she called priests "her beloved sons." I really thought she would be unhappy with me or scold me in some way. She didn't. She just showed me the school yard as it was today, concrete and stone, just like a car park. "See!" she said. "It's gone and it no longer has any power over you." Mary gave me love, peace and understanding, and an ice-cream.

I felt so special. We never had real ice-cream as kids because we were too poor. The ice-cream represented so much, and Mary knew it. I felt loved and accepted by her. I no longer felt any anger, hatred, fear or revenge toward the teachers. I understood they were doing their best and the harshness of the memory had gone.

As a result of these experiences in his early, formative years, John now realised why he didn't like being around priests throughout his life, as they represented the authority figures who hurt him so badly. He also realised why he had developed an uncooperative attitude towards those in authority. This, of course, damaged his relationships with those he worked with. John also realised that this buried anger had vented itself from time to time in sarcasm and criticisms of others and even 'setting people up' to get back at them. He had enjoyed the satisfaction he felt when they were uncomfortable!

Since this healing, John has been aware of many changes for the better. The most noticeable change has been with priests. He now feels comfortable with them and no longer feels angry, fearful or revengeful in their presence.

A victim of one's own anger
A friend of mine was noticing how tense she was recently. Her face looked tight and hard. She asked for help to find the root cause of her problem. It didn't take long for her to be aware of the weaker aspect of herself which she realised she was angry at and which she hated as it made her feel miserable and like a nobody. She had repressed this aspect not wanting to experience these feelings of anger.
She said she felt tired a lot of the time and had poor health.

She now wanted change and was ready and open to be guided by Wisdom to reveal his truth and presence to this 'weaker' side of herself. As she experienced a Presence and light, the anger and hardness melted away. She sensed herself becoming whole. She no longer felt divided against herself. Her face became softer and her body relaxed as she experienced peace and freedom. Instead of hatred for this aspect of herself, she now felt compassion.

Please be aware if you need to resolve any anger towards yourself, and if you have judged or blamed yourself when you have not lived up to your expectations or those of the world. Ask for Wisdom's perspective!

Brief practical guidelines on how to deal with anger constructively

o *Explore your anger and all other associated feelings and beliefs about yourself thoroughly.* This helps unload what is inside you and makes space to hear Wisdom's perspective. If you are unable to sense or hear anything that releases you, ask Wisdom to reveal any other blockages within you. The powerful information in the Chapters on Blockages and Obstacles or the Healing Meditation can also be of great help to experience Peace.

o *Relinquish anger from minor offences* and if necessary ask for Wisdom's perspective on the offense. You can often feel an immediate release.

o *Resolve the anger in your mind's eye* through the Three-Way Perspective exercise. This usually works well to resolve anger. It is *always* done under the guidance of the Divine Counsellor for the good of all. All you have to do is be the observer and accept what is revealed.

1. Ask the Divine Counsellor to bring the person you are angry with, or who is angry with you into your mind's eye. Tell this person how *you were left feeling and believing* about yourself as a result of what happened. Express every feeling and, if necessary, tell them what you would like to do to them (so you completely release every bit of anger in a safe way).

2. Ask the Divine Counsellor to reveal *what they would say or do in response* to what you have shared. Look at them in your mind's eye as you listen to them.

3. Ask the Divine Counsellor to reveal anything else that is necessary for you to see about the person, yourself or the situation. Usually all anger is replaced with compassion.

- *Ask for the grace to forgive.* If you have tried all the above suggestions but you still can't forgive then ask Jesus for his capacity to forgive. This has completely released people from their anger and hurt when abused. I remind them that Jesus knows what it is like to be abused and even murdered unjustly in the most horrific way, but that he rose again, and so can they.

- *Pray for the person.* You should be able to pray for the person who has made you angry. Although we can hate what people *do,* we are asked to *love our enemies and even pray for those who persecute us.* Now I understand why … because this way of responding keeps us free from acting or responding just as badly as those who hurt us. I have just heard how two policeman have just been shot in retaliation for the way they hurt some people. This only perpetuates anger and hurt.

Some wise instructions regarding anger

- *When we are slow to anger we have greater understanding.* I believe we can become slow to anger as we resolve any repressed anger from the past. If we become *aware* too of what we are thinking and feeling when someone abuses or offends us, we will be able to choose how to deal with the situation appropriately rather than react. This is being responsible and self-controlled. There are some situations though where I have had to distance myself from people and situations until I become centred and at peace before responding.

- *Be angry but don't do any harm otherwise you may be harmed and don't let the sun go down on your anger.* Remember to deal constructively with your anger so you do no harm to anyone, including yourself. Resolve your anger within the same day. Don't go to sleep on it or you will be restless. Avoid letting your anger turn to hatred and revenge. Also avoid dumping it on others or turning your anger on yourself or your problems and sufferings will multiply.

- *Let go of all bitterness, anger and slander,* and be kind to one another, tender-hearted, forgiving one another. When you let go of your anger, make sure you resolve it completely. You must *be empty before you can be filled* with the grace to be tender-hearted and forgiving.

- *A soft answer turns away anger but a harsh word stirs it up.* This is great advice. Try it and see. When someone is angry at you next time, try being silent and do not react. If you do speak, respond softly. Be aware of the results.

Remember you usually can't have a constructive conversation with another person when they are angry. All I do is repeat back to the person what they have said to me, saying I hear their perspective. I don't bother giving them my perspective unless they genuinely and respectively want to listen.

Will you join me in using anger constructively, applying whatever you read that relates to your situation? This will lead you down the path to peace, despite the circumstances, as you will feel equipped and empowered whenever you encounter anger within yourself or other people. Now that's truly powerful!

27

How to 'Really' Forgive

I have often heard people say, 'I have forgiven,' but in actual fact when they think of the person and situation where they felt hurt, they still get upset or want to retaliate. Others have shared that they want to forgive but just can't. What I share has made it possible for many to 'really' forgive and experience peace where there was none and compassion where there was anger, resentment and even hatred.

The power is beyond oneself to 'really' forgive.
This story is typical of those who came to us seeking peace and freedom from a situation that still troubled them significantly. Sue remembered the time her father abused her, leaving her feeling dirty, ashamed, guilty and helpless. She believed in some way she was responsible because she didn't do anything to stop him. She then realised she had felt frozen from fear which made her feel completely powerless.

    I asked Sue if she wanted to forgive. She said 'yes,' but she just couldn't completely forgive. I silently asked for Wisdom to help me at that point and then these words flowed through my mind: 'Sue can use my capacity to forgive when I was being crucified.' When I repeated what I had just heard in my mind, I then asked Sue if she would accept this capacity from Jesus to forgive. The moment Sue said 'yes,' her face softened and she began to cry tears of relief. It was a sacred moment. After a brief time she shared that she saw in her mind's eye that she wasn't alone at the time of the abuse and had a sense that Jesus had suffered with her. When I asked how she felt in the memory, all the negative feelings and beliefs had dissolved! We were both grateful beyond words. Sue left feeling free and at peace.

Anyone from any background can ask for the same capacity and power Jesus had to forgive when he was being abused and crucified unjustly to flow through them to the person they want to forgive. This is where you can really experience the power to forgive.

Gaining three perspectives

Dennis told me twice to 'shut up' at a dinner party. I could feel anger rising inside me so I decided to visit the ladies room instead of reacting out of anger. Although I knew this was the language used by him at work (he was a truck driver) and that he had a good heart, I still felt upset. When alone in the ladies room, I asked the Divine Counsellor to help me resolve my feelings with the Three-Way Perspective Exercise.

- *The first perspective: mine!* I asked the Divine Counsellor to bring Dennis into my mind's eye. As I looked at him, I expressed my feelings of anger and resentment and told him I could have hit him over the head as I felt disrespected and treated like I was nothing.
- *The second perspective: Dennis's!* Again, I asked the Divine Counsellor to show me in my mind's eye how Dennis would respond. As I focused on him and listened, I sensed he didn't mean to hurt me. I saw him feeling embarrassed and ashamed. The anger within me dissolved and was replaced with peace.

o *The third perspective: the Divine Counsellor's!* I asked the Divine Counsellor to show me how he would have me see the situation. I then saw how Dennis had been feeling bad about himself after what happened that day. I then felt compassion.

Resolving pain, hurt and unforgiveness in memories
Hanna had been overwhelmed with emotions and an inability to forgive her father. He had verbally abused her all her life and as a result she had been left feeling like she was of no value with no voice or rights. She said she had done all she could to forgive him but was still so very angry. As we asked the Divine Counsellor to bring her father into her mind's eye, she was able to release all the feelings of anger, rage, revenge and even feelings of murder at her father that had never been expressed. She said she had gone on to experience unhealthy relationships with other men in her life.

She then drifted into a blank area of her memory that held a feeling of helplessness. As this area of her memory was heard, she was willing to receive help from her Creator. This area of her mind experienced Light and a Presence and as a result she no longer felt helpless but empowered.

When Hanna looked again at her abusive father in her mind's eye, she felt at peace. She was able to forgive him as she now felt sorry for him. Peace flooded her whole being. She knew too that there now was a possibility of attracting a man who would respect and love her in the future.

Forgiving on the spot!
Once I had worked through many of the areas of my life using the above ways to come to a place of forgiveness, it became easier to exercise forgiveness 'on the spot' to others and myself when necessary. The more I realised how *I had received a load of mercy and*

forgiveness it made it easier to pass it on to others. Self-knowledge is very humbling … and is also good for the soul and relationships. On the other hand, self-righteousness—always needing to be right—tends to destroy relationships! I want healthy relationships. What do you want?

True justice and forgiveness
Jane said to me, 'If I forgive my friend, it feels like she just gets away with the insults and that seems unjust.' What Jane didn't realise was that we all reap what we sow. Justice will be done, i.e. we *all* eventually experience the consequences of our actions, both bad and good. For example, on reflection, I became aware of how I had suffered the consequences of my judgements by being judged by others. We can also attract injustice by the way we unjustly treat ourselves or others.

True justice and real victory for me is letting go of any desire to retaliate, but rather using the power I have to resolve my feelings and thoughts and enter a place of Presence and Peace, despite what has been done or said. It's like living in the world but not of the world. I now understand that people often don't 'see' or 'know' what they are doing in many cases and need to unfortunately suffer the consequences of their actions to wake up to what they were doing, just like I had to! We can become better or bitter. What do you choose?

The amazing benefits of forgiving
When we 'really' forgive, we let go of many toxic, negative emotions such as anger, resentment, hatred, rejection and judgement to name but a few. They act as an invisible, heavy weight on us. Harbouring these emotions within ourselves creates poisons that begin to destroy our body, mind, heart and spirit. Our mind becomes clogged with negative thoughts, which often flow out to others in the way of blame, criticism

and gossip. We tend to then attract what is in us; it is just a law of life. Depression and other feelings of despair can take root and strangle the life and love inside of us.

Every area of your life will improve as you forgive. You will then become more understanding, compassionate and healthy as well as attract good things into your life. Growth is usually another offshoot. I have also seen people being released from excruciating back pain, stomach pain and chest pain as they have forgiven and dealt with all the negative feelings and thoughts within themselves. Surely for these reasons alone, it is worth choosing to forgive!

Three-way forgiveness
It is necessary sometimes to not only forgive others, but also ourselves and maybe even God. God doesn't need or require our forgiveness, but harbouring un-forgiveness towards God will harm us. Many people have discovered that they haven't forgiven God, but have judged and blamed him for not being there for them.

I encouraged one young lady to express her anger and rage at God in her mind's eye (to bring release and see the truth). When she had finished telling God what she had felt and thought, the image she had thought was God changed into a grotesque figure. She screamed in terror. This had been a counterfeit image of who she thought was God. She then realised it hadn't been God but the deceiver she had been listening to. She asked for forgiveness for her judgements, forgave herself and the other people who had hurt her. I then asked for the Spirit of Truth to be revealed and she came into a place of Peace.

Forgiveness, mercy and unconditional love
I felt bad when I let my father-in-law down one day. When I apologised and asked for forgiveness, he just smiled gently and said all was well. I felt unconditionally loved at that moment. I knew then

how others could feel when I forgave them. As I asked others to forgive me for any hurt I had inflicted, I experienced such gentleness and mercy from them that I was amazed. Walls dissolved and respect developed.

I had a powerful image come to mind that may help jog your memory on the importance of forgiving. I saw a strained, tense hand clenched in a fist as it held on to unresolved hurt. It looked like skin and bone—lifeless. Then I saw the hand open up wide, relaxing, letting go and forgiving. I saw all the associated pain and hurt (which looked like muck) dissolve away. I then realised that the hand was open to receive good things.

Will you ask the Spirit of Truth to show you who you need to forgive so your life and your relationships will grow and even flourish? What do you have to lose apart from unnecessary pain and baggage? You then will be open to receiving good from all things.

28

Questions That are Empowering and Life Giving

The power of questions vs. statements and instructions
I have learned what a subtle yet profound difference it makes in my relationships when I ask questions such as, 'What do you think?' instead of only making a statement that can imply that what I say is right. When I have been on the receiving end of a dogmatic statement, I feel flattened and think, 'What's the point of having an opinion as this person is only interested in what they believe.' I then feel I can't be bothered talking with them! Ever felt like that yourself? Try asking others what they think and see what happens. They usually become very alive and empowered.

Do you hate being told what to do? Most people do. But when people ask us something in question form, it can engage us in conversation and develop a relationship—that is providing they ask us with genuine interest. I was recently asked to help Tim who had felt the need to deal with some difficult issues in a committee he was involved in. I suggested that he present his concerns into questions, giving them a moment to think and reflect. The next day he said that this approach had been very effective.

Bill, who loves to have debates and enjoys luring people into heated discussions, often began his conversation by asking me questions. But in this case, I could *feel*—and see by his distorted face—that I was being lured into one of his games to have a heated debate, one that he intended to win. Over time, I would ask, 'Are you genuinely interested in my point of view or do you just want to inform me of what you believe is right?' This would disarm him and he would soften. The 'lion' in him would become a lamb! So when asking questions, it is important to have a genuine attitude of heart that is going to build rather than destroy.

Instead of telling four-year-old Tom, 'You are a bully' when he pushed his little two-year-old brother over, I looked him directly in the eyes (with an attitude of building rather than destroying) and then asked these questions very firmly: 'How would you like me to do that to you? How would it make you feel?' Tom's eyes became large as he listened to me and very quietly answered, 'No, I don't want you to do that to me.' I would then say, 'Then treat others how you want to be treated, okay?' I would always get a 'yes.' Little Tom was not judged or blamed by me, but rather given an opportunity to become aware of the consequences of his action and I could feel respect building between us.

When we need help or assistance, if we ask respectfully 'I'd love some help when you are free' instead of, 'I need help now!' builds relationship. I wonder what attitude you have when speaking to your children, friends, husband or others? Try asking questions that invite possibilities of cooperation, despite what has happened in the past. And please let the past go so the present and future can change!

When a child shows you something they have done, value the child more than what they are showing you. Being present to them is more important than the quality of work. I remember a lady sharing how her mother always made alterations to her drawings. In the end she just stopped drawing because she was left feeling what she did was never good enough. Engage and encourage them by asking, 'Did you enjoy doing this?' or 'Would you like to tell me how you did this drawing?' This attitude and way of being applies to any age group and situation, particularly if you are a leader, allowing others to learn, especially from their mistakes.

Here are some other empowering questions:
- 'What do you think?'
- 'Are you genuinely interested in my point of view?'
- 'Would you like me to help you?'
- 'How would you feel?'
- 'Would you be able to help me?' Instead of telling or instructing others, ask them respectfully.

Questions that invite other people to have a voice and an opinion

Sharing our thoughts and opinions is important to developing relationships, but what is just as important is listening to other people share about their lives. To open the door for the other person to share, we can ask, 'What's happening in your life?' Then listen! This shows that you care about them.

When my teenaged children shared things that were going on in their life, I used to give them my opinion as I wrongly presumed they wanted my wisdom. This annoyed them because I hadn't asked, 'Would you like me to comment on what you said?' When I began to ask this question, they still said 'no thanks' (for over two years!), but I respected their wishes and learned to listen to them. After about two years, they began to *ask* for my point of view. Respect had been established and they were genuinely interested to hear my perspective. Those two years of listening were a turning point in our relationship.

Questions can help or hinder

I hear many people, especially mothers with young children, asking children the question, 'What's wrong?' Sometimes there's nothing 'wrong' at all! I remember a child sharing how he would make up a story about what was *wrong* as he felt this is what the mother expected! We could instead say, 'What's happening?' Can you *feel* the difference in these two questions? One assumes something is wrong and the other is just a general, open question.

Whenever I feel cranky and off centre, I have learned to ask the 'cranky part' of me: 'Okay, I understand you're cranky so what else do you feel and what are you thinking?' As I listen to this 'part' of me, peace comes.

I often hear people say 'one part of me wants to go, but another part of me is resisting!' As these people are not single minded and committed, they end up divided, full of confusion and tension. So whenever you feel this way, stop and listen gently and thoroughly to the 'part' of you that is resisting or frightened. Just by doing this can bring peace and unity within. This also prevents us dumping our cranky attitude on others.

I recommend you asking yourself some questions next time you're out of sorts and apply what I have shared. You may then experience how freeing and empowering it is.

Questions to ask when anxious or upset
When there is drama going on in your life, there can be a tendency to think a lot of negative thoughts which only compounds your fears and tensions. I used to have very frightening and negative questions going on in my mind when my teenagers were late coming home, such as, 'I wonder if they are ok?' or 'Have they had an accident?' and so on. As a result of these unanswerable questions, I began expecting the worst. When they arrived home, I would be in a very anxious, angry state even if they hadn't been harmed. This caused everyone to be further upset.

I realised I needed to change so I decided to deal with these bombarding negative thoughts by asking and then thanking God for sending his angels to protect and return my children home safely. I would then experience peace and sleep soundly until they arrived home.

In other upsetting situations, I have learned to ask: 'What good could come from this circumstance?' or 'What can I learn from this situation?' These questions change my focus and open my mind to look for the good in each circumstance. My family now also asks these questions. We all have discovered what a difference it makes. I feel entirely different as a result.

Other the years I have heard many people share how powerless they feel in certain situations, believing they couldn't do anything. They have been unaware of what they *can* do which is to ask Wisdom questions such as, 'How would you have me see the situation?' or 'What should I pray for?' Listen and apply what you hear and see the empowering results.

Questions for direction in life
Whenever I need some direction in life, I begin to '*ask* in prayer and thanksgiving' believing the answer will be revealed at just the right time. Being thankful releases tension and I am more open to hear and receive the answers to my question. To gain clarity, it is also helpful to ask yourself the question, 'What are the advantages and disadvantages?' when considering a particular decision in life. Never ever make any life-changing decisions when you are in a negative emotional or mental state. Always wait until you are centred and at peace before making these decisions.

These questions may also bring clarity for your direction in life:

- What do I *love doing* that brings life to me and others?
- What *comes naturally* to me? (referring to your gifts and talents)
- Where could I *use my talents*?
- Who *should I contact* to find out more information on the particular direction being considered?

When you allow time to *listen to the answers to these questions,* they will usually be creative, insightful, freeing and empowering. If there are no doubts, you can consider committing yourself 100% to this direction in life. I also ask Wisdom to guide me and go before me. I have then found doors begin to open up fairly effortlessly to this direction in life.

May you come to enjoy asking questions that are empowering and life giving and experience the difference it can make to your relationships and your life in general.

29

Freedom from Stress … Practical Keys

The following practical suggestions have helped many people, including me, experience real relief and true freedom from stress.

Listen to that 'part' of you that feels stressed…without judgement!
When you become stressed, listen to that part or aspect of yourself that is stressed. Although at first it may feel like it is every part of you, in my experience it is just *a* part of you. Ask the Divine Counsellor to reveal all your feelings and thoughts and acknowledge each one (this allows you to become present to yourself and bring everything to the surface). Then ask the Spirit of Peace to reveal his truth, i.e. his perspective.

This has helped me to release stress in many situations and to be filled with Peace. The first time I became aware that I could actually talk to 'parts' or 'aspects' of me was when I was driving off to present a talk and I felt stressed. I realised I felt frightened, resentful and angry at myself for agreeing to give the talk as I doubted I would be good enough. After listening to these feelings and thoughts and accepting them, I invited the Spirit of Truth to give me his perspective. As a result of listening to myself without resistance, and accepting Truth's perspective, all the stress I had felt dissolved. I was then able to present the talk from a place of peace.

Explore and express: write, confront or draw
When your stress is unresolved by the above exercise, the following brief exercises may help you:
Write down every feeling and thought you may have had, exploring them thoroughly, no matter how bad they sound … BUT don't send this paper to anyone; simply destroy your notes. This process will help you to listen to and connect to yourself and empty all you have thought and felt, making space for another life-giving perspective. Then ask the Spirit of Peace what he would write back to you. Let whatever comes to your mind flow through to your pen.
Confront the person you struggle with by asking the Spirit of Truth to bring all who stress you into your mind's eye. Look into their eyes as if they were present and then express all your feelings, thoughts and beliefs to this person as a result of what they have or have not done. Only so that any unresolved anger is dealt with and released, ask the Spirit of Truth to reveal what you would like to do to them. This releases anger in a safe way, which prevents you from hurting people either emotionally or physically in reality. Then ask the Spirit of Truth how they would respond and listen to them. Remember this is only ever done in your mind's eye so you are released from stress and come to peace. Lastly, ask the Spirit to reveal anything else you may need to know. You will have gained three perspectives, yours, the other person's and the Spirit of Truth.
Draw using coloured pastels, crayons or pencils. Allow yourself to take the colours that appeal to you and let your hand go. This helps when you can't identify your feelings or thoughts and allows you to express and release what you feel. I still have the first 'freestyle feeling' drawing I completed many years ago. The colours say a lot about where I was at that time. There was a great deal of red and black drawn! It helped me experience some release at the beginning of my journey to Peace.

Some other simple ways to de-stress
Choose at least one of the following suggestions that appeal to you and do it! Then see how you feel. Use anything on this list when appropriate in the future.
- Get your hands into the soil—garden, dig or weed. It has certainly 'grounded' and de-stressed me.
- Make time to do something you've always wanted to do but never allowed yourself to do.
- Go dancing! I wanted to Latin dance, but although it seemed impossible, I took the first step (no pun intended). It brings me fun, joy and life and a total change of focus from everyday situations.
- Plan a picnic with a friend and enjoy nature.
- Soak in a warm bath, perhaps with bubbles and candles.
- Go for a long walk in the park or by the beach. Learn to become a companion to yourself.
- Make a list of all the *good things* that are in your life. Every day, be thankful for three things and consider adding another one to your list. See how this action changes how you feel. I read how a young woman began to photograph one thing she was grateful for each day for a whole year. She put them in a scrapbook, and she said this exercise changed her life. Thank Wisdom in advance for turning *all things to good*, despite how you feel.
- Take time to be still and allow the Source of Love to touch every part of you. Persevere, as I learned to do, until you experience Peace.
- Make a decision to declutter your life and home.
- Do less when tired or rest so what you 'do' will be fruitful for you as well as others. Rest until you are no longer exhausted,

tired or restless.
- Always ask for Wisdom's perspective whenever you become stressed. Memorise and repeat a text from the Word of God that speaks to your heart. This I believe invokes the very presence and power of Peace, Presence and Power. I used to repeat these words when stressed: 'Whenever I face trials of any kind, I consider it nothing but joy because the testing of my faith produces endurance and let endurance have its full effect so I become complete lacking in nothing.' I didn't feel full of joy at the time I might add, but I persevered with these words until I actually felt joy and eventually became more complete, lacking little.
- Give up controlling, struggling and battling and instead allow Wisdom to guide you and change your circumstances. He will be responsible for helping us in our battles if we ask and thank him … and get out of the way.
- Do not allow external things to rob you of the Presence and Peace within you, such as:
  - other people changing
  - your success levels
  - how much money you have
  - your children growing up
  - people leaving
  - people acknowledging and affirming you
  - having the right clothes, car and appearance
  - having a happy, healthy and successful family.
- Seek your happiness first in the One who is the source of all good things. There can be no stress when you feel secure and remain in the presence of Peace. Otherwise, you will be controlled by these things and situations and end up on a

rollercoaster ride of emotions.
- Live guided by Wisdom instead of living life your way.
- Trust in Wisdom in all circumstances despite not understanding, which is faith in action, and then go with the flow of grace.

Body, mind, heart and spirit de-stressing exercise

I recommend applying this exercise before you get out of bed and before you go to sleep. It is also valuable to use before you make any major decision or have to deal with people or circumstances that usually make you feel stressed. It brings you into the present moment and shows you how you can reconnect to the powerful Source of peace within you.

- ASK the Divine Counsellor to reveal what state you are in (mind, body, heart and spirit). Begin with your mind, then focus on the other areas *one at a time*.

- OBSERVE and ACCEPT what is revealed in each area. You may be given an image, a feeling or a sense of what state you are in in each area. It can be subtle. Just accept what is revealed. The following are examples of what you may have a sense of in each area of your being as you observe what is revealed:

    Body: Your body may have an area of pain, tension or heaviness

    Mind: Your mind may appear scattered, blank, dark, grey or racing. There have been occasions where people have observed blankness or darkness in their minds. Just accept what is revealed and again observe what happens as you invite the Spirit of Peace to enter these areas. This blankness or darkness is usually a part of one's memory in which the Healing Meditation in Chapter 16 will help. If there is no change for the better, you may require some assistance from an experienced facilitator.

Heart: Your heart may appear to be broken, raw or shattered.

Spirit: Your human spirit may appear flat, lifeless, grey or dull.

- INVITE the Divine Counsellor, the Spirit of Peace, with his powerful healing presence, into each area and *observe what happens*. Allow yourself to be still and enjoy the change for the better.

GIVE THANKS! When unable to resolve stress
My favourite words in these circumstances were 'take over' Wisdom. When I said and meant this, my stressful circumstances were changed for the better. If necessary, ask Wisdom to guide you to an appropriate person who may be able to help you face the source of your stress and begin to experience peace. Your stress could be rooted in memories that are unresolved and require clarity, peace and healing. When the relevant root memory is revealed and healed of stress, which will usually have similar negative feelings and beliefs as in the present stressed area of your life, you should feel great release and freedom.

I encourage to you to see stress as an opportunity to learn about yourself, how to change your ways and to reconnect to Peace within.

30

Change Your Focus and Change Your Life!

Jenny was *always* busy. If she wasn't constantly active and responsible for everyone and everything, she felt guilty and unacceptable. She remembered that as a child she only felt noticed and valued for what she *did* rather than for *who she was.*

I asked if she would allow the Divine Counsellor to show her how this left her feeling in her life. She saw an image in her mind of chickens with their heads *focused* on the dirt, scratching endlessly. She also saw another image in her mind of herself whizzing around and around in circles, going nowhere. She realised that is just how she had felt in life. She felt exhausted from just watching this image!

She was then willing to *change her focus* from trying to gain acceptance from others and instead focus on and listen to the Divine Counsellor's perspective. As she became still and listened, she became aware of a Presence and experienced a deep knowing that she was of value and acceptable *without doing or achieving anything.* She let go of the past and felt a deep peace.

Some years later, Jenny reflected back to this time in her life remembering what her life had been like at that point—out of control! She then realised how almost every aspect of her life had slowly and gently changed for the better since the moment of *changing her focus* and listening to the Divine Counsellor and his truth.

How many people in the world believe that they are only worthwhile or acceptable if they achieve something or have something like money or position? What do you believe and *where are you focused* for your worth and value?

Who or what do we focus on in life for our happiness and self-worth?

The word focus means a number of things, but I particularly want to hone in on the aspect: 'a central point … to concentrate.' So let's look at some of things I have seen people focus and concentrate on and which can become central to their worth, value and happiness:

Achieving

Being active and achieving is meant to bring us life and enjoyment as we use our gifts and talents for the benefit of ourselves and others. However, when we focus and rely upon our achievements to *prove* that we are 'good enough' or 'acceptable,' we often don't feel satisfied even after we have achieved our goals. On the other hand, if we *don't achieve* what we wanted, we can feel disillusioned, exhausted and even depressed, as Jenny and many others like her experienced.

Family

We need to care for our family, but when what our family becomes our *prime focus* for peace and happiness, we can become *co-dependent, controlling* and *obsessive* about what they do. This way of acting usually leads to resentment, anger and abuse. We can become victims and doormats which will destroy, not build, healthy relationships.

Ann believed her mother was never there for her and didn't feel provided for in the way she had wanted. As a result of this hurt, she said she would make sure she would be there for her children and her grandchildren. However, this led her to be often exhausted and fed up because she is constantly helping her children and grandchildren. Her focus for peace and happiness is totally on her family. Her responsibilities only continue to grow and she is often overwhelmed. Her husband isn't happy either as her focus is always on the children. Ann is beginning to experience anger and resentment at the way she is being treated and is realising that change needs to occur. Sound familiar?

Ourselves
Caring for our health, bodies and looks is vital for our well-being, but when we become *focused* and *obsessive* in any of these areas, it can cause problems of all kinds. Dianne is a young woman who became obsessive about her looks and body. She was always focused on her stomach and could only see it as huge—in reality it was tiny! She went to the gym and dieted, but would then binge on junk food. She was very critical and judgemental about her body and hated herself when she didn't look 'right.' She was often unhappy and depressed. She said she couldn't 'control' herself.

Some years later as a result of becoming a model she discovered a healthy way of maintaining her weight. She shared how she began to *accept and care for her body* instead of hating it. By eating five small, healthy meals a day she kept her metabolism functioning at its optimum. She said she no longer focused on her weight as it was no longer a problem. She never felt hungry and rarely thought about her weight. What a change as she changed her focus to accepting her body and treating it with respect.

Others
Enjoying other people's company is important, but when our lives revolve around them, and we *focus* on them expecting them to fulfil our needs, we set ourselves up for disappointments. Mary believed her family would be there for when she was going through a very stressful

time in her life. However, when she expressed her feelings and thoughts, they just ignored her pleas. She left feeling angry, hurt, alone and betrayed. On the way home, the emotional pain overwhelmed her so much she thought of driving into a telegraph pole on the way home to end the pain. But then she *focused* on her children at home and instead drove home to them. It was a moment of saving grace. There are many people that don't survive this kind of onslaught of emotional pain.

How to change your focus and change your life
- Whenever you feel upset with yourself or others, struggling or out of control emotionally, it is a wakeup call to stop and *focus on listening to yourself* thoroughly, as you would with a little child. This *active* listening, without judgement or expectation, can begin to help.
- Share how you feel when exhausted or upset with a *trusted friend or professional counsellor* can help change your focus. But I have found that taking time to be still and share my feelings with my Divine Friend helps most. My focus changes as I listen to Wisdom's perspective and experience Truth.
- Only make life-changing decisions when you are at peace and have listened to yourself thoroughly, other people and then to Wisdom. Then your life should change for the better.

As I write this chapter, I realise how grateful, and even emotional, I feel about the changes that have occurred in my life as I changed my focus to listen to the Divine Counsellor, the Spirit of Truth.

31

The Power of Decisions That Can Change Your Life

Life-changing decisions can have the power to bring us either fulfilment and life or stress and regret. I have discovered that the majority of people that have come seeking freedom have made decisions, usually forgotten, that have led them down the path of stress and regret.

Where do decisions come from?
Decisions usually come from a need to move forward in one direction or another or to protect ourselves. One such example was when Jude told me she had made the decision never to go away on holidays at Easter time. When I asked her why, she said it was safer at home as there were a lot of road accidents at Easter and she wouldn't put herself at risk of this danger. She looked frightened as she shared, and I felt sad as I thought of all the fun I and others had experienced going away together at this time of year.

Decisions can be as simple as deciding what time to get out of bed, what to wear, what to eat or what arrangements to make for the weekend. All decisions have consequences, either bringing more or less life. Many decisions come from:
- what we experience in a situation, either in the present or past;
- the associated feelings;

- our beliefs, perceptions and judgements about ourselves, others or a situation;
- our reactions and ways of coping to protect or defend ourselves.

Decisions that bring stress and regret

Example 1:
Jane remembered a situation where her teacher ridiculed her in front of the whole class when she responded to a question. As she remembered the incident, all the feelings of being ashamed, embarrassed, belittled and stupid (her belief) flooded back to her as though it had just happened. Jane then remembered *making the decision* to never answer a question in class again so she would never feel like that again. Jane could now see with clarity why she always felt paralysed and unable to respond to questions throughout her university years. She also realised the stress she had carried all these years as a result of that decision and regretted allowing that teacher's behaviour to influence her. Jane decided to renounce the decision never to answer questions and forgave the teacher. She then realised how light and free she felt!

Example 2:
Lewis had a great relationship with his mother until he entered his teenage years when there were many situations where he believed his mother was not being real and honest. As a result of frequently feeling frustrated, angry, and powerless, he *made the decision* to never discuss things with his mum again. He exercised the only power he felt he had left as a young man. Sadly, years later, he shared with me how he hadn't felt close to his mother since that decision. However, in recent years he decided to be open and honest with his elderly mother about

how he felt. As a result, a healthy respect began to grow between them and she stopped trying to protect him by telling him what to do.

Other decisions that can bring stress and regret are:

- 'I'll never forgive.' Many people do not realise that unforgiveness poisons not only the mind, body and spirit but also our relationships. We retain what was done to us and it often leads to emotional and physical disease. I remember a young girl who wanted to forgive her father for abusing her, but just couldn't. I asked her if she would allow the power that Jesus had to forgive when he was being crucified to flow through her. She agreed and was then able to forgive. I know it is possible to forgive anyone for anything with God's grace, but it is always important that we share how we felt, what we believed and experience the truth first. Many people have shared that they felt if they forgave the person who hurt them, the person would get away with the offence, not realising that *everyone* eventually reaps what they sow.

- 'I'll never trust anyone again.' As a result of this decision, relationships suffer as trust is missing. This decision acts as a barrier in relationships. Many people have complained of their sense of aloneness and lack of intimacy in relationships as a result. People often retreat from life to some degree to protect themselves. One lady made this decision as a young teenager because of her trust being betrayed. She came to see that this had prevented the intimacy her husband wanted. The decision had formed a protective wall between them. She then experienced Peace in her memory, renounced the decision, and later rang to say she and her husband had got back together again.

- 'I will never tell anyone.' This decision is often made as a result of abuse. The person has remembered being threatened in the abuse and told never to tell. Although they have come seeking our help, they are often unable to speak or share until we discover they made the decision 'never to tell anyone' and let go of this decision. There is always an immediate release and the ability to speak and experience deep release.

- 'I'll make everything all right.' People have made this decision to be responsible to make everything all right usually as a result of their earlier life being painful or difficult. Those who have shared this have felt overwhelmed, burdened and stressed as they have decided to take on this role which is almost impossible to sustain. Their shoulders and back ache as a result, until they let go of this decision and role. I have often found that the belief of being 'responsible' can be linked with the belief 'it's my fault' in some situation in the past. These people are rarely appreciated, are often used and taken advantage of and have little joy, as life itself has become a burden. Expectations of themselves and others are unreasonably high and tension, fears and stress in general are often constant companions.

- We are making a decision *not* to make a decision when we procrastinate. When we struggle and agonise over making decisions, even seemingly insignificant decisions, we often do nothing! Invariably, it is because we feel frightened of what will happen if we 'don't make the right decision.' Usually this is as a result of some previous experience when we believed we were wrong and were blamed. Thus we are fearful of making a mistake or getting it wrong. Many people I have seen in this situation often feel paralysed, until they face their fear of being blamed or being wrong and experience Truth.

Obviously, it is wise to take adequate time to discern what to do when making any life-changing decisions. This is different to procrastinating. A practical way to decide what to do is to make a list with three columns: advantages, disadvantages and consequences. This can bring clarity if we do not have any underlying fears and false beliefs from previous painful experiences.

Once we have listened to our feelings and beliefs about ourselves or life, all we have to do is renounce decisions that create stress and regret and if necessary decide to forgive ourselves or others. The relief and release that people experience mentally, emotionally, physically and spiritually is life changing. They always walk away feeling light and free, feeling free to make decisions from a place of peace.

Decisions that bring fulfilment and life
- Decide to forgive … forgiveness is a decision. Chapter 27 in this book shares more information on how to 'really' forgive.
- Decide to face your fears, asking for Truth and Presence to be revealed. The fears dissolve as Truth is revealed.
- Decide to use *all* your gifts and talents no matter what people say or whether they appreciate you or them. Not using your God-given talents is robbing yourself, the world and God who wants all of us to flourish.
- Decide to unconditionally love others, although you may dislike what they do! Asking Unconditional Love to flow through you makes it easy!
- Decide to replace a bad habit with a healthy habit.
- Decide to listen to and obey the wisdom given in ancient Scripture; the laws and principles apply today just as in the past. I know from experience that they are a gift so we know the way to live in peace, freedom and fulfilment.

All decisions can be an opportunity from which to learn and grow.

If you discover you have made decisions that have robbed and trapped you, acknowledge them and let them go. Then be conscious of making decisions in the future that will improve your life in general and influence relationships for the better.

I hope you come to know and experience that you are *always* loved unconditionally no matter what type of decisions you make. I now see myself as a child in this amazing universe learning from everything, especially how to make decisions that will lead to freedom, peace and fulfilment. I hope that you will do the same.

32

The Power of Expectations

Expectations that lead to disappointments
Have you ever felt let down by other people or been confused and disappointed? Well that's exactly what I experienced with some people who had made a commitment to me but hadn't followed through with their promise. I realised I had *expected* them to do what they said. I felt disappointed and disillusioned. I decided to ask Wisdom to give me his perspective on the situation as I didn't want to remain feeling that way. As a result, I came to see the situation with a new perspective i.e. that the people involved were overwhelmed by their present situation.

I was also made aware of the times I have let people down—for instance, the numerous times I was late picking up my children from school. I had reasons, but that did not change the fact that they had *rightly expected* me, their mother, to be on time waiting for them at the conclusion of school. They later shared with me how they felt disappointed and disillusioned, believing that I didn't care about them. These insights immediately softened my heart. I was humbled and asked them to forgive me. All their feelings of disappointment and disillusionment dissolved. Thank God for his perspective and mercy! *Expectations* stem from what we believe will happen as a result of what people tell us they will do and also from past experiences. When we have been let down by others in the past, we can begin to believe and *expect* we will be let down again in the future. More often than not what you believe comes to be and we get what we expect! This can lead to further distrust and we can become cynical. I've heard people say, 'why would I expect others to be there for me because they never have in the past!' Relationships can be negatively affected as we close ourselves off in the hope of protecting ourselves from being disappointed again. The net result though is it closes us off from being open to learn from every situation and closes the door on the possibility of change for the better.

Some expectations can be: that people will here for you; that your mother and father will support you; that your spouse will be trustworthy; that others will treat you as you have treated them; that your children will be there for you as you grow older. The list goes on. When have you been disappointed as a result of your expectations? Just pause for a moment to discover the answer.

One day, I asked Wisdom to show me what we were supposed to have instead of expectations as I had often been left disappointed. What then came to my mind was to have hope. As I pondered the word hope, it felt soft in contrast with the sharp feeling around expectations. As I decided to give up expectations, I began to place my hope not in myself, others or things, but in the One who created everything and who could guide me to make wise decisions.

Most of my life I expected that if I did the right thing, we would all be happy. I had no idea then of the burden and expectations I had placed on myself, but I realised something wasn't 'right' when people took advantage of me and used me like a doormat. I was left exhausted and drained as a result of the decision I had made to be available to help anyone at any time. I didn't know how to say 'no.' I had no idea then that my expectations were founded on my underlying beliefs, needs and decisions.

I became aware during a Healing Meditation that as a young child I believed I was wrong and felt responsible because it seemed to be my fault. As a result, I felt alone and frightened. My way of coping was to become responsible (a role) to make sure everything and everyone was all right. This, of course, was impossible, but I only came to realise all this as a result of the consequences: my exhaustion and times of burnout.

As I waited to hear my Creator's truth, I experienced Light and Presence. I then knew I wasn't wrong or guilty and that it wasn't my responsibility to make everything all right! This experience on reflection released me from the pressure of my unrealistic expectations to meet other people's needs and for them to meet my often unrealistic needs. As a result, some unhealthy relationships dissolved whilst others became stronger. What a relief!

Are you aware of any negative beliefs about yourself or unmet needs that have led you to unrealistic expectations of yourself or others?

Life-giving expectations

Experience has shown me that when I have an expectant faith in the One who created me I am never disappointed. But it has taken me many years of clinging on to hope, trusting and believing in faith that 'all would be well' despite what I was experiencing. Faith I learned is the substance of things *not seen* but the *evidence of things to come*.

I became aware too that doubt had often robbed me, as it has others, leaving us believing nothing would change and opening the door to despair. Doubt robs us all from experiencing truth, unconditional love, mercy and forgiveness. Faith in God though brings life in its fullness. Abraham is one of the most remarkable examples of *expectant faith*, despite what seemed impossible. He believed that God would honour his promise and give him descendants, as many as the stars. Abraham *decided* to have faith in God's promise, even though he had to wait in hope until he was very old to see the evidence of this promise. Sarah, his wife, was then many years beyond child-bearing age and to many people it would have seemed impossible for her to become pregnant. But she indeed became pregnant and gave birth to Isaac which from a human perspective had seemed impossible.

No wonder it is vital that we gain God's perspective in life. Otherwise, we can stress ourselves on our journey trying to figure out situations we often don't fully understand, and we can try to fulfil our needs through our own strength alone, as I used to do. I hope though that we all choose to have hope, believing and trusting, with an expectant faith, that our Creator will guide us on to the path to life in *every* area of our life.

33

How to Gain an Empowering Perspective

The origins of developing perspective
We all have experiences, some we would see as good and others bad. These experiences cause us to form a view and belief about ourselves, people, things and life. This is where our perspective comes from. Unfortunately, many of our experiences create beliefs about ourselves or life that are distorted and untrue and can disempower us and alter the course of our life by how we respond.

One such example is Lilly's experience with dogs when she was three-years-old. She was on a farm when a young, large, playful dog suddenly appeared in front of her. He jumped up on her in a playful manner that knocked her to the ground. She was shocked and terrified. From that point on, Lilly perceived dogs as terrifying animals and avoided them at all costs.

Difficult or disastrous situations transformed by perspective
Some situations in my life used to look like disasters until I learned to ask the questions, 'What could be good about this situation? How do you, Wisdom, want me to see this situation?' This changed my focus from what was wrong to what good could be coming from the situation. As I listened to the response to my question, I would always

gain a whole new positive perspective, which began to change my life. I remember listening to a young man, Nick Vujicic, on television who was born with no limbs. After sharing how difficult his life had been growing up, he went on to say he eventually *made a decision* to inspire others by having a healthy perspective on life rather than live in self-pity. He touched my heart as I listened to him. Nick eventually wrote a book called *Life without Limits* and is now married, about to become a dad, and has travelled the world inspiring people with his positive perspective on life, despite what has happened.

We can do the same no matter what the difficulty, particularly when we can ask for the Spirit of Wisdom to help us, gaining his perspective, which is exactly what Nick did.

John shared with me an example of him going from feeling powerless to empowered when he had changed his perspective after a recent visit to his financial consultant. He had been told the devastating news that his superannuation had halved in value as a result of the global financial crisis. He had been planning to retire in a few years but now believed he had no other option but to keep working well past the age of sixty. As a result he felt trapped, powerless and despondent.

However, within hours of this meeting, John said he had seen the situation from a different perspective, and as a result actually felt empowered rather than trapped and powerless. He became aware of the many people who had also lost much of their money but were retired. Although he felt for these people, he realised how grateful he was that he had the opportunity to continue working for as long as he wished to build up his superannuation.

The keys for gaining a life-giving perspective
Always allow yourself to express your perspective and feelings, even when negative or depressing. Accept your perspective. Do not make it

right or wrong. Just hearing yourself begins to make space for another perspective. Then ask for Wisdom's perspective which will always bring life. Listen to what comes into your mind. You may hear words, see an image or just have a sense of what is being given to you. Then become aware of how you feel, as what comes from the Spirit is always encouraging even when corrective. Sometimes I feel led to open up the Word of God and ask to be led to the words I need to read. They always inspire me and change my perspective.

I particularly love the words in Matthew 7:24, 25 that say 'everyone then who *hears these words of mine and acts on them* will be like a wise man who built his house on rock. The rain fell, the floods came and the winds blew and beat on that house, but it did not fall because it had been founded on rock'. When I reflect on how unstable my life used to be, I now see and experience the truth of these words. I no longer fall apart as a result of people's bad attitudes or comments, but instead feel a deep peace and security within.

It took time and perseverance to gain my perspective because I had to *learn to listen* to myself. Over time, I gained confidence in listening to Wisdom's perspective. The Three-Way Perspective exercise described in the Healing Meditation Chapter, Chapter 16, is also very helpful in gaining clarity and peace as you not only gain *your* perspective, but the *other person's* perspective as well as the *Divine Counsellor's perspective* (the real truth).

How to avoid arguments using the power of perspective

Whenever I spent time with James, he always loved to ask me questions. I felt he was trying to lure me into a debate. His eyes would light up and he actually snorted in excitement with the possibility of a heated debate beginning in which he would always try to win. Once I was in the ring of the debate, it was like I was having punches thrown at me. He only listened to me in order to tear down any perspective I had. As you may have gathered, he was very aggressive.

In the past I had no idea how to handle or avoid this situation. I always left feeling exhausted. He had to be right it seemed! Finally though, I became aware that I only had to listen to his perspective, without struggling, agreeing or disagreeing as in this arena there was no possibility of having a civil conversation. I would just repeat back to him what he had said, so he knew I had heard him and acknowledged that I heard *his perspective*. I sometimes said, 'I have a different perspective.' Over time, he stopped trying to bait me into an argument. Remember that it takes two people to argue! Try this powerful way of dealing with aggressive people.

Other examples of the power of perspective
I once received a beautiful gift of handcrafted, dried flowers from a dear friend. I said to her, 'These are just like you!' Her response was, 'You mean all dried up!' I said, 'No, I meant they are beautiful just like you!' Clearly, we weren't on the same page!

Have you ever made a comment to someone and they have taken it the wrong way? Rather than get upset, it is *vital you first acknowledge their perspective* so they know you have listened to them, even if you don't agree. Then, as I have said before, ask if they are open to listening to your perspective. This is a respectful way of dealing with these situations that can make a huge difference to developing healthy relationships.

Blockages to obtaining a life-giving perspective
When Jody came asking for assistance to find peace, she discovered she had hidden anger, resentment, hatred, revenge, unforgiveness, rejections, judgments and doubts blocking her from seeing clearly. She believed everything was her fault and that she was responsible for

everything that went wrong. She also felt worthless. As we allowed time for her to listen to herself, her perspective, so she could become aware, acknowledge and accept all her feelings and beliefs, bringing them to the surface, she was then ready to listen to her Creator's perspective.

As she listened, her face lost all the tension and became peaceful and serene. She shared that she experienced Light and a Presence. When I asked if all the beliefs were true in this place, she realised none of them were relevant anymore. They had dissolved. She could 'see' the truth in the Light which totally changed her perspective of herself, others and life.

Jody's hidden feelings and beliefs are some of the most common blockages to gaining a life-giving perspective. There are many other common negative beliefs that people have about their worth and value such as 'I'm stupid'; 'I'm a failure'; 'I'm no good'; 'I'm hopeless'; 'It's my fault' and 'I don't deserve anything' that need to be acknowledged. Then there is space to hear and experience Light and Truth. Please see Chapter 33 for further information on other obstacles and blockages to gaining a life-changing perspective.

We can choose either a negative or positive perspective

The consequences of actions, reactions and decisions made from a negative perspective lead down a path that creates a bad attitude, stress, exhaustion, disorder and disharmony in one way or another. Therefore, being aware of negative feelings and beliefs is essential so we can ask for a life-giving perspective in every situation before we react and make potentially damaging decisions.

I choose to listen thoroughly to my perspective now, giving myself a voice, but then always ask for Wisdom's perspective when making decisions or whenever some situation occurs which tries to tear me down. Will you do the same? Give it a try and see the difference.

34

The Power of Attitude

I heard an extraordinary story that inspired me. The man in the story, who I will call Joe, developed an enduringly *positive attitude* despite extraordinarily difficult circumstances. His mother was a prostitute and his father was a pimp so life had been anything but ordinary. On top of that, as a young boy, he had an accident in which his foot was smashed to a pulp and had to be amputated. Yet during all these trials, he must have eventually *made a decision* not to focus on what had happened to him, but to focus on what he could do with his life despite his background and a missing foot.

  He decided to become an athlete and aimed to run in a disabled event. Eventually he was fitted with the first artificial foot to be produced and later decided to compete in the Para Olympics. He was successful in reaching his goal and competed extremely well. Life only became better for him because of his *life-giving attitude, focus and decisions*. Imagine what could have happened if he had felt sorry for himself and used his disability as an excuse not to become the best he could be. What might happen in our lives and those around us if we all decided to have a *good attitude* about all the difficult circumstances and focus on what we can do?

  As I reflect back over my life, I now see how my attitude in many situations only caused me more pain, separation and grief. When people expressed opinions opposite to what I believed, I would feel personally offended. I believed they were wrong and I was right. This would lead me to 'stinky thinking' as I would go over and over the conversations justifying my anger and resentment. My attitude towards these people was cold and defensive and whenever we were together the atmosphere between us was full of tension. This would often leave me with the PLOMs. What does PLOM mean? The Poor Little Old Me syndrome! When I was in this mindset (which is all it is), life seemed really bad, hard and unfair. I now realise with this attitude I repelled people and attracted people with the same bad attitude as myself. Do you ever suffer from the PLOMs?

Underlying causes of bad attitudes
Underlying our bad attitudes is the way we perceive the world, situations and ourselves and the resulting beliefs we develop. The foundational beliefs from which we live our lives are often not true, and everything in life becomes distorted and adversely affected. Past experiences can be triggered making us react out of hurt whenever something similar in the present reminds us of past painful experiences. Beliefs can stir up negative feelings and lead us to have unrealistic expectations which lead on to disappointments. The decisions we then make often only trap us further.

What has helped many people experience freedom from unresolved pain and beliefs from the past has been to allow the Divine Counsellor to bring to the surface any unresolved areas of our past. Chapter 16 contains a step-by-step guideline that will lead to an attitude of gratitude. It also helps to practice asking the question, 'What could be good ...' about certain challenging circumstances, rather than looking for what is wrong.

Effectively handling bad attitudes

When confronted with another person's bad attitude, here are some suggestions that have made a huge difference in my life:

- Be aware that you have a choice on how you respond to circumstances. Responding with a bad attitude is like putting petrol over a fire! Responding with a good attitude in a negative situation should bring good results. Even if it doesn't, you will have retained your dignity and remained in control of your emotions instead of allowing your emotions to control you!
- Observe the consequences of bad attitudes. How are you left feeling for instance when you are in the presence of someone with a bad attitude? Usually it repels us. Being aware of how you felt may help you develop a life-giving attitude, so you don't influence people negatively and repel them.
- Look after yourself as we can develop bad attitudes when we become tired, cranky and out of balance. Become aware of when you feel this way and make a decision to take time to rest your body and nurture your soul to avoid having a bad attitude.
- Deal with the upsets in your life quickly and effectively. Otherwise, we can bottle up resentments and then our attitude changes with these unresolved feelings. I think road rage is a good example of what I am talking about. The slightest mistake can unleash people's rage and pent up anger showing the worst attitude possible. When people are enraged, it isn't the time to sort out anything. It's better to say you are sorry they are upset and depart! Recently though I encountered someone with a good attitude when I almost caused an accident. I was very grateful. We can change our world with our attitude—for better or worse.
- Can you have an attitude of forgiveness towards those who have treated you badly? I believe it is almost humanly impossible in

some circumstances, yet when people have been willing to allow the power of Jesus' forgiveness to flow through them to their abusers, it has dissolved any unforgiveness, released the associated pain, restored their dignity and bought peace. The change in these people and their lives has been profound.

If anyone could have had a justifiably bad attitude, Jesus could have. After all, he was asked to die for other people who were often ungrateful and would ultimately be the ones to put him to death. That's a big ask! But his attitude was to forgive those crucifying him unjustly, as he realised they didn't know what they were doing ... or to whom. With this example, he demonstrated the power of an attitude of forgiveness, despite injustice, as he literally rose above their murderous attitudes and then did the impossible, physically rose again.

- Avoid complaining and blaming. Instead you could adopt the attitude Paul and Silas had after they were slandered, attacked and thrown into prison unjustly. They prayed and sang hymns to God despite what happened. Then there was a sudden earthquake. The prison was shaken. Their chains fell off. The doors were opened. And, which was probably the point of all their suffering, their jailers were converted! We sometimes can't change what happens to us, but we can change the way we handle it by having a life-giving attitude. Instead of feeling trapped or 'chained up' in our circumstances, we could do what Paul and Silas did. It is *our choice*. What type of attitude do you have when treated badly?

If you need further help in relation to changing your attitude after what I have shared, remember that it is available if you ask Unconditional Love to take over. You will receive power and an ability beyond yourself to overcome your bad attitude. This isn't something I've read about; it's what I have experienced.

35

'What if...?' A Powerful Question

How you respond to the question 'what if...?' can change the course of your life. If you do nothing else after reading this chapter, begin becoming aware of the times you either think or hear the words 'what if...' and how it leaves you feeling.

Possibilities and lost opportunities
What if you were considering a new possibility in your life? It could be in any area such as a relationship, business, study, a trip or something you have always wanted to experience or achieve. Let's use a relationship as an example for this topic.

John was attracted to a young woman at work and thought about asking her out on a date to get to know her better. But he began to think, '*What if* she doesn't accept my invitation?' He then began to feel frightened of possibly being rejected and feeling stupid. He then decided it was too risky and didn't extend the invitation. That was a lost opportunity.

On the other hand he could have thought '*What if* she accepts my invitation?' This perspective would have encouraged him to extend the invitation which could have opened the door to other possibilities. When you ask yourself 'What if ...' when considering a decision, does it lead to possibilities or lost opportunities?

Asking 'What if ...?' from a foundation of fear, doubt or faith

Asking 'What if...?' from a fearful perspective closes doors, but it does more than that; it can actually attract the very thing we fear as Job in the Bible discovered. He said 'that which I feared came about.' In other words, what we focus on, and what is in our mind can come to be as, to some extent, we can create it with our thinking as mentioned in Chapter 4—Transforming Life by Transforming Thoughts and Beliefs!

An example of what I am saying is when Jan told me how she almost had an accident one Easter. She also said she had made the decision to never go away at that time because she said, 'I won't take the risk because *what if* I had an accident?' which revealed a fear of being hurt. Sadly, fear of being hurt was controlling her in this instance. I left her hoping she didn't attract what she feared.

Asking 'what if ...?' based from *doubts* usually makes us procrastinate over decisions because we can be frightened of making the wrong decision. This can be because of past, negative experiences, but fortunately they can be released by the Healing Meditation described in this book so doubts no longer control your life.

These words of wisdom in Mark 11:23 tell us '... if you do not doubt in your hearts, but *believe* that what you say will come to pass, *it will be done for you.*' What extraordinary power we have if we *believe in faith* and don't doubt!

Asking 'What if ...?' can reveal deep-seated fears that can be dissolved!

If fear is crippling your life, this can be dissolved, but first the *belief* causing the fear needs to be revealed. This is where asking the question 'What if ...?' can quickly reveal the source of fear.

This is what happened in Lilly's situation when she came for help. She shared how she had wanted to be a doctor all her life, but she had been devastated after she failed the entrance examination to medicine.

So I asked the Divine Counsellor to reveal to Lilly *What if* she never became a doctor?' A memory then came to her mind of when she had had an accident. She could still feel the fear and devastation and the belief that she was all alone, as though it had just happened. She realised that shortly after the accident she had made the decision to become a doctor to prevent others feeling this loneliness, fear and devastation So the devastation Lilly had felt after failing the entrance examination had triggered off the unresolved fear and devastation felt in that childhood memory.

As I asked the Divine Counsellor 'How true is it that Lilly was alone in the accident?' Lilly listened and observed the memory. She then became aware of a Presence and saw Light and realised that she hadn't been alone. All the devastation and fear dissolved. Although she had no idea of what the future would bring, she left in peace. In fact, many years later, Lilly became a doctor, a specialist. How different it may have been if she hadn't been released from her deepest fears.

What about you? Which path has the question 'what if…?' led you down? Has it been one of possibilities and success or lost opportunities and failure because of fears? It isn't too late to face your fears and journey on in peace.

Questions that can change your life
Many years ago, I never thought of considering the following questions. Unfortunately I was too busy and focused elsewhere, running in the opposite direction, until I crashed! I know now they can open our minds to possibilities:

- *What if* I faced my fears and experienced truth and freedom?
- *What if* I learnt how feelings and beliefs could lead to freedom?

- *What if* I could make a difference in the lives of others?
- *What if* my weakness could be turned into strengths?
- *What if* I could be released from the pain of past memories?
- *What if* I could discover Peace, Presence and Power within myself?
- *What if* I could learn how to attract good things into my life?
- *What if* I could learn how to free myself from stress?
- *What if* I developed a healthy attitude?

If I can experience the reality of all I mention here, I know anyone can. So despite where you are in your life, I encourage you to ask the One who has the power within you to accomplish what you never dreamed was possible with your life.

36

How to Attract Good Things into Your Life

Have you ever thought that *we* can attract situations, things and people into our lives, like a magnet, by the power of *our* thoughts, beliefs (either conscious or subconscious), words and actions? I hope, as a result of what you read, you will come to know and experience the power you have to attract good things into your life which in turn can flow on to those around you.

Your words can reveal what you're thinking, believing and attracting

When I hear people say they hate themselves, that they are an idiot, not good enough, hopeless or a failure for instance, I wonder if they know they open the door to attract more of what they have said from others. *As you judge so will you be judged is a law of attraction.* I wonder if you are aware of what you say and what you attract from others, whether it be positive or negative? Judgements are like a dead weight on our being and life becomes hard.

One day I became aware that I was saying to myself repeatedly, 'I feel so tired.' I then became conscious that I felt even more exhausted as a result of what I was saying. So I asked the Spirit of Life to flow through every part of me to refresh and renew me and began *thanking him in advance for renewing me.* As I did this, I actually felt better. I was amazed how powerfully my thoughts and words attracted either tiredness or energy! When my husband is tired, he now says, 'I am in need of refreshment.' It makes me laugh. It's interesting how you can actually 'feel' the heaviness or lightness in words.

Even changing the word 'suffering' to 'opportunity' when I was being challenged made a *huge* difference. It still didn't mean that I 'enjoyed' the challenge, but I began to focus on what I could learn from it. This book is a product of what I have learned from my own experiences and other people's, showing how powerfully we can *begin to attract good things* out of challenging or difficult situations. Life-giving language has a powerful effect on us and others. We often attract what we say because it comes from what we *think* and *believe*. And *as we believe, so will it be done* … another powerful law of attraction.

We are invited to ask for what we want

We are invited to *ask* for what *we want* in prayer and thanksgiving. Any good parent wants to give good things to their children so how much more would the One who created us want to give us good things! Asking builds our relationship and thanking builds our belief, faith and gratitude. This way of being usually *attracts more good things*.

On reflection, I now realise that some of the things I had asked for eventually came to be, *but* it took many years for me to be open to receive them. There were so many deep-seated fears and negative beliefs that were still *attracting the very thing I didn't want*. As the blockages of fears, doubts and negative beliefs dissolved, I became open to receiving. I then attracted many *good things* into my life.

I used words of affirmation for what I wanted to attract into my life many years ago. However, I began to realise I felt uneasy about these affirmations so I asked Wisdom to show me why. Then I heard in my mind, 'You haven't asked me about what to ask for.' So I went through the affirmations asking Wisdom's perspective on them. I could see clearly how to adjust each affirmation. Then I felt at peace about each one, most of which have now come into being. Asking Wisdom *what specifically to ask for* in circumstances can be very enlightening and brings us into line with the will of the Creator of all good things.

Ask for what you want … not for what you don't want!
Many people actually ask for what they *don't want*. Saying: 'Please don't let little Johnny get *hurt*' is focusing on what we *don't want* from fear, instead of asking 'Please keep little Johnny *safe.*' Can you 'feel' the difference? If you ask a little child *not* to step into a puddle, usually the child steps into the puddle because that is where we focus their attention. Instead, we could ask them to 'stay on the dry part of the path.' **Do you focus on the positive or the negative when you ask for what you want?** Become aware of what you ask for and see what you attract.

I discovered you can attract the type of day you want when you first wake up in the morning. I even ask the Creator of my day how he would like me to see it. On one occasion, I heard the word 'delightful.' So I thanked him for the delightful day ahead and I entered the day focused on and looking forward to a delightful day. And that's what I experienced.

Why we don't attract what we ask for
Sometimes we don't attract what we want because we are double-minded, unsure and doubting. If we are not 100% committed to what we ask for, this undermines the power of our asking, attracting and receiving.

For instance, Jan asked that a man come in her life as a friend, but nothing ever seemed to happen in this regard. She felt frustrated. After gaining clarity through a Healing Meditation, she discovered a part of her actually couldn't stand men and in fact hated them! She was double-minded. Part of her would attract men and the other part would repel them; she was sabotaging her heart's desire. Jan resolved her feelings and experienced the truth in this part of her and is now wholehearted about meeting the type of man she wants in her life.

Janice had to leave America for a position in Australia. When she tried to arrange all her affairs the week prior to leaving, everything went wrong and she wondered why. But then she realised she *wasn't totally committed* to moving to Australia and she had been doubting her decision. Part of her wanted to go, but another part of her was hesitant. The moment she let go of the doubt and committed 100% to the move to Australia, she completed in one day what would normally have taken four days to accomplish.

Do you believe good things will happen in your life?

I encourage you to believe the best so you can attract the best outcome from *all* your experiences. Many people have believed deep down they *don't deserve good things* because of past experiences. I invite these people to listen to the Spirit of Truth and his perspective. This blockage then *dissolves* and then they are *open* to receiving good things freely, if they don't doubt!

When you are not experiencing good things in life become aware of what you are *expecting and believing*. Is it for a positive or negative outcome? If you are reflecting on past *negative* experiences and projecting them into the present and future, you usually attract more of what you focus on. Instead, you can learn from these past negative experiences asking the life changing questions: 'What good could come out of what happened; what can I learn; how would you, Spirit of Truth, have me see the situation?' You will have then changed your focus from 'what is wrong' to 'what good can come from the situations.' Then see what you attract.

We attract what we give

As you give so will it be given to you is another law of attraction. I now realise I used to give to others but expected something in return. When I didn't get back what I gave, I would be unhappy. Once I learned to give freely, then I discovered *it is in the act of giving alone that I received,* attracting happiness and satisfaction as a result of making a difference in another person's life, even by a smile or a word of encouragement.

Some people have shared they feel they *haven't anything to give.* If you feel this way, then one simple solution can be to ask the Creator of all good things, who is within you, to *release through you* what you need so you can give to others. You will then realise the truth of '… the Power at work *within us* which is able to accomplish abundantly far more than we can ask or imagine …'

I invite you to persevere in asking for the quality you need, be open to receiving it, then share it with others.

37

How to Attract the 'Right' Friends and Partner

Let's first understand fully what the word 'attract' means. The *Oxford Dictionary* states it is 'to draw towards itself by *unseen forces*: a magnet attracts iron; to get the attention of; to arouse the interest or pleasure of.'

We tend to attract, or draw to ourselves, others who have similar underlying attitudes and beliefs about themselves or life. For instance, I now realise that my husband and I are very similar in the way we are both very responsible and that we have both had high expectations in the past trying to get things or ourselves 'right.'

We can also be attracted to others because they have something we lack. My husband and I are quite different in other ways. I tend to be very creative, spontaneous and sometimes scattered whereas he is very ordered and structured. These differences when used appropriately have balanced and completed each other. But we had to learn over the years to be tolerant and patient, instead of being frustrated.

Discovering what 'right' means in relationships!
When I thought about what the 'right' person might mean to me, I realised I am drawn to people who are gentle, kind, fun-loving, sincere and real. As I share this with you, I realise these are many of the

qualities my husband has! As a teenager, I thought he was 'hot' because he was good looking as well so good looks also attracted me at first. However, good looks weren't enough for me as shown by the fact that my relationships with a few other good looking guys never lasted. Now I realise they didn't have the other qualities that I was attracted to in a person.

I remember my husband and I meeting a guy I will call George. We both thought he looked like an unusual character at first, and we certainly did not feel drawn to him. However, we ended up playing tennis with him and through this experience got to really know him. We discovered he had the most delightful, funny personality, with a passion for life. We became the very best of friends and have shared our lives for over 30 years! You've heard it said, 'Don't judge a book by its cover.' It's always wise to open the cover and check what's inside!

So what does 'right' mean for you in this context? What qualities do you value in another person? Write them down before you continue reading so you are aware of them. Are there any people in your life at present that have these qualities?

The difference between 'needs' and 'wants'
When we look at the word 'need' from the perspective of 'something necessary for us to live,' I believe we need the people in our lives that will help us grow and develop into the very best we can be as human beings, through the good times and especially the tough times.

When we look at the word 'want' from the perspective of 'desiring or wishing for something we lack,' we are no doubt aware that many of us 'want' a lot of things from life and other people. If we *want* and *expect* people to *fulfil* us, they can feel under pressure. We can become demanding and then disappointed and the relationship usually suffers.

Do you believe receiving what you 'want' from others is the key to your happiness and freedom?

I heard about a lady at a very important luncheon being asked the question, 'Does your husband make you happy?' As she paused to answer the question, the lady was aware there were others listening into the conversation waiting for her answer. She then said, 'No, my husband doesn't make me happy; my happiness is up to me.' If you were asked this question, how would you reply?

Letting go and developing a 'safe' space for honest relationships
I had to let go of what I wanted from others before they felt 'safe' to be open and honest in our relationships. This then developed true intimacy with a number of people, something I had always wanted. However, before I could *honestly* let go of what I wanted, I needed to listen to all my negative feelings and beliefs, my perspective, before I could gain Wisdom's freeing perspective.

As I changed, most of my relationships improved; however, some relationships dissolved since I wasn't giving them what they wanted. I realised we had been in an unhealthy relationship where I had been 'people pleasing' and trying to 'keep the peace.' I wasn't being authentic with these people and I had attracted people that weren't being authentic with me.

Do you think people feel 'safe' to be open and honest in your relationships?

Obstacles to attracting the 'right' friends or partner into your life
We either repel or attract others by the way we are 'being,' which comes from what we are thinking. We create an atmosphere around us which either creates an inviting, safe space or one that is tense and uninviting. Be aware of what you experience in the weeks to come and sense the atmosphere we or others create.

The following list contains some of the things we do that create tension and obstacles and can repel others rather than attract them. It also contains suggested solutions. I have seen the power, both negative and positive, of the following:

Issue: Being critical and judgmental of ourselves or others.

Solution: Focus on the *good points* you can see in others and yourself. A positive change should occur in your relationships.

Issue: Not being honest about what we are really thinking and feeling and having unresolved negative emotions, thoughts and beliefs.

Solution: Ask the Divine Counsellor to help you to listen to all your feelings and beliefs and then ask for his truth about your worth and value. You may be triggered by a past experience that can be resolved leaving you feeling secure.

Issue: When we or others try to manipulate, control or dominate another person because we want something, feel insecure or doubt the relationship.

Solution: Let go of these ways of being and apologise to anyone if necessary for this way of acting. There is no love or respect in manipulation, control or domination! Use the Healing Meditation to release you from everything that would act as an obstacle to fulfilment, security and love.

Issue: When we *conditionally* love others or can't forgive.

Solution: Take time to gain three perspectives as mentioned in the Healing Meditation. You will often 'see' the people differently as a result. If you still can't forgive, ask the capacity Jesus had to forgive, even whilst being murdered unjustly on the cross, to flow through you. It is amazingly powerful.

Most people want to attract into their lives friends or a partner that are loving, caring and respectful. But we often need a capacity beyond us to develop these qualities and attitudes because of our past or present difficult circumstances and relationships. This is where you can ask Wisdom to show you how to develop these qualities, asking for his capacity of unconditional love to flow through you. I've done this in difficult relationships and experienced great results. Remember too to set healthy, respectful boundaries in relationships so you are respected. For further help with this, read Chapter 22—Relationships with Healthy Boundaries.

The bottom line is, we attract what we think and believe as well as how we act to some degree. Allow any negative feelings or thoughts of any kind to lead you to discover Truth's perspective deep within and see the wonderful people you will then attract into your life.

38

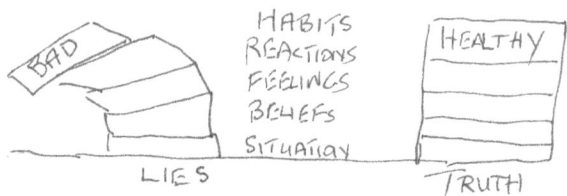

How to Develop Healthy Habits

Habits are like a bundle of *conditioned reflexes* which we can be *unaware of* or *believe are outside of our control,* which is untrue. To change them, we need to become aware of our habits and their consequences so we can take responsibility for any bad habits and replace them with healthy habits that will bring peace, order and purpose.

    Let's begin with an example from my life. As I finally settled down to write this chapter of the book, I realised that I have a bad habit of putting off writing articles and seminar material to the last possible moment. As a result, I put myself under pressure as well as the person who is waiting to print the article on time. I find myself getting distracted and doing anything else but the thing I need to be doing! If in fact I didn't have a deadline, I could see how easy it would be for me not to write at all. I wouldn't then have to research the work and reflect on it.

    I asked myself why I do this, and the answer that came back is that a part of me *believes it's too hard and doubts I can do it.* There was even a slight fear of being stupid. I remembered someone very close to me often saying how stupid they were so their belief had influence me somewhat. So one part of me wants to prepare the articles and another part resists. I am in fact being double-minded and consequently disempowered. So after listening to myself, I turned to the Source of real power within, asking for help and grace in my weakness. I then experienced Peace as the negative beliefs and doubts lost their power over me and what seemed hard became easy. Now I write from a place of Peace, which is great especially as this book is called Peace, Presence, Power!

I wonder if you have a bad habit that creates tension and stress in your life? This is also what I experienced with another bad habit of always being late for appointments. I found it hard, or almost impossible, to change this bad habit, until I was eventually made aware of the underlying cause. I realised that as a child I *believed* I couldn't waste time because I would somehow feel bad. So to avoid feeling bad, I had developed the habit of being super busy, using every single moment to accomplish *something*. But then I would always be late for appointments, which made me feel guilty and bad anyway. I was trapped in this cycle, until I experienced release from this foundational *belief* of being bad in the childhood memory. I then felt free, like invisible chains had fallen off me, from my unrealistic expectations and was able to allow plenty of time to get ready and arrive at my appointment on time, with grace and ease. What a difference this made to my life, reducing the stress and pressure my old beliefs and subsequent habit had created.

I also became aware that I had the bad habit of often talking about other people's flaws. I didn't realise then that I was actually pulling them down and that I would attract back to myself what I was giving out! When I asked Wisdom to reveal why I did this, I saw this way of acting somehow made me feel superior and better than them. How wrong I was! I then decided to develop the healthy habit of looking for people's good points so I could encourage them and build them up instead. What a difference that made to my relationships!

Will you be open and ask Wisdom to show you any bad habits that are causing stress in your life so you can change them?

How to gently discover and change bad habits
Developing the healthy habit of being present and aware is vital to changing any bad habit. Then slowly but gently we can make a change for the better by:
- *asking Wisdom to reveal any bad habit* that is creating negative results;
- *deciding to change one bad habit into a healthy habit* one at a time, and acknowledging the results and how this makes you feel.

I realised that unless I changed my ways i.e. my negative beliefs, actions and bad habits, I would always end up with the same negative result. So I made a *decision to give up the habit* of excuses, blaming, complaining, judging and criticising as this behaviour always disempowered or destroyed me or other people. In its place, I developed the habit of being responsible for what I said and did. I then became more conscious of the law of sowing and reaping, getting back what we give out. What a difference this change made in my life. Will you *make a decision* to change for the better?

A lot of people have a bad habit of *worrying.* Underlying worry can be doubt, a lack of faith and trust especially in the One who can bring good out of *all* things. The habit of worrying actually makes the situation worse, but it is not the worry that is the problem, but rather *continuing to entertain the negative thoughts and beliefs* that cause the worry, allowing them to settle in the harbour of your mind. As most of us, to some extent, experience what I call free radicals, 'negative thoughts,' trying to attack our minds, how can we develop healthy, constructive habits of dealing with them?

We can develop the habit of observing, instead of accepting, any worrying thoughts and letting them *pass by our mind*. That enables us to refocus and fill our mind with life-giving thoughts. Another powerful and easy way to deal with worrying thoughts is to take them to Wisdom and ask for his truth and perspective. When I do this it stops me from struggling with the worrying thoughts and, as I listen to what comes to my mind, Peace replaces worry. It is brilliant! If certain negative beliefs and thoughts still keep reoccurring in my mind, I use the Healing Meditation in Chapter 16 which brings my mind into a place of peace.

Developing the habit of asking empowering questions instead of disempowering questions will change your focus, perspective and life. As a result of asking myself, 'What can I do to help bring order into my preparation for a seminar?' I realised I needed to put time for writing into my diary. This simple step developed the *healthy habit of planning* which helped me meet the printer's timeline and avoid the stress I used to create for myself.

If I fail to meet my deadlines, which still occurs on occasion, another empowering question is, 'What can I learn from failing to meet my deadlines and what can I do about this?' This is a much better solution than beating myself up through self-criticism. I have also developed the *habit of being grateful* for many things, but especially with people who are patient and forgiving when I don't do what I say. This in turn reminds me to treat others with the same attitude in similar circumstances.

Healthy habits that will bring life
Will you consider developing healthy habits over time that will energise, enlighten, bring joy and make a difference? Here are a few suggestions:
- making time to be still for at least 10 minutes a day, when you

- can pray, reflect or meditate, so you become present to yourself and the Presence and Power within you. *You reflect who you spend time with.* This habit has changed my life!
- being thankful for at least five things per day;
- replacing junk food with whole natural food;
- exercising each day in whichever way is appropriate;
- drinking at least eight glasses of water a day;
- reading inspirational, life-giving books;
- listening to TV programs, CDs, podcasts and other types of media that encourage and teach you;
- making time to rest, relax and enjoy nature and life in simple ways.

I encourage you to choose *one* of the above suggestions to begin with or make up your own list of the healthy habits you want to develop and work on *one* for a month or two until it becomes a habit.

I recently read a book about Tom who had a life-changing experience after a brilliant Light penetrated the cell he was in whilst in solitary confinement. After this experience he felt and acted totally different and was then placed in a cell with an elderly prisoner who became his mentor. This elderly man, who had served his sentence but was too old to leave jail, showed Tom how to change bad habits into good habits. He suggested making up two lists, one with his bad habits and one with his good habits. He was then to focus on one bad habit and begin to change it so it ended up on the good habit list. The elderly mentor said it was important that *this project be treated like a game and it would become fun.* Sometime down the track, Tom noticed that the long list of bad habits had become very small and the list of good habits had grown. He then began to mentor other people as he felt led and most of their lives were changed for the better.

So you could have the same attitude and have fun changing bad habits into good habits as Tom did. Remember to focus on one bad habit at a time and that you can ask for assistance from the Helper of all helpers, the Divine Counsellor. Enjoy the journey of discovery and empowerment and be your own best encourager!

39

Empowering Destiny Keys

Here are some very practical and powerful destiny keys that can make a great difference in your life. So you don't become overwhelmed by trying to apply these destiny keys all at one time, I recommend you focus on the one key that stands out to you until it becomes part of your life and is making a difference. Then move on to the next key that you want to apply to your life. Remember that new habits take many weeks to develop, but with the help of your Creator even this becomes easier! I find if I ask the Divine Counsellor for help, it is *he* who makes me not only *wish for* but also *carry out* what pleases him. The results always bring life.

Discover which empowering destiny keys could make a great difference in your life:

- *Acknowledge and accept your gifts and talents* no matter what others or you think about them. Then use them for the good of everyone. This will bring you and others life. Please don't bury them out of fear of failure, but rather learn from any failure. Remember it is false humility to deny the gifts you have been given.
- *Reject rejection!* Stop worrying about what other people think about you! Be yourself, for those who matter don't care and those who care don't matter. You will then feel free to go in

the direction of your heart's desires. So let no-one and nothing stop you from your destiny to flourish and be fulfilled.

- *Take 100% responsibility for your life.* You either master life or it masters you! Stop blaming and complaining and start changing—either yourself or your life. I wasn't aware of how much energy I used to waste on blaming and complaining instead of using it on what I could do.
- *Tap into the Source of unlimited creativity and wisdom within yourself* instead of journeying on your own because we are limited. You have a Divine Helper within you with an unlimited well of wisdom, creativity, love and guidance whenever you need it. In fact, when I have no idea which direction to go, I have often said 'Take over Wisdom!' and the results are wonderful! The direction I was to take in my life, my destiny, slowly and gently became clear and doors began to open effortlessly in this direction.
- *Associate with honest, encouraging people.* Share your dream only with people you can trust will hold it respectfully.
- *Learn, learn, learn ... from everything.* Allow everything that happens to you be an opportunity to gain helpful information. Make the most out of *everything*.
- *Create your world each day* by what you think, believe, say and do. Every day can be seen like a blank canvas on which you create your life. It is your choice how you paint your day with your attitude and perspective, despite what happens!
- *Make the pathway clear* so you can gain clarity about your destiny. Deal with any unresolved emotional or mental baggage from the past so it doesn't influence your present and future. Ask the Spirit of Truth to show you if there is anything you are holding onto that is preventing you from moving

forward. The Blockages and Obstacles Chapter may help in this regard.
- *Face your fear.* Feel it and move forward anyway in the direction of your destiny with Wisdom's guidance.
- *Ask for advice or constructive comments* from people who have gone before you and whom you admire. One suggestion is to ask someone to evaluate your work on a scale of 1 to 10. If it is less than 10, then ask the person how it can be improved. You will gain valuable information that you can act upon.
- *Develop healthy habits.* Remember 90% of behaviour is habit. Focus on developing one healthy habit at a time until it becomes part of your way of living. Chapter 38 gives you some very practical ways to develop good habits.
- *Start today with one small step* towards what you feel destined to achieve. If you fail or get stuck, remember you can start again tomorrow! Always keep in mind though what is of greater importance is how you are 'being' on the journey and if this brings life to others and yourself.
- *Persevere and be determined in what you set out to do.* Once you know what you what to achieve, these two qualities will make all the difference in achieving your goals. It is like taking an axe to a large tree. If you keep chopping at it, even if your swings are slowly taken, the tree will eventually fall and you will have achieved what you started.
- *Check the 'seeds' you are planting,* if you're not feeling fulfilled and happy as you will reap—receive—what you sow. What kind of seed are you sowing?
- *Be balanced in your life.* We are meant to enjoy life as well as use our gifts and talents. Be aware of any warning signs that tell you to take time out to *recover* physically, emotionally,

mentally and spiritually. From a physical point of view, remember to drink water as even a little dehydration can decrease your mental clarity by up to 30% and make you feel low. Also be sure to move by walking, dancing, playing tennis, swimming or whatever brings life to your mind, body heart and spirit. I love Latin dancing and hope to dance 'til I die. Making time for building healthy relationships is also important. What do you love?

Ultimately, I believe our destiny is not *just* to use our gifts and talents, but primarily *to allow ourselves to be loved unconditionally.* Then from this secure foundation we can give back what we have received.

I believe our Creator's desire is to *accept him* for who he is—Unconditional Love—and to accept *his* plans for us as his children, *his* works of art. Once we 'know' who he really is, we become aware of our dignity and our common destiny. *We will know then we are loved 'anyway' as a gift to the world and be our very best, unburdened and unafraid.*

I once read that the purpose of God's presence is for our *total flowering in existence.* So for me this says that He who holds us in existence desires our full development in being. I know now that for the good of all Unconditional Love is willing to supply whatever is needed for our complete fulfilment no matter who we are or what we have or have not done. Enjoy the adventure and see the results of applying these destiny keys.

40

Angels and Their Power to Help

I had never thought much about angels until I became aware that throughout the Bible they played a major role in many ways. After reading these stories and becoming aware of their roles, I decided to ask my Guardian Angel for help. What a change occurred!

I began by asking my Guardian Angel to help me pause before reacting when confronted with a difficult situation. It doesn't sound like a big request, but it made a huge difference in my relationships. Prior to asking for help, I had often over-reacted, making matters worse than before which often left me feeling guilty and bad. I knew I was entitled to have a voice when hurt, but I didn't know then, in the early days of this journey, how to communicate my feelings constructively.

After asking for help, a change occurred effortlessly in me. I had a moment to pause and become aware of anger and resentment rising up within me. I knew not to react then because I had already experienced the awful consequences. What I did though was process my negative feelings and beliefs. Only when I calmed down did I approach the person to discuss the issue. I realise now I had begun to become responsible for myself and the way I was acting. Thank God! I learned how to 'really' listen to myself first and then listen to other people's perspective, allowing us to agree to disagree. As I changed so did my relationships.

I also discovered that as many unresolved feelings and beliefs in memories were healed, I reacted less and less. One example of such a healing, where an experience with an angel helped me, was a memory that came to the surface during a Healing Meditation. I was about three-years-old in this memory. I saw myself as a child in front of John, who was an authority figure in my life. As the three-year-old Helen looked at John, she sensed a huge, dark, frightening presence behind him that terrified and overwhelmed her. The person who was facilitating the meditation asked the child in this memory if she would like help. She said yes as she needed a very powerful protective person to help. She didn't believe God was strong enough, in her child's mind, so she was asked if an angel could come to protect her (children relate more to angels than God we have discovered over the years). Little Helen said yes. At that moment a large angel appeared behind her in the memory.

When the facilitator asked little Helen in the memory if she still felt terrified, overwhelmed and powerless, she said no. She said she felt protected and safe. Then when she looked at John, she realised the dark frightening presence behind him had disappeared. John now looked tired, slumped over and weak as though he needed help. Little Helen now felt compassion and wanted to help John, but this responsibility felt too heavy for her. She was then asked if she would allow the angel to help John. As she said yes, she felt a weight of responsibility lift off her back and then felt light and free.

As I observed the transformation in this memory, I became aware as an adult I could feel the same freeing release. I have never forgotten this encounter with the large protecting angel guarding and helping me. It was very real. I then asked my Guardian Angel to make me aware to always call upon him whenever I felt a need.

Whenever I see others struggling, I am reminded to ask God to send his ministering angels to help them. I did this in Janet's case as she and her husband had a massive argument and she had been left believing the situation was hopeless as he would never change. As she unloaded all her negative emotions and thoughts and came to peace, I said I would ask God's angels to go before her and minister to her husband as she returned home. She discovered a very calm husband and peace was restored. She was amazed! This has occurred in many similar situations, so I am never left feeling helpless as I know I can always ask for the angels to help in whatever way is appropriate.

Most people are open to angels helping them
Many people who have come seeking clarity and peace in their difficulties are not open to help from God or Jesus because of the pain they and others have suffered and the bad experiences with religious people or organisations, which is understandable. But most people are open to angels guiding them to experience Truth. This then helps us meet people where they are.

When people haven't been able to trust enough even to listen to Truth's perspective during a Healing Meditation, the moment I invite the angels to surround them there is an immediate softening. They tell me they feel protected and that they are then willing to listen to Truth's perspective. When they hear Truth in their mind, the fear, trauma, darkness and negative feelings and beliefs just dissolve away leaving Light. People share that they experience a Presence and feel at peace. Again I am grateful that the angels make people feel safe and protected; otherwise, we would have difficulty helping them.

Personal stories about angels helping in everyday situations
The following people share their stories where they believe angels

have transformed situations that could have been disastrous, brought peace when the opposite was expected, and protected and helped in many other ways.

Angel train!
As my son's best friend, who was 17, left to go overseas, I gave him a card wishing him a great trip adding that if he ever needed help he could call upon his Guardian Angel. When he returned home some 12 months later, he couldn't wait to share the following story.

He said that in journeying through a foreign country on his way home to Australia, he and two girls became stranded on a railway station in a small town. They were told by the railway assistant that there were no further trains that night. It was very dark and they felt very vulnerable and scared. There was a bad feeling about the town. They didn't know what to do. He said he then remembered what I had written in his card about asking his angel for help when in need so he asked for help straight away. Within minutes, they saw a light in the distance down the railway tracks. They realised it was a train. It stopped at the station and, apart from the driver who welcomed them aboard, there was no one on it. They were very grateful. He said it 'blew his mind' that there were no further trains expected, but right after asking his angel for help a train was provided, it seemed, just for them! He said he will never forget the experience.

Peace and sleep, despite the dangerous circumstances
At the age of 18, one of my daughters decided to take on a part-time evening job as a waitress in a night club in a very undesirable part of Melbourne. There was little my husband and I could *humanly* do after trying to talk her out of the job because she was legally an adult. She usually finished at about 3.00 am and a bouncer would walk her to her car in the parking lot under the railway bridge. Can you imagine how dark it was and how we felt as parents? So many thoughts came into

our heads. Would she get home without being attacked? Who would she meet in this 'dive'? Would drugs be offered to her? Would she make friends with people with the 'wrong' values?' These sorts of questions bombarded our minds. After leaving this venue, she went on to yet another night club.

It may sound crazy, but throughout this whole time my husband and I would go to bed and sleep peacefully. This was a result of the choice we made. We could either entertain terrible thoughts, worry, get agitated, lose sleep and become frustrated and angry at our daughter thus destroying our relationship or ask the angels to take care of her and the whole situation. So of course we asked the angels to take care of her. We both then experienced peace, despite the circumstances, and were able to sleep peacefully until her safe return. It was truly amazing.

Our daughter later told us that both night clubs had been selling drugs and she discovered there had even been a shooting at the last club. This knowledge made her quit, never to return to work in night clubs again!

Sharing how life can change ... with the angels' help
Earlier on in my life, I tried unsuccessfully to share with my children and other people how life can change for the better, but many haven't been interested. In fact, they just tuned out! I sometimes felt disillusioned and disappointed, but this taught me to 'really' listen to people first and foremost. Then, if appropriate, I would share my thoughts. But when I asked the angels to be present to me and those I met, I noticed even a greater shift. I realised I relaxed and let go of my expectations. I felt I could just 'be' as I had asked the angels to be in control of what happened. On one such occasion the most remarkable change occurred. People came up to me, instead of me approaching

them, and instead of me asking them questions, they asked me questions allowing me to naturally share how my life had changed for the better. A family member told me later a number of people spoke glowingly of our time together, which hadn't been the case in the past. I wonder what would happen if you also did the same?

Saved by an angel
Ursula, who had been a Director of Agape Encounter, shared how she'd catch the tram outside St. Patricks Cathedral after mass to go to her workplace in Collins Street. One morning, as she walked towards the tram, she suddenly felt herself falling. She came so close to the asphalt she thought it would touch her nose, but then she felt something strange happen. Someone seemed to be picking her up and putting her in an upright position, yet there was no physical person present!

Later on she reflected on what happened and realised that she certainly couldn't have saved herself. She believed God must have had a hand in the situation by sending one of his angels to protect and save her.

Rescued from the Pit
One day, Dorothy was verbally abused by someone close to her. As she was meeting with her team members, being a Director of Agape Encounter, she was able to share how this abuse had left her feeling devastated and even destroyed. She was then led through a Healing Meditation, during which she saw, in her mind's eye, an image of a part of her being trapped in a pit with snakes all around. She said in this image she was terrified and couldn't move. When asked if she would like someone to rescue her, she said yes. Then in her mind's eye she saw an angel appear who brought some light into the pit. Then more angels appeared who covered up the snakes. Then there was a

sense of more and more angels lifting her out of the pit. She said she felt lighter as though she had wings and was able with their help to get out of the pit. At the top of the pit, she became aware that this part of her memory was somehow separate so she asked the angels to bring that part back to her. When they did this, she felt more complete and stronger. All the negative feelings had disappeared.

When she revisited the recent situation of verbal abuse, it was just a memory, with no power to harm her. The negative feelings of devastation were no longer relevant. There was just peace and Dorothy was grateful and thankful for her special angels. She had also become aware of other similar memories of devastation where she sensed the angels laughing and chattering, waiting to put her back together after being shattered. You could visibly see the transformation in her whole being from devastation to peace.

'I was lonely and didn't belong.'
One day Edna, who is also a Director of Agape Encounter, allowed the Holy Spirit to bring forth any memories that needed healing. She said she saw in her mind a bright, sunny bedroom. There was a rose pink quilt on the bed. The curtain had the same shade scattered through the design on them. Under the window stood a child's table and chair and on the chair sat a teddy bear. It was her bedroom when she was a child. She remembered spending many happy hours of play in this room.

One day the family dog was given away to her dad's friends in a hessian bag and she can remember feeling disturbed. The next morning the furniture truck arrived outside the house and men began busily loading their furniture, including all Edna's furniture from her bright sunny bedroom. She saw herself standing on the front lawn watching the van drive away with it all.

She remembered her mum closing the front door and then walking together to the train station. Edna could see, in this memory, bombarding her mum with questions as they travelled to the city, but her answers didn't satisfy Edna's puzzled mind. She remembered alighting at Middle Park Station and walking down the street until they came to some terrace houses. One of them she came to realise was to be their new home. The family lived upstairs in a one bedroom home. Edna remembers having no bedroom of her own anymore, but a bed that was put up for her every night in the hall. She played on the veranda when it was fine or on the floor of the lounge in winter. She missed her friends, as there were no children living near the new house. Edna was very lonely and felt as though she didn't belong. This belief and the feelings associated with it have been with her ever since, until the encountering prayer ministry.

Edna was asked by the facilitator of the Healing Meditation if she wanted some help in this memory. As she said yes, she became aware of four small angels coming to play with her. What a happy scene it was, as she saw them laughing and playing with little Edna. The feeling of loneliness disappeared and Edna no longer felt as though she didn't belong. She was at peace in this memory and felt grateful to God for using his angels to bring healing.

Bringing help in a potential disaster

A few years ago when one of my children made a mistake during her first week of work, her boss was furious and verbally abusive. She was devastated at his reaction but had the courage the next day to acknowledge the mistake whilst also expressing her concern over the language he used. He listened to her and apologised for his language. She was setting healthy boundaries even at the young age of 19, which was quite courageous.

The following week my daughter made a huge error on the

computer and all her employer's clients were sent the wrong statements. It was a disaster. In panic, she rang her dad who immediately prayed that the angels would be present when the boss returned. After the previous experience, you can understand her nervousness. When her employer heard the news, his first reaction was to ask what she had done to rectify the situation and he was not abusive. After explaining what she had done, he congratulated her and said he was confident that in a few months he would be able to go on holidays. He said not only was she aware of the huge mistake she made but was competent enough to rectify it. What a difference in attitude! I have seen and heard of many situations where change *seemed impossible* until the angels were asked for their help.

Paul who was a director of Agape Encounter shares his experiences
Protected from a large falling tree ... I was driving my car during a windy and rainy night when my passenger suddenly shouted, 'Look out!' Startled, I said, 'Look out for what?' because I couldn't see anything, but at the same time felt the steering wheel in my hands turn sharply to the right. As my car was travelling at some speed, I slammed on the brakes thinking something was wrong with the car. I didn't know why it had suddenly veered to the right.

As I skidded to a halt on the opposite side of the road, a large number of leaves and small branches crashed around my car. Then I realised a very large tree had fallen down. It went across the fence, footpath and road. It was huge! The trunk stood around eight feet high off the road and the length must have been about 120 feet. I believe that my angel had grabbed the steering wheel and taken over, steering me out of harm's way. He could see what was about to happen. This tree would have crushed the car with my passenger and me inside had I kept driving. God certainly sent an angel to guide, protect and help us that night.

What if my car hadn't stalled? When I was running a taxi truck business, I was in the routine each morning of letting the truck idle to warm up while I did my checklist which took a couple minutes. One particular morning after completing the checklist, I started to back out of the driveway when suddenly the van stalled and stopped dead. As I turned the key in the ignition and tried to start it up again, I happened to glance in the side mirror and saw a small child peddling his bike away from the back of my van down the driveway and onto the footpath. I had no idea the child was there as he was in my blind spot. Wow! All the 'what if's …' started to run through my mind. What if the van hadn't stalled for that moment? What if I'd run over the child? I couldn't stop thanking my angel believing he help prevent a disaster.

Red lights and a large truck … I was driving along Barkers Road heading towards the Glenferrie Road intersection, probably going too fast, when I heard the words 'slow down.' Thinking that there must have been a policeman nearby, I did as the prompt suggested. I slowed down as I approached the intersection even though I was facing a green light. I was about 30 metres from the intersection when suddenly coming down the hill on Glenferrie Road was a large truck that went straight through the intersection and the red light. If I hadn't heard and responded to those words 'slow down,' I could have been killed. I had to stop the car for a while because I was shaking so much from shock. I am sure the warning was from my faithful Guardian Angel who I call Benny, as I now know his voice.

How angels helped people throughout the centuries

Angels can go before us … When Abraham was well advanced in years, he made his servant go to his country to get a wife for Isaac. But the servant was concerned that the woman wouldn't be willing to follow him back to the land they were in. Abraham said, 'The Lord, the God of heaven, who took me from my father's house and from the land of my birth and who spoke to me and swore to me, "To your offspring I will give this land, *he will send his angel before you,* and you shall take a wife for my son from there."' You can ask God to send his angels before you too in your life today, as I do, and see the difference it makes.

Angels protect and deliver ... 'The angel of the Lord encamps around those who fear him and delivers them' (Psalm 37). This type of fear is a healthy, respectful fear: fear of being separated from God's protection and love.

As you have read, I invited the angels to protect and deliver my daughter from the night clubs, and they did, and we were also left in peace in the meantime. Even the other day my daughter was thrown off her horse head first into a tree and although shocked and shaken she had been protected from a serious accident. A few days later my husband fell off the ladder as he was beginning to come off the roof, and apart from some bruising, he also was protected. Again I am so very grateful. You too can ask for protection every day for your family from the angels of the Lord.

Angels can provide for us ... When Jezebel sent a messenger to Elijah threatening to kill him, he became afraid and fled for his life. He went into the wilderness and sat down under a solitary broom tree. He asked that he might die, telling the Lord to take his life away. It would seem that he was very depressed and feeling hopeless. He fell asleep under the tree and then suddenly an angel touched him and told him to get up. He looked and there at his head was a cake baked on hot stones and a jar of water. He lay down again and the angel of the Lord came a second time and again touched him telling him to get up and eat, otherwise the journey would be too much for him. On the strength of that food, Elijah travelled for forty days and forty nights. You can read this in 1 Kings 19:5-8.

This reminds me of the times when I feel I can't get out of bed in the morning. But when I ask for energy to be provided I have experienced a change within minutes and feel completely energised to actually jump out of bed. Both my husband and I are amazed but again grateful. Would you ask for what you need and be aware of what happens?

Angels can instruct and release us ... When Paul was imprisoned, an angel of the Lord appeared and a light shone in the cell. He instructed Peter to get up and the chains feel off his wrists. Then the angel told him to get dressed and follow him. They went past the guards and through the iron gate that opened in front of them. When they were outside, the angel suddenly left him.

As we have facilitated Healing Meditations, we have heard many people describe images in their mind's eye of being alone, trapped and powerless in dark pits or cages, which I related to. Then many have a sense of angels being sent into these places to help and freedom is experienced! When in need, would you listen to the prompting of Wisdom and his angels and be aware of the release you may then feel?

Angels can comfort us in our fears ... When Paul was taken as a prisoner by ship to Rome, they encountered a violent wind and were pounded by a storm for many days. When they had been without food for a long time, Paul stood up and told the men that they should have listened to him and not set sail from Crete, but went on to urge them to keep their courage as he knew there would be no loss of life. He said, 'For last night there stood by me an angel of the God to whom I belong and whom I worship and he said, "Do not be afraid, Paul: you must stand before the emperor; and indeed, God has granted safety to all those who are sailing with you"' (Acts 27). Next time you feel you are in a storm in your life, will you call upon an angel of the Lord to help bring you through safely?

Angels can direct us ... In Acts 8:26-40, Philip was directed by an angel of the Lord to go to a particular place. He went, despite not knowing why he was to go. As a chariot came along, he was directed to go and join the person in it. That person was having trouble understanding the Word of God and Philip was able to assist him. The man then asked Philip to baptise him. As soon as Philip had done this, he was snatched away and found himself in another place. Because he was available and responsive to an angel of the Lord, this man was instructed in the Word of God and baptised.

This reminds me of the time I was having a meditation time during which I felt directed to go and see a particular lady and tell her that God loved her. Thankfully, I had the courage to go and share these words with her as she was desperate and had been walking around the house saying to God that he must hate her as everything in her life was so bad. If some direction came to you, would you be open to following through and seeing the results?

Angels can serve and help ... It says in Hebrews 1:14, 'Are not all angels spirits in the divine service, sent to serve for the sake of those who are to inherit salvation?' In other translations, the word serve is replaced with help. I find this fact very comforting.

When God's angels don't seem to respond
People have told me that when they ask for help nothing has happened. I related to what they said because earlier in my life when I asked for help for my daughter when she was dangerously ill, it seemed that I wasn't heard. However, I now realise not only did my daughter recover fully, but I also was released from deep-seated fears that were controlling our lives.

Some people ask for the things *they* want, but God's angels only obey the *will of God* who is Love. Therefore, he only responds out of love giving us what is best for us long-term. Isn't that what a loving, wise parent would do?

Although we can ask for help, we can also be divided within ourselves. Part of us can want what we have asked for, but another part of us believes we don't deserve it. Experiencing Truth in this case is imperative so we can be wholehearted in asking and open to receive help.

Understanding Angels

Fallen angels

This is not easy to write about because I am aware many people don't want to know about such things as fallen angels. And I certainly recommend never focusing on the darker side of life, as we attract what we focus on. But I share this information so we are aware that there are such things as fallen angels.

At first they were good angels, created naturally good by God, but they became evil by their own doing. Isn't that what happens now when people who were born good choose to do wrong and evil things? Out of their free will these fallen angels radically and irrevocably rejected God and his reign. Remember again here that the word God means Love. So they rejected Love. Despite what you may think, I know now that Satan can come disguised as an angel of light. People who have been angry at God during a Healing Meditation have expressed their rage only to discover that in fact they had been deceived. Many people are unaware these days that there is a great difference between fallen angels and angels of God! That is why it is wise to ask God to send *his* angels! If you find all this too much to handle, just ask Wisdom to bring understanding so you are free of fear and informed.

God's holy angels

Angels are servants and messengers of God and his saving plan. They are purely spiritual with intelligence and will, but come in human form at times. God gave them great wisdom, power and holiness. They were created through and for him and have been present since creation. They know and love God.

Angels can be known by proper names to indicate their powers and their work. When angels come to minister to us, even the names by which we know them are taken from their ministry. Michael means 'who is like God'; Gabriel means 'strength of God' and Raphael means 'healing of God.'

It is the angels who proclaimed the good news of Christ's birth and resurrection. It is angels who led Adam and Eve out of paradise after they disobeyed God. They protected Lot, saved Hagar and her child, prevented Abraham from sacrificing his son, led the people of God, announced births and callings and assisted prophets. They protected Jesus when young, served him in the desert and strengthened him in his agony in the garden.

And for all of us, I believe these comforting words to be true: 'Take care that you do not despise one of these little ones; for, I tell you, in heaven their angels continually see the face of my Father in heaven.' Many of us haven't been aware or else have forgotten this truth. People who had been abused as children have often encountered angels or a sense of their presence in these memories which brings such a release of all the shame, false guilt and lies. They leave after a Healing Meditation feeling restored, safe, protected and free as they know they are no longer alone.

Because of what I and others have experienced and shared, I hope that you will come to know you are never powerless because you have the power to ask the angels to help you or other people. My hope is that you will share this information with the children in your lives, who can then call upon their angels whenever they need help, protection or guidance.

41

When 'It' Seems Impossible!

Having a clear picture of what you want makes 'it' possible
Judy shared with me how she'd been trying to find a suitable job for some time without any success. When I asked her if she was clear about what she wanted, she looked surprised and said, 'What do you mean?' I asked her did she know where she would like to work. She said she hadn't given it much thought until I asked the question. 'Twenty minutes from home by car would be great,' she said 'but I *don't believe* there are any positions that close to home.' I then asked her what hours she would like to work. Judy again said she hadn't thought about that either. In other words, she hadn't begun to create a clear picture of what *could be possible*. She paused for a moment and then said with a little 'doubting' type of laugh, 'Well, ideally, I'd like to work half days during the week!' (which came across to me as 'Get real Helen. You can't just think about what you want and then get it!'). So I suggested that now she was clear about what she wanted, we could both ask our Helper and the angels to find such a position, if appropriate. Within days of this conversation, Judy had not only found a position with the exact requirements she had asked for but was employed by this organisation.

This is a perfect example of what can become possible when you are totally clear about what you want and then ask for some Divine help! I always suggest adding the words 'if it is appropriate' when asking because what we ask for may not be in our best interests.

Being *open* to other points of view and what 'is' possible
Have you heard people say 'it will never change' or 'he or she will never change?' It is a statement coming from what they believe as a result of their past experiences, personal efforts and then failure to bring about change. This belief *doesn't* allow for possibilities or change. In a sense, we act like we are the 'all knowing one,' instead of going to the One who truly knows all! A quick way to remove this *restricting blocking* belief is to ask Wisdom, 'How true is it that "it" will never change?' and listen. When you still can't sense a freeing perspective usually the belief that 'it' will never change comes from an earlier unresolved memory. This is where the Healing Meditation can bring clarity and an openness to what 'is' possible.

Tilly rang yesterday saying she was desperate. She said she had tried to deal with the negative feelings and beliefs she had in relation to her present situation and gain Wisdom's perspective, but nothing changed. So I asked her how she was left feeling. She said she felt frustrated, trapped, frightened, angry and powerless, believing she had no purpose and no value. No wonder she was desperate! Then as I invited her to let go and drift into these feelings she became aware of a memory that was filled with darkness. She felt this memory occurred when she was 13-years-old.

All the same feelings and beliefs that she had recently experienced were also in this dark memory. The 13-year-old girl in the memory was willing to trust only the angels to give her their point of view, their truth. At that point, the darkness dissolved along with all the negative feelings and beliefs and the memory was filled with light. She realised how peaceful and secure she now felt and that the situation that had triggered all the dramatic, negative feelings and beliefs no longer concerned her. This aspect of her memory that had been disconnected from the adult Tilly now felt at one with her. She felt a greater wholeness. She was amazed and I was very grateful. From this place of peace Tilly was then open and able to see what was possible in her life.

Everything is possible for the one who believes!
Fiona believed her husband would never change as a result of the years of tension and verbal abuse that occurred off and on in their relationship. She eventually had an emotional breakdown as a result of further abuse at work and it seemed her life as she knew it was collapsing all around her. However, she rang for help as she was now ready to face her deepest fears and take responsibility for what was going on in her. After observing traumatic memories and all the relevant negative beliefs and feelings, guided by the Divine Counsellor, she experienced a Presence and felt great release, peace and sense of security within. One of the biggest blocks were rejection, judgement and hatred of herself because of what happened to her as a child. So the door within her was open to other people rejecting and judging her.

She went on to develop a deep personal relationship and profound belief and trust in God and everything in her life began to change for the better. Over time, she realised how secure she felt and the fears that had controlled her no longer existed. The verbal abuse from others also stopped and her relationship with her husband is now better than it has ever been. She knows now without doubt *that everything is possible* for the one who *believes in God for help*. Feeling free within, she realised how much energy she had to put into her garden and writing, something she had always wanted to do.

Other powerful, practical keys that make 'it' possible
- Changing one's focus from what is wrong to what is right attracts more of what is right!
- Nurturing a daily attitude of gratitude for even little things.
- Asking questions that lead to empowering answers such as: 'What *can* I change?'; 'What *can* I learn from the situation?' and 'What *can* I do?'
- Persevering in believing and *always* letting go of doubt so the door of your mind is *closed* to torment and procrastination!

How would you feel if you discovered 'it' was possible?
Discovering how you would feel if 'it' was possible is important, as we are attracted to those things, people or circumstances that we believe will make us feel happy. The good feelings also motivate us and can even drive us to take action towards what we desire. This is the power of association. For instance, if you did get the job you thought was impossible, perhaps you'd feel excited and satisfied. If your children began to do the things you had always hoped they would, you would probably feel relieved and at peace. How would you feel if you experienced what now seems impossible?

I learned though that when we *rely upon 'it'* to feel relaxed, look good, be happy and have some peace, we are taken on an emotional rollercoaster ride. This reliance can lead to addictions of one sort or another which usually destroys our health and relationships.

It took me a long time, and much disappointment, before I finally realised I must *never rely upon* someone or something for my source of satisfaction, happiness and peace, but rather rely upon the One who I discovered is the source of all I was seeking.

All I ever desired was within me instead of without. What a discovery! When I remain conscious of and in the Presence, I feel whole and complete. The feeling I experience of peace and contentment is priceless. I no longer *want something* so I can feel some way and feel freer to use my talents in whatever way is appropriate to help make this world a better place.

Interestingly though, I am now doing things I would have once thought were impossible. But I never directly sought them. If tomorrow the things I am doing stopped I know I would still feel content in the Presence within, my real home.

My hope is that we all come to experience this deep abiding contentment within so we can feel safe and free to explore what 'is' possible with no attachment to 'it' for our happiness. That which seems impossible often happens then almost effortlessly or we are content anyway.

42

How to Maintain and Retain Peace, Presence and Power

If we maintain our car with regular check-ups in order to keep it operating at its best, then surely we need to have regular check-ups to become aware of how we are running. Although I have had many experiences where I felt Peace beyond understanding, remaining and retaining a centred, peaceful place has required frequent check-ups and maintenance! Here are some of the tools that help me maintain and retain Peace, Presence and real Power in my life.

Tune in and tune up daily to reconnect and be refuelled!
When: First thing in the morning, and last thing at night, take a few minutes to do this powerful reconnecting and transforming exercise. Then we enter our day connected to ourselves and to the One who created the day! That's powerful. I also use this exercise *whenever I am upset or scattered and need help to return* to a centred, peaceful state.
Why: Because of the benefits of this simple, yet powerful exercise. It will make you *aware* of the state you are in. It will help you reconnect you to yourself before you breakdown. Then *you can receive transformation* in each area of your being.

How to prepare: Allow five to 10 minutes.
This exercise can be done in bed or wherever will best enable you to become centred and present to the Presence.
Take a few deep breaths.
Always be the observer throughout the exercise, allowing the Divine Counsellor to reveal the state of your being and to transform it ... truly 'tuning' you up!
The state of your being can be revealed as 'a sense' or 'image.' Just accept what comes to you as an observer.

I recommend throughout the exercise you use *the name you relate to*, i.e. Divine Counsellor, Spirit of Peace, Love, Life or Truth for example. From my perspective, these names all relate to one and the same Presence, the Author of Life, but I mention this because some people cannot relate to certain names because of their past painful experiences.
Suggestion: I recommend closing your eyes during this meditative exercise as it prevents distractions.

Body, mind, heart and spirit reconnecting, renewing guideline
It is *vital* to ask the Divine Counsellor to reveal and release as follows:
Body
- *Reveal* the state of my **body** (e.g. tired, heavy or painful in some area) ... Pause and observe.
- *Release* your Spirit of Life into my body ... Pause and observe the change (the negative feelings can dissolve leaving peace).

Mind
- *Reveal* the state of my **mind** (e.g. it could be scattered, racing, dark, blank, or in some other state)... Pause to observe.
- *Release* your Spirit of Peace into my **mind** ... Pause to

observe the change (it can become still, calm and centred).

Heart
- *Reveal* the state of my **heart** (e.g. broken or flat) …Pause and observe.
- *Release* your Spirit of Love and healing into my heart …Pause and observe the change (healing and wholeness can be experienced).

Spirit
- *Reveal* the state of my **human spirit** (e.g. flat, grey or lifeless) … Pause and observe.
- *Release* your Spirit of Life into my spirit … Pause and observe the change (you can experience your spirit become filled with Light and life).

Be aware, now, of how you feel at the conclusion of the meditative exercise. Usually people feel refuelled and renewed. I also recommend surrendering the day and situations to Wisdom's guidance. Then at the conclusion of your day observe how your day has evolved. Usually I find my day flows and has been life-giving in some way.

Another benefit of this exercise is that we become aware of where we need to change. For instance, I realised how often I was exhausted. I was being given a warning to slow down, respect my body, take time out and enjoy life. I then saw how I had placed myself under pressure from my unrealistic expectations. This unchecked could have led me to experiencing burnout yet again. When that occurred in the past, it left me feeling lifeless, grey, disconnected and depressed. This made me vulnerable to becoming ill as well. I wonder if you relate to what I have shared and if you are aware and connected to how you are looking after yourself?

As a result of tuning in and becoming aware of my exhaustion, I let go of my *decision* to be available to all those who felt broken. Then I committed my time to Wisdom asking that I be available only to those he wanted me to help! This simple decision on reflection, bought wonderful order and peace into my life. I then had time to exercise and look after my health and my family were much happier as my phone stopped ringing so frequently. Now there is a natural flow and order to assisting people through presenting seminars and other appropriate times. I am very grateful I tuned in and reconnected to where I was at so I could change my ways.

Sometimes when our body breaks down, we need the help of professionals as did my friend Jean. The doctor discovered she had a cancerous growth. I shared with her how we can also help our bodies by beaming Love into the part of our bodies that are in need. (Most people hate the parts of them that are struggling which can prevent recovery!)

When Jean had the operation to remove the cancerous growth, the physician said that they had trouble finding the growth as it had completely disappeared. They were dumbfounded. Jean shared how she decided to beam love into the cancerous growth for the two weeks prior to the operation and see what happened! She is very well now and living life to the full. *Love* can cure all types of diseases. There are other examples of physical healing in Chapter 12 on Healing of Body Pain. But keeping balanced and in tune with every part of ourselves and the Spirit of Life, I believe, can prevent us from breaking down in one way or another.

Making time to meditate ... spending time in the Presence
Another way to maintain and retain Peace is to make a decision to take at least 10 minutes daily to be still, meditate or pray. Following the reconnecting meditative exercise is a perfect time to do this, often remaining in stillness in the Presence you may have entered. You will eventually reflect, like a mirror, who you spend time with. And in this case you can experience Peace beyond understanding and true

contentment. If you persevere, this in time will reflect and change your outer life, as it did in mine. This special time also helps develop an intimate relationship with the Presence.

How different was my experience though when I didn't make time for the One who created my day; it would never be as peaceful or 'flow' and I wasn't as present or mindful to what I was thinking, believing or how I was acting. I was out of control in a sense! But even this was good, because it made me turn back to my Divine Counsellor within me to address my negative feelings, thoughts, beliefs and reactions and then become aware of Truth and Presence again as mentioned in the Healing Meditation chapter. Knowing where to turn and how to reconnect to Peace when I break down or am weak in some way has been powerfully reassuring for me.

The next step to maintaining and retaining Peace, Presence and Power is to *practice* being aware of the Presence and Peace with me in the moments of each day, learning how to see everyone and everything through his perspective. This is in contrast to how I used to live years ago, only seeing everyone and everything through my perspective and running life my way, which definitely didn't always bring peace.

Avoid doubting to retain Peace
Although many people have had extraordinary breakthroughs and release of pain in memories, I have seen them begin to doubt what they have experienced as being real. At the moment of doubting, confusion replaces Peace and they begin to feel insecure yet again. Many have shared they doubted because it was difficult to *believe* the Peace and Presence in the memory was real or would last. They are often blown away by the extraordinary release they experienced so simply, after years of trying to personally resolve them.

However, the moment I again invite them to let go of doubt and ask them to listen to the Truth in the memory, they realise again that only Peace instead of fear is present in the memory. So to retain Peace, *always let go of doubt*, and then ask for the Divine Counsellor's perspective and truth.

Taking 'true' responsibility for our lives
I believe that we become powerful, in the truest sense, when we take responsibility for our lives, including our thoughts, words, actions and reactions. We can't change others, but we can change ourselves. Our aim should be to grow up in every way despite our circumstances for the good of everyone. Everything that I share in this book has been part of what I have learned as a result of taking responsibility for my life. Here are some of the keys that I have learned that helped people maintain and retain connection to Peace, Presence and Power:

- Be aware when you are challenged, before reacting and responding.
- Recognise if the problem belongs to you or another person. If it is the other person's problem, you can leave it for them to sort out! If the problem belongs to you, then acknowledge this fact and deal with it constructively.
- Name and own every feeling.
- Recognise what you believe.
- Ask the Divine Counsellor to reveal his truth.
- Ask Wisdom to guide you and take over in every situation.
- Thank the Advocate and Defence Attorney for bringing justice.
- Decide to persevere until you become complete, lacking nothing!
- Choose life-giving attitudes and be aware of your motives.
- Avoid these destructive reactions when challenged by circumstances:
    - losing control (if you do lose control, just apologise!)

- abusing, judging and condemning yourself, others and God (instead let go of all you have said and done and ask for forgiveness).
- manipulating and controlling others to get what you want (discover what you really need and want within you).
- using food, drink, drugs or sex to make you feel better (rather discover the Comforter within and the Peace beyond understanding that will satisfy every part of you).

Here are some other daily actions that have made a huge difference in my life and that can help us retain and maintain being centred, happy and peaceful!

- Begin to do random acts of kindness: a word, a smile or a card. It will bring life to others and yourself.
- Forgive, making sure you not only listen to all that you have felt and believed but also listen to the Spirit of Truth's perspective. Allow Jesus' capacity to forgive on the cross to flow through you so you can really forgive. You then release yourself and others from past negative experiences.
- Focus on what you want, not on what you *don't* want when asking in prayer and thanksgiving, rather than in prayer and anxiety, which is doubting.
- Develop the habit of being thankful at least five times daily.
- Remember what is important is the journey, not the destination!
- Remember the friends you choose will influence you. Choose wisely.
- Begin to treat life as an adventure of learning and growing rather than a struggle and challenge.

- Use all your gifts and talents, no matter how humble they seem, to make a difference.

I believe the purpose of God's creative presence in us is our total flowering in existence and our full development in being. Once upon a time if I had read this statement, I would have asked the question 'then how come I'm not experiencing this in my life?' The information in this book now shares the answers to this question gained over 28 years of experience which has been life-changing for many.

I recommend you read the chapter that appeals to you first and take out one suggestion you feel is appropriate for your life, applying it and then observing the wonderful changes that occur. Take time and be gentle with yourself as you learn and grow over time as I have. Perhaps you could see this book as a compilation of recipes with the ingredients for creating a life that makes a real difference to you and others.

All real and lasting progress lies in *daily surrendering* to Unconditional Love's *creative action* within me so this can then flow through me to *create* a better world. And when I make mistakes, I see them now as an opportunity from which to learn and if necessary experience mercy and forgiveness.

I believe we can become co-creators with the Creator of all the Universe within our scope and for me that's real power. But if we are serious, it means taking time out from our busyness to build an authentic, open relationship where we are humble enough to ask for what we lack, listen, and respond out of love. This is what I have learned to do and the results have been extraordinary. *Would you consider doing the same and seeing the results?*

And finally I have come to know, as I hope you do, that Peace, Presence and real Power is always available within everyone to help all of us on the journey to truth, real life, peace and even joy!

Will you join me?

Expanded Contents

SECTION 1   PEACE

1—Overcoming Struggles—An Adventure Begins!   21
- Discovering a powerful Friend to bring order out of chaos
- We're not just a body, but a soul and spirit.
- What do you do when overwhelmed?
- Discovering the path to life when struggling
- Recognising the path to destruction when struggling
- How to grow personally from every struggle
- The power of perspective to defuse a battle
- Regaining clarity, peace and unity

2—Understanding Feelings and Using Them Constructively!   33
- Anger
- Frustration
- Rage
- Hatred
- Murderous feelings
- Fear
- Feelings of being numb or frozen
- Sadness and grief
- How feelings can lead to awareness, healing and peace
- Some steps to discover the Truth which dissolves negative feelings
- Three-way Perspective Exercise: a powerful freeing meditation
- Feelings and everyday life
- Let your experience help others
- The ultimate role model
- Discovering how you deal with your feelings
- Rejoice and be thankful (You have to be joking!)

3—How Negative Feelings Can Lead to Peace 49
- 'Over the top' emotions
- Why we bury our feelings
- Other consequences of burying our feelings
  Sudden outbursts of anger or rage
  Depression
  Physical Depletion
  Trapped and stuck in hurt

4—Transforming Life by Transforming Thoughts and Beliefs! 57
- I was unaware of what I was thinking–I just reacted!
- My first attempt to transform my mind was totally unsuccessful!
- Past unresolved experiences were controlling my mind!
- Transformation needed at a deeper level
- Release and blessing
- Changed from a snake into a lamb!
- Allowing our mind to be guided in a superhuman manner
- The influence of our formative years on our thoughts
- No more 'struggles' with negative thoughts
- Daydreaming?
- Out of one's mind … blank, dark, grey areas of one's memory
- Finding life hard and difficult!
- Where is your mind focused?
- Some keys to retaining peace of mind
- Another key is not to worry!
- How creativity can flow from your mind
- What you believe will be done for you!

5—Blockages and Obstacles—Discovered and Removed! 72
- Lack of Awareness
- Judgements, condemnation, rejection and hatred
- Control
- Pride

- Fear
- Death wishes and 'not wanting to be here'
- Not forgiving
- Decisions and inner vows
- Logical thinking
- Roles
- Denial
- Doubt
- Unresolved memories
- Blank, dark, grey areas of our mind
- Generational influences

6—Resistance and its Influence on Your Life   87
- How resistance, based from fear, can stop the flow of life!
- Some signs of resistance
  Tension
  Fears
- How to deal with resistance constructively
  Become aware
  Face your fears
  Get realistic
  Always listen to yourself and others
  Accept the situation
  Gain a life-giving perspective

7—From Breakdowns to Breakthroughs   92
- A new perspective on breakdowns
- Keys to breakthroughs

8—How Fears, Terrors and Trauma Can Dissolve!   96
- My way of coping with tension and fears
- How do fears start?
- Healthy and unhealthy fears

- Fear and abuse
- Fear and disasters
- Religious fears
- Demonic fears
- Fear of people
- Effects of fears on our bodies
- How fear and body pain can be released
- Using the power of the Word—the Truth—to dissolve fears
- Circumstances that can cause trauma and shock

   Abuse
   Accidents
   Operations
   Death
   Wars
   Other occasions when we can experience trauma and shock
   My experience of being released from trauma, shock and terror
   How I now see fears, trauma and shock

9—Finding Your 'True' Self Versus Roles and Masks   111
- Foundation for our true self
- Dissolving the barriers

   Roles and masks we create
   Negative actions and reactions
   Negative emotions
   Negative beliefs
- Getting to know your 'whole' self … body, mind, heart and spirit
- Spiritually: our human spirit
- Physically: body
- Mentally: mind
- Emotionally: heart

10—How Being 'Right' Can Be 'Radically Wrong'   121
- The results of needing to be 'right'
- How to experience freedom

11—The Power of Words 126
- The power of negative words
- How to deal with negative words
- The power of life-giving words
- Creating the life you want by your words
- Speak your truth in love

12—Healing of Body Pain 134
- The influences of feelings and beliefs
- Healing our bodies naturally
- Healing and forgiveness
- Divine healing—beyond human understanding
- All were healed and evil spirits were driven out
- Renew your strength
- How to stay young and strong
- Life and healing for our flesh
- Fountain of life
- A daily check up

SECTION 2   PRESENCE

13—Discover What You 'Really' Want 145
- What do you want right now?
- When we get what we want how do we feel?
- How do we feel when we don't get what we want?
- The consequences of reacting negatively when we don't get what we want.
- Creating space for what you 'really' want
- Discovering what you 'really' want within yourself

14—Discover True Treasure   146
- My treasure bought displeasure!
- True and lasting treasure
- Discovering your treasure

15—Discovering the Loving, Powerful Presence Within   154
- How the Presence has been experienced
- Asking the Presence to take over!
- Life becomes easier and lighter
- Qualities of the Presence
- A barrier to experiencing the Presence—our distorted perception
- Beliefs, terror, trauma and shock act as barriers to the Presence
- Promises given by the Presence … my Divine Friend
- Lovingly corrected
- A solid, secure foundation
- Sensing myself, the created within the Creator, as one!
- Abiding with the Presence
- Does the Presence leave us?
- What helps us to discover and maintain this Presence?
- How making a decision to be still changed everything

16—The Healing Meditation—A Step-by-Step Guide to Peace   168
- The Healing Meditation Step-by-Step Guide
  Preparation
  Identify what needs to be resolved.
  Emotions/Feelings
  Thoughts/Beliefs
  Listen to the freeing Truth.
  The Three-Way Perspective Exercise: resolving anger, hurt and conflict
- Experiencing Peace, Presence and Power

17—True and Lasting Happiness   173
- Discovering your perspective about happiness
- Making space for a new perspective on true happiness
- The source of happiness
- A simple way to discover true happiness despite where you are at!
- Practical tips to discover and maintain true happiness

18—The Power of Love Languages   180
- Discovering another person's love language
- The benefits
- The different types of love language
  Words of Affirmation
  Quality Time
  Receiving Gifts
  Acts of Service
  Physical Touch

19—Becoming Free To Be Me!   186
- Blockages and obstacles to freedom
- Different types of fears
- Roles and Masks
- Doubts
- Trauma
- How to remain free

20—How 'Really' Listening Melts Hearts   193
- What prevents authentic listening?
- Authentic listening
- Listening to yourself
- How to listen to quiet/shy people
- Do we listen to people who never stop talking?
- Listening to the One who created you and the Universe
- Some practical tips on how to be an authentic listener
- Be encouraged even when you fail to authentically listen

21—How to Develop Healthy Relationships   199
- Being open and honest about relationships
- A time to speak
- A way to speak
- Be aware of your body language
- The "I" word
- The power of asking questions
- Listen to others
- Let your words be like gifts
- Qualities required for developing healthy relationships
- Do you have a healthy relationship with yourself?
- Becoming present to yourself and the power of your Creator
- Body, mind, heart and spirit reconnecting meditation
- What is your relationship like with others?
- Three Way Perspective Exercise
- What is your relationship with God like?

22—Relationships with Healthy Boundaries   209
- Being calm, centred and consistent
- Setting appropriate time boundaries
- Agreements and consequences
- No boundaries = chaos!
- Listen to and accept no when appropriate
- When fear threatens to overwhelm you from setting healthy boundaries
- Some fears and false beliefs about setting boundaries

SECTION 3   POWER

23—Powerfully Resolving Conflicts   219
- Conflict stoppers!
- How conflicts can be constructive

- Express your feelings
- Anger in conflict
- How do you respond to conflicts?
- Allow yourself space and time to heal
- Consequences of conflict, resolved and unresolved

24—The Power in Acknowledging, Allowing and Asking to Receive 227
- Allowing and Receiving

25—The Power of Curses and Blessings! 231
- What is a curse anyway?
- What is the 'something' that causes evil or harm?
- Wishing evil is the same as cursing others!
- How blessings occur
- Helpful hints to receive blessings: the 5 Rs
Realise
Repent—Say sorry!
Renounce
Receive
Restore
- Generational release

26—Using Anger Powerfully and Constructively 241
- Justifiable anger
- Murderous anger turned to compassion
- Unresolved, accumulated anger is like a bonfire ready to be ignited!
- Suppressing anger
- Victims of other people's anger
- A victim of one's own anger
- Brief practical guidelines on how to deal with anger constructively
- Some wise instructions regarding anger

27—How to 'Really' Forgive   253
- The power is beyond oneself to 'really' forgive.
- Gaining three perspectives
- Resolving pain, hurt and unforgiveness in memories
- Forgiving on the spot!
- True justice and forgiveness
- The amazing benefits of forgiving
- Three-way forgiveness
- Forgiveness, mercy and unconditional love

28—Questions That are Empowering and Life Giving   259
- The power of questions vs. statements and instructions
- Questions that invite other people to have a voice and opinion
- Questions can help or hinder
- Questions to ask when anxious or upset
- Questions for direction in life

29—Freedom from Stress … Practical Keys   265
- Listen to that 'part' of you that feels stressed … without judgement!
- Explore and express: write, confront or draw
- Some other simple ways to de-stress
- Body, mind, heart and spirit de-stressing exercise
- When unable to resolve stress

30—Change Your Focus and Change Your Life!   271
- Who or what do we focus on in life for our happiness and self-worth?
  Achieving
  Family
  Ourselves
  Others
- How to change your focus and change your life

31—The Power of Decisions That Can Change Your Life   275
- Where do decisions come from?
- Decisions that bring stress and regret
- Decisions that bring fulfilment and life

32—The Power of Expectations   281
- Expectations that lead to disappointments
- Life-giving expectations

33—How to Gain an Empowering Perspective   285
- The origins of developing perspective
- Difficult or disastrous situations can be transformed by perspective
- The keys for gaining a life-giving perspective
- How to avoid arguments using the power of perspective
- Other examples of the power of perspective
- Blockages to obtaining a life-giving perspective
- We can choose either a negative or positive perspective

34—The Power of Attitude   290
- Underlying causes of bad attitudes
- Effectively handling bad attitudes

35—'What if…?' A Powerful Question   294
- Possibilities and lost opportunities
- Asking 'What if …?' from a foundation of fear, doubt or faith
- Asking 'What if …?' can reveal deep-seated fears that can be dissolved!
- Questions that can change your life

36—How to Attract Good Things into Your Life   298
- Your words can reveal what you're thinking, believing and attracting
- We are invited to ask for what we want
- Ask for what you want … not for what you don't want!
- Why we don't attract what we ask for

- Do you believe good things will happen in your life?
- We attract what we give

37—How to Attract the 'Right' Friends and Partner   303
- Discovering what 'right' means in relation to friends and a partner!
- The difference between 'needs' and 'wants'
- Letting go and developing a 'safe' space for honest relationships
- Obstacles to attracting the 'right' friends or partner into your life

38—How to Develop Healthy Habits   308
- How to gently discover and change bad habits
- Healthy habits that will bring life

39—Empowering Destiny Keys   314

40—Angels and Their Power to Help   318
- Most people are open to angels helping them
- Personal stories about angels helping in everyday situations
  Peace and sleep, despite the dangerous circumstances
  Sharing how life can change … with the angels' help
  Saved by an angel
  Rescued from the Pit
  'I was lonely and didn't belong.'
  Bringing help in a potential disaster
  Paul who was a director of Agape Encounter shares his experiences
- How angels helped people throughout the centuries
- When God's angels don't seem to respond
- Understanding Angels
  Fallen angels
  God's holy angels

41—When 'It' Seems Impossible! 334
- Having a clear picture of what you want makes 'it' possible
- Being open to other points of view and what 'is' possible
- Everything is possible for the one who believes!
- Other powerful, practical keys that make 'it' possible
- How would you feel if you discovered 'it' was possible?

42—How to Maintain and Retain Peace, Presence and Power 339
- Tune in and tune up daily to reconnect and be refuelled!
- Body, mind, heart and spirit reconnecting and renewing exercise guideline
- Making time to meditate … spending time in the Presence
- Avoid doubting to retain Peace
- Taking 'true' responsibility for our lives

Afterword

Many times I have thought 'what a journey!' And I wondered how life and situations could possibly change for the better. But as you have read, I made a *decision* to persevere and endure through whatever came my way, clinging to the hope that life would change for the better and through it all I would one day become complete lack nothing—which many times seemed laughable. Without the Presence, his power, wisdom and unconditional love, I would not have seen such results in myself and in other people's lives and the turnarounds, which often occurred when we felt powerless.

The experience of 'feeling' complete occurs in the Presence, where I and others have felt like we lack nothing. This then acts like a solid foundation, a rock, from which to live life, making a difference. This doesn't mean that I rely on this feeling, but I remember in whose Presence this occurs and where I can come again to experience a peace beyond understanding.

So I encourage you to make the same decision to persevere with the guidance of the Presence who is within you, who will empower you, and go before you if you ask and allow and then begin to see life as the greatest adventure of all.

I would love to hear about your experiences as a result of what you learn and apply from this information. Just email me on peacepresencepower@hotmail.com

www.ingramcontent.com/pod-product-compliance
Lightning Source LLC
Chambersburg PA
CBHW071854290426
44110CB00013B/1136